Taxation and Development
Lessons from Colombian Experience

Written under the auspices of
The Center for International Affairs
Harvard University

Taxation and Development

Lessons from Colombian Experience

Richard M. Bird

Cambridge, Massachusetts   Harvard University Press   1970

For Marcia

Contents

Tables

Concern with fiscal problems in poor countries long antedates
the modern flood of development literature. Development finance continues to be the subject of many books, articles, and
reports by fiscal experts. Yet most of these studies take little
account of the results of the intensive theoretical and empirical work on economic development during the last two decades.
Similarly, many development economists tend to view the financial side of the development process as secondary, a mere
veil obscuring the "real" forces which determine the rate and
character of economic growth. My aim in this book is to help
bridge this unfortunate gap between fiscal expert and development economist.

My principal thesis is that tax policy in a developing country
ought to be considered as an essential instrument (or set of
instruments) of development policy. The proper nature and
task of the fiscal system in any country, however, depends not
only on the appropriate development strategy for that country
but also on its peculiar economic and institutional structure
and on the objectives other than economic growth which must
be considered in formulating tax policy.

To design a tax reform for a developing country without a
coherent analytical framework, blurred and uncertain though
it may be in parts, is to risk the unconscious use of often inappropriate models based on the experience of developed countries. It is true that the objectives of economic policy are seldom
spelled out explicitly enough in any country to be of much
operational use, in part because there is seldom any political
advantage in such precision, which may well alienate support
but will be of little use in attracting it. Even if meaningful
policy targets can be determined, the tax adviser is often at a
loss to attach more than the most casual quantitative weight-
ing to the targets and achievements of the tax system. This is
the case because of the statistical lacunae characterizing most
developing countries as well as the inadequacy of our knowl-

edge, theoretical or empirical, on the interconnections of financial and growth variables. Yet, despite these problems, the task of specifying the appropriate policy framework and fitting the best feasible tax system within it is crucially important both for meaningful tax reform and for efficient use of the relatively few policy instruments available to the government in most poor countries.

I have attempted this task for Colombia in the present book at two levels. The first level has to do with the proper macroeconomic task of fiscal and tax policy—a complex question indeed in the particular situation of Colombia today but one which is treated only briefly in this book. The second level of discussion, and the main focus of this study, concerns the *structure* of taxation. Although conditioned in part by the appropriate aggregate level of taxation, tax structure reform is in itself a complex and important subject.

The design of tax structure policy is characterized by apparent conflicts of ends (for example, faster growth vs. more equal income distribution) and by a resulting need for compromises and trade-offs in the tax structure, all within the constraint on feasible alternatives imposed by institutional limitations. My contention is that the tax structure provides not one but many policy instruments, so that by judicious design it is often possible, even in an administratively underdeveloped country like Colombia, to approach such nominally contradictory ends as growth and greater income equality simultaneously.

The study is organized in six chapters. The first two provide the descriptive and analytical setting for the more detailed tax analysis of the next three, and the last chapter sketches some broader considerations affecting tax reform in Colombia. Chapter 1 sets forth the task of a development-oriented fiscal system in Colombia, with special stress on the interaction of economic growth, inflation, and income distribution. Chapter 2 appraises the structure and recent performance of the Colombian public sector in the light of this task. Chapter 3 shows how the heavy reliance on direct taxation desirable in Colombia can be made consistent with dynamic private sector growth. Chapter 4 considers some tax effects on resource allocation in more detail, concentrating on indirect taxes and on tax incentive policy. Chapter 5 turns to the important state and local levels of government in Colombia and urges much more use of the property tax and more self-financing of urbanization expenditures.

The sixth and final chapter suggests a strategy of tax reform, given the administrative and political constraints of the Colombian environment. An important theme of this book is that the tax policy appropriate for a given country at a given time is determined by the economic, political, and social circumstances of the country. It follows that, as these circumstances change, the appropriate tax policy will also change. Tax reform is therefore a never-ending process, not something that can be brought about once-and-for-all and then forgotten. A key idea in the proposed strategy of tax reform is thus the need for building the process into the decision-making structure of the government—that is, "institutionalizing" tax reform. This strategy, like the analysis in the book as a whole, is presented in a partial and limited—one might equally say cautious and pragmatic—way. The conclusions reached are in some respects conventional and in others not, depending on which conventions one believes.

Most of the data and many of the ideas in this study derive directly from my interpretation of Colombian experience in recent years. Although much of the analysis should be equally relevant for other developing countries, particularly in Latin America, no systematic attempt has been made to test the generalizations derived from Colombian experience against data from other countries. In short, the book is an example of that common hybrid, the generalized case study, with the defects (and virtues) of most of its breed.

Three specific limitations deserve brief mention. First, although two of my main arguments—the dependence of the proper tax structure for a country on its particular institutions and problems and the potential importance for development patterns of the details of tax structure—require me to devote considerable attention to a few quantitatively minor tax problems, I do not pretend to provide a detailed study of all aspects of Colombian taxation. One reason for not going into more detail is to keep the book moderately readable by other than tax experts. Equally important, such a study would be largely redundant in view of the recent publication of a *Fiscal Survey of Colombia* carried out for the Joint Tax Program of the Organization of American States and the Inter-American Development Bank by a fiscal mission directed by Milton C. Taylor. Much of the detailed analysis in the Taylor Report is complementary to the present study, which concentrates on a few of the more important issues and relates them to the general development problem and to each other. The weakness of the *Fiscal Survey* from the present point of view is that its hundreds of generally sensible recommendations on tax reform are not related in any coherent way to the postulated framework of tax policy.* The assumed goals of the system— (1) more revenue, (2) more private saving and investment, (3) more equitable income distribution, (4) reduction in luxury consumption, increase in exports, and more efficient resource use, and (5) neutrality, simplicity, feasibility, and flexibility—are not consistently related to general development policy, and the inevitable conflicts and trade-offs between these objectives are never explicitly discussed. It is on precisely these points that the present study focuses.

A second, related limitation is that the empirical evidence advanced in support of the different propositions in this book varies greatly in quality and in quantity. While I have tried to rely on "facts" whenever possible, I have often had to fall back on judgment and simple analysis in order to reach any conclusions. Furthermore, my descriptions and prescriptions may in some respects already have been overtaken by events. I have generally tried to take into account information avail-

---

* Milton C. Taylor *et al.*, *Fiscal Survey of Colombia* (Baltimore: Johns Hopkins Press, 1965), p. 20. For a more extensive survey of the reports of fiscal missions in Latin America, most of which suffer from a similar defect, see Richard M. Bird and Oliver Oldman, "Tax Research and Tax Reform in Latin America—A Survey and Commentary," *Latin American Research Review*, III (Summer 1968), 5-28.

able to me up to the end of 1967; occasionally, however, this means the effective cut-off date for conditions and actions to which the information refers is as early as 1963 or 1964.

Finally, it has sometimes been argued that a tax adviser is not doing his job properly unless he considers not just how to raise funds but also the purposes for which the funds will be used.† There is much to this argument. I am in full agreement with the common contention that present public-expenditure patterns can and should be greatly improved in Colombia. The theoretical and practical merits of explicitly connecting revenues and expenditures are also great in Colombia, as is indicated with respect to primary education in Chapter 5 of this book. Nevertheless, the underlying assumption in the study as a whole is that the structure of government expenditures is determined independently of tax structure. It is as legitimate (and necessary) in this field as in any other to discuss only selected issues and to take other factors as constant. On the practical side, while it is true in Colombia, as in most countries, that a great deal of present public expenditure is wasted, it is equally true that improved expenditure allocation cannot usually be expected unless total expenditure is rising in real terms. There is, I think, good reason to expect that any government which is capable of raising real revenues in the ways proposed in this book will be a government which will spend the increases in ways relevant to and helpful for development.

The original stimulus for this study was my two-year experience at the Colombian Ministry of Finance in 1964–1966 as an adviser on tax and fiscal policy with the Colombia Advisory Group of the Harvard University Development Advisory Service, a part of the Center for International Affairs. My greatest debt is to the numerous colleagues, both Colombian and foreign, who helped me learn-by-doing during this period: among these colleagues Miguel Bermúdez, Richard Bilsborrow, Lauchlin Currie, John Delaplaine, Harold Dunkerley, Solón

---

† For a strong argument to this effect, see Wolfgang F. Stolper, *Planning without Facts* (Cambridge, Mass.: Harvard University Press, 1966), p. 45.

Garcés V., Rafael Isaza G., Bengt Metelius, Guillermo Mojica, Dick Netzer, Francisco Pineda M., William Rhoads, Olaf Saetersdal, Mario Salgado C., Miguel Sandoval Z., and John Sheahan deserve special mention. I am also indebted to Albert Berry, Anthony Churchill, Peter Griffith, Karsten Laursen, Jonathan Levin, Richard Mallon, Richard Musgrave, Oliver Oldman, Gustav Papanek, William Rhoads, John Sheahan, and Robert Slighton for useful comments on and discussion of earlier drafts of parts of the book. Although many of the ideas in this book, good and bad, originated with these and other students of Colombia and of taxation, those from whom I have learned would not necessarily agree with my conclusions, which remain, of course, entirely my own responsibility.

In May 1968, after this manuscript was essentially finished, I had the privilege of returning to Colombia briefly to assist Professor Richard A. Musgrave in setting up an ambitious research program dealing with many of the problems discussed in this book. The program was part of the work of the Technical Commission on Tax Reform headed by Professor Musgrave and set up at the request of President Carlos Lleras Restrepo. In the course of this visit I profited greatly from discussions with the members and staff of the Commission—in particular, Richard Musgrave, Abel Cruz Santos, Carlos Echeverri, Humberto Mesa, Oliver Oldman, Alan Peacock, Paul Senf, Eduardo Wiesner, Federico Herschel, Miguel Urrutia, Aníbal Gómez, Joaquin Bohórquez, Richard Slitor, Melvin White, and Andrew Quale—and from preliminary work done for the Commission to update and improve this study in a number of respects. It is a rare privilege indeed for an author to have his work, published or unpublished, subjected to such an intensive scrutiny by so able a group actively interested in learning from it, and I can only hope my work proved as useful to them and to Colombia as their advice and comments have been to me. The Commission's report was released as this book went to press; it is summarized briefly in Appendix C.

The Development Advisory Service, through funds provided under a United States Agency for International Development research contract, and the International Tax Program of the Harvard Law School made it possible for me to spend much of my research time in 1966–1968 working on this book and provided a stimulating environment in which to work.

Earlier versions of portions of Chapters 4 and 5 appeared previously in the following articles: "Sales Taxation and Development Planning—Colombia," in Gustav F. Papanek, ed., *Development Policy: Theory and Practice* (Cambridge, Mass.: Harvard University Press, 1968), pp. 239-266; "Local Property Taxes in Colombia," *Proceedings of the 58th Annual Conference of the National Tax Association, 1965* (Harrisburg, Pa., 1966), pp. 481-501; and "Financing Urbanization in Developing Countries by Benefit Taxation: Case Study of Colombia," *Land Economics*, XXIII (November 1967), 403-412 (© 1967 by the Regents of the University of Wisconsin). I am especially indebted to William G. Rhoads, coauthor of the last-named article, for permission to use our joint work in the present book. A preliminary version of Appendix B was published as "Coffee Tax Policy in Colombia" in *Inter-American Economic Affairs*, XXII (Summer 1968), 75-86.

R. M. B.

Toronto, Canada
August 1968

One | Public Finance and Economic Development

1 | Public Finance and Development in Colombia

In 1966 there were about 19 million people in Colombia with an average per capita income of around U.S. $325. From 1950 to 1965, the Colombian gross domestic product in real terms almost doubled; corrected for changes in the terms of trade as well as in domestic prices, gross national income increased by 82 percent in this period, for an average annual rate of increase in income of 4.2 percent.[1] At the same time, however, the population was growing at an average annual rate of about 3 percent, so that for the period as a whole per capita income rose, on average, only 1 percent a year.[2] Since 1954, with population increasing more rapidly and output more slowly, it is possible that the per capita income of most Colombians has hardly increased at all. This growth performance, poor by any standard, is almost certainly well below the potential of the Colombian economy.[3]

Not only has the rate of growth been low, but it has also been very irregular and subject to substantial year-to-year fluctuations, chiefly as a result of changes in the terms of trade. In Colombia changes in the terms of trade are virtually equivalent to changes in the export price of coffee, since coffee still accounts for two-thirds of export earnings despite a considerable expansion of other exports in recent years. The average coffee price reached its postwar peak in 1954, with a much lower secondary peak in 1964.[4] The pattern of changes in gross domestic output and income throughout the period followed closely that in coffee prices, export earnings, and the capacity to import, with high coffee earnings leading to high imports, high investment, and high growth rates. Perhaps the most dramatic evidence of the close connection between imports and growth came with the sharp fall in coffee prices in 1957 and the consequent absolute decline in per capita real output and income.[5] Both the internal price level and the external balance of payments were also sharply affected by this episode. From 1950 to 1956 prices rose only 5 to 7 percent a year, and the external current account was in balance. Since 1956, however, there has been a considerably higher (though uneven) rate of inflation, with the consumer price index more than doubling from 1958 to 1965, and repeated balance-of-payments crises leading to major devaluations in 1957, 1962, 1965, and 1967. Concern with economic instability as manifested in these monetary problems dominated economic policymaking in Colombia during the late fifties and early sixties.

Colombia's economic performance since 1950 has also been responsive to changes in agricultural production. Despite the marked decline in the share of agricultural production in the national output in recent years and the equally marked rise in the share of manufacturing production (some of which consists in processing agricultural commodities), agriculture is still by far the most important production sector in Colombia, accounting for 32.5 percent of output in 1965.[6] Although the fall in agriculture's importance in the national economy accelerated after 1958, there was also a considerable slowdown in manufacturing expansion and a fall in construction activity in these years, in large part because of the limitations on imports and on public investment, limitations brought about by the fall in export earnings and the related inflation.

Although agriculture is not nearly as important in Colombia as it was ten or twenty years ago, over half the Colombian people are still directly dependent on agriculture for their living, and the active rural labor force constitutes perhaps 55 percent of the economically active population.[7] Most of these people are engaged in low-productivity activities on small plots, generally owner-occupied. Although there has been rapid migration to urban areas in recent years—the twelve largest cities alone more than doubled in population from 1951 to 1964—nonagricultural employment opportunities have risen only slowly, in part because of the import-investment problem. Perhaps only about one-fourth of the additions to the urban labor force have been employed productively in recent years. The rest have gone to swell the ranks of the unemployed and the almost-unemployed, especially in the service and artisan industry sectors. Rapid expansion of population, slow growth of agricultural output, an increasing move to the cities, and a severe lack of urban employment opportunities thus characterize the Colombian economy today and would leave Colombia with a very difficult economic situation in the next few decades even if the employment problem were alleviated by a relaxation of the import constraint on manufacturing expansion. Except for a few years in the early fifties when coffee prices

Table 1. Colombia: Supply and use of resources, selected years, 1950–1966 (percentages).

	1950	1954	1958	1960	1962	1964	1966
Supply							
Gross domestic product	81.6	78.8	85.8	85.1	85.4	83.7	83.7
Imports	18.4	21.2	14.2	14.9	14.6	16.3	16.3
Use[a]							
Private consumption	61.9	59.4	62.9	60.8	63.4	64.7	64.2
Government consumption	4.8	5.5	5.0	4.9	5.2	4.9	5.1
Gross fixed investment	15.4	20.1	13.8	15.6	15.4	14.4	13.2
Inventory changes	2.5	−0.1	2.2	2.0	0.7	1.8	3.8
Total domestic uses	84.6	84.9	83.9	83.3	84.7	85.8	86.3
Exports	15.4	15.0	16.1	16.7	15.3	14.2	13.7

Source: Calculated from data at 1958 prices in Banco de la República, Departamento de Investigaciones Económicas, "Cuentas nacionales, 1950–1961" and "Cuentas nacionales, 1960–1966" (both mimeographed; Bogotá, n.d.).
a Figures may not add to 100 percent because of rounding.

were high and capital-goods imports high also, the share of fixed investment in the final supply of goods and services (gross domestic product and imports) has fluctuated within narrow limits around 15 percent since 1950 (Table 1). Imports have provided a more or less constant proportion of final supply, especially since 1956. The composition of imports, however, has continued to alter as a result of import-substitution policies, with the share of capital and intermediate goods continuing to rise in accordance with the long-run trend (Table 2). Private consumption tended to rise over the period, especially after 1960, reaching a peak in 1964. Government consumption, on the other hand, first rose, then fell, then rose slightly again, following much the same pattern as imports and invest-

Table 2. Composition of Colombian imports,[a] 1925–1965 (percentages).

Period	Consumer goods	Machinery and equipment	Raw materials, fuels, and intermediate goods
1925–1929	43.5	32.2	24.3
1930–1938	45.4	21.4	33.2
1939–1945	30.1	21.6	48.3
1946–1953	22.5	36.6	40.9
1954–1960	12.0	38.2	49.8
1961–1965	10.6	39.5	49.9

Sources: For 1925–1953, United Nations, Economic Commission for Latin America, The Economic Development of Colombia (Geneva, 1957), p. 37; for 1954–1960, John Sheahan, "Imports, Investment, and Growth—Colombia," in Gustav F. Papanek, ed., Development Policy—Theory and Practice (Cambridge, Mass.: Harvard University Press, 1968, p. 95; for 1961–1965, unpublished study by Departamento Administrativo de Planeación.

a The classification of imports in the different sources may vary slightly and is in any case inherently arbitrary.

ment, in large part because of the dependence, direct and indirect, of government revenues on the relatively small external sector.

The increase in consumption means that domestic saving tended to fall over most of this period. If the average savings ratio is low and falling, the marginal savings ratio must be even less than the average: a recent study estimated the long-run marginal propensity to save out of disposable income is only 1 percent.[8] This low marginal-savings ratio, combined with a high marginal propensity to import and no growth in export earnings, reflects the fact that Colombia in recent years has not been able to sustain an adequate growth rate for long out of its own resources.

The Economic Problem: Diagnoses and Prescriptions

This dismal picture has stimulated quite different diagnoses and prescriptions for Colombia's economic ills. These analyses fall into three categories: those focusing on the shortage of foreign exchange, those focusing on internal development problems, and those focusing on monetary variables. These different (though related) emphases, each of which can claim some support from respectable sources both within and outside Colombia, lead to quite different policy conclusions in some respects.

The major official document produced in Colombia itself analyzing the economic problem and prescribing a way out of it is the 1962 General Plan of Economic and Social Development. This Plan laid down a series of aggregate growth targets for the 1961–1970 period and suggested, in much less detail, how these targets might be achieved. It soon became painfully clear that no important Plan target for the first part of the period would even come close to being achieved. From 1961 to 1964, for example, gross domestic product grew at 4.4 percent, not the planned 5.6 percent; investment failed to rise from 18 to 24 percent of output as planned; per capita consumption rose 10 rather than 6 percent, and per capita savings fell compared to the planned increase of 100 percent. Sectoral rates of growth were less than targets in all sectors. Public investment amounted to less than two-thirds of Plan levels, with education and health—the only sectors set out in detail in the Plan itself—being especially low.[9]

It is not entirely fair to consider the Plan a failure, however, since neither had it been designed to be implemented nor had any real attempt been made to implement it. The Colombian General (or Ten-Year) Plan was nothing more than a generally well-organized preliminary attempt at quantifying and coordinating possible goals for economic policy. Since the Plan apparently had no real support in the government and did not set forth the policy choices that had to be made to achieve the targeted goals, its failure to have any impact on the decisions of the operating agencies of government is hardly surprising.[10]

The development strategy of the Plan was essentially that the persistent trade gap had to be closed in order to achieve an adequate growth rate. The main instrument used to reduce imports relative to exports was a protective trade policy designed to foster import-substituting industrialization. At the same time the Plan called for a considerable expansion of savings (especially public savings through increased tax revenues) in order to take advantage of the new investment opportunities that would thus be generated.

The crucial importance of closing the foreign-resources gap was also emphasized in a more sophisticated econometric exercise carried out under the auspices of the Agency for International Development in 1964.[11] With AID the proposed solution shifted, however, from an attack on both the savings and foreign-exchange problems to one on the foreign-exchange problem alone. In this analysis the *only* way in which domestic economic policy could increase Colombia's growth rate would be by increasing exports (and thus imports) or by reducing the imports needed to maintain a given rate of growth. Any attempt to save more than the investment level permitted by imports was said to lead not to an increase in the growth rate but to unemployment and under-utilized capacity. Only when increased foreign-exchange permitted more imports of capital goods (and of intermediate materials) could production and investment, according to the 1964 analysis, be expanded.[12]

This conclusion, though certainly true to some extent, is overstated. Simple econometric studies are interesting as examinations of past events but may sometimes be dangerous guides to the future. The interest of economic policy is in changing structural relationships, not in assuming they will prevail forever. No economy is so rigid that there is no scope for altering structural coefficients, and there is in fact a good deal that Colombian economic policy can and should do to raise the rate of growth attainable at any given level of imports: for example, by altering the relative prices of imported and domestic capital goods, thus stimulating more import substitution in the capital-goods sector, or by altering the allocation of investment, or by stimulating the expansion of exports. Furthermore, even increases in domestic saving, by cutting down the consumption of both imports and exportables, would, at least up to a point, free some foreign exchange for investment.[13] In short, while the analysis of the real external gap focuses on a central problem of Colombia's development, it neither precludes domestic economic policy from an important role, nor would the resolution of the foreign-resources shortage solve all the country's development difficulties.

A second approach to Colombia's development problem is to start from two obvious real internal difficulties—low agricultural productivity and rapid population growth. This approach leads to different policy recommendations. A dramatic proposal along these lines which has been widely discussed in Colombia in recent years is the so-called Currie Plan.[14] The central idea of this scheme is to stimulate even more the already large farm-to-city migration and to concentrate the reduced agricultural population on a smaller number of production units which would then be mechanized and automated as much as possible, thus increasing the transferable agricultural surplus. The influx of "excess" agricultural labor (estimated at up to a million workers) into the cities would be absorbed by massive, labor-intensive public works and housing projects of the low import-content, learning-by-doing variety. This investment would in any case be needed to provide cities in which the migrants could live. Once this "big push" was over, in perhaps two or three years, a new market would have been created, production for which would absorb the labor force freed from the public works program. A "breakthrough" from the infamous circle of low productivity – low income – low investment – low productivity to sustained growth would have been made.

The attractiveness of this gigantic mobilization and transformation of society as a conceptualization of a once-and-for-all attack on the internal factors holding back growth in Colombia is obvious. The aim of the Currie Plan is to increase greatly the number of new nonagricultural jobs and to raise the consumption of the poor, not to raise the growth rate of the gross domestic product as such. Its success would seem to depend on (1) the existence of idle capital equipment which can be put to work with the idle labor to increase output without new investment or imports; (2) increased substitution of labor for capital in nonagricultural production; (3) increased availability of foreign exchange (through exports and aid) to sustain the growth process, at least after some brief initial period; (4) in the long run and as a result of increased urbanization, some decline in the rate of population growth; (5) increased saving to hold back inflation (because of the expanded investment); and (6) a disciplined, well-run directing effort and widespread popular response.

This is a formidable list of requirements. An equally formidable list of criticisms of the Currie Plan may be put forward. For example, while it is true that there appears to be much idle industrial capacity in Colombia, most of this capacity exists in the wrong industries (nonwage good) and cannot be of much help in this program. The (inadequate) evidence suggests that it takes at least a generation for urbanization to lower birth rates. The massive increase in saving needed cannot be achieved without major (and most improbable) institutional changes, and in any case more saving, after some point which would soon be reached, needs to be matched by increased availability of foreign exchange in order to carry out the large investment in complementary capital needed to transform the country. Competent observers—and official policy as pursued through Instituto Colombiano de Reforma Agraria (INCORA), the agrarian reform agency, which is attempting to rearrange labor in rural areas rather than encouraging it to leave—disagree completely with Lauchlin Currie's diagnosis of how to solve the agricultural problem, stressing the lack of entrepreneurial capacity in agriculture and the huge investment needs. Finally, the political and administrative apparatus in Colombia is inadequate to the task of managing such a "war economy" for any period of time, and the needed sense of national integration and dedication to the task at hand does not seem to exist as yet.

For my purposes, no final decision on these weighty matters is needed, since a tax policy can be devised which reconciles the major apparent conflicts between the "foreign-resources gap" analysis and Currie's structural analysis. Some aspects of the Currie Plan are almost surely correct and have important implications for economic policy. As argued earlier, structural coefficients—the capital-output ratio, the capital-labor ratio, the import-investment relation—are just not as rigid as an econometric investigation, which necessarily reflects the distortions induced by past policy, would make it appear. Government policy can and should do much not only to increase exports, to reduce import dependence, and to increase saving but also to improve the quality of investment and to alter the choice of technology by private entrepreneurs in both industry and agriculture. Similarly, urbanization expenditures such as those entailed in the Currie Plan, most of which would be incurred anyway in the course of growth, can and should be financed by self-generated saving to a much greater extent than is now true. Also, the pattern of final demand can and should be altered by tax policy to achieve these ends as well as to give more of the benefits of growth to the masses and less in the form of import-intensive luxury consumption to the rich.

In short, though the foreign-exchange constraint is without doubt the dominant proximate factor blocking growth in Colombia today, a great deal can be done along the lines indicated by Currie to alter the structure of the Colombian economy both to loosen this constraint and to achieve a healthier pattern of growth in general. Public finance, like other instruments of development policy, should therefore work on all fronts at once.

The third strand of analysis and policy arising from the experience of the last two decades is the focus on monetary problems, both internal (inflation) and external (balance-of-payments difficulties). It is worth separating out these monetary symptoms from their underlying real causes since it is in fact emphasis on the monetary variables which has dominated Colombian economic policy in recent years. The real trade gap has been tackled by import-substitution policies and by efforts to get more foreign aid; the real internal problems of poverty, poor agriculture, and unemployment have been virtually neglected; the monetary problems, internal and external, have been so pressing (and so emphasized by the international lending agencies) that almost every policy measure taken in the last few years—devaluations, tax increases, credit restrictions, import licensing, tariff changes, price controls— can be traced directly to an attempt to do something about either inflation or the balance of payments.[15]

The main pressure behind budget changes in particular has clearly been the pace of domestic inflation, which has led to budget deficits and still more inflation in a typical vicious circle. Owing to the inelasticity of the revenue system and its cyclical dependence on import availability (see Chapter 2), a recurrent critical need for new taxes and increased rates of old taxes resulted from this process. There was hardly ever any consideration given to the allocative effects of these tax changes. Tax policy was not thought of at all as an instrument for altering relative prices and inducing desired changes in the economic structure, and any such effects taxes may have had were unintended.

Since 1950 the Colombian government has employed an amazing variety of economic policies but employed them almost entirely for the limited purpose of coping with balance-of-payments difficulties and domestic inflation. The recurrence of these problems indicates that the effort was not successful. Other development efforts (conducted mostly through an array of autonomous public agencies and institutions) suffered by contrast. Without disparagement of the very real desirability of curbing inflation and of restoring some degree of equilibrium to the external balance, future fiscal and tax policy in Colombia must take a more active and conscious role in the allocation of resources if the growth rate is to be accelerated, whatever the development strategy followed.

The Distribution of Income

Taxation in a developing country is not only a means of providing public savings and of correcting imperfections in the price system: it is also a major means of effecting any income redistribution thought desirable. The role of taxes in achieving economic equality is sometimes considered as important as their role in achieving economic growth. This question deserves special attention since many see a necessary conflict in the degree to which these two goals can be achieved —a conflict well expressed by W. Arthur Lewis: "The less developed countries have awakened into a century where everybody wishes to ride two horses simultaneously, the horse of economic equality, and the horse of economic development. The U.S.S.R. has found that these two horses will not go in the same direction, and has therefore abandoned one of them. Other less developed countries will have to make their own compromises."[16] The central concern here, of course, is the effect of income redistribution on the level of capital formation.

To appraise the tax structure of any country one must have at least some idea, in quantitative terms, of the distribution of income—preferably both by income classes and by factor shares. This knowledge is particularly important when the government must decide on the distribution of tax increases as is almost certain to be essential in Colombia in the near future.

While information on income distribution is no better in Colombia than in other poor countries, fortunately enough data exist to serve as a first step in the appraisal of the appropriate distributional role of the tax system. The great inequality of income is strikingly evident in the 1961 figures carefully assembled by the Joint Tax Program mission.[17] Table 3 indicates that about 13 percent of income in 1961 went to the top 1 percent of the labor force, 29 percent to the top 5 percent, and 42 percent to the top 10 percent; on the other hand, the poorest 65 percent of the labor force received only 26 percent of total income.

Table 3. Income distribution within the labor force, 1961.

Income class (pesos)	Number of persons (thousands)[a]	Cumulative percentage	Estimated income (millions of pesos)	Cumulative percentage
0– 1,000	555.2	11.06	416.4	1.92
1,000– 2,000	1,463.5	40.22	2,195.2	12.06
2,000– 3,000	1,220.4	64.54	3,051.0	26.16
3,000– 4,000	488.7	74.28	1,710.4	34.06
4,000– 5,000	186.0	77.99	837.0	37.93
5,000– 6,000	158.2	81.14	870.1	41.95
6,000– 7,000	137.0	83.87	890.5	46.06
7,000– 8,000	115.7	86.18	867.8	50.07
8,000– 9,000	106.9	88.31	908.6	54.27
9,000– 10,000	100.6	90.31	955.7	58.69
10,000– 12,000	176.8	93.83	1,944.8	67.68
12,000– 13,000	57.9	94.98	723.8	71.02
13,000– 14,000	40.2	95.78	502.5	73.34
14,000– 15,000	29.5	96.37	427.8	75.32
15,000– 16,000	24.5	96.86	379.8	77.08
16,000– 17,000	19.7	97.25	325.0	78.58
17,000– 18,000	16.5	97.58	288.8	79.91
18,000– 19,000	13.3	97.85	246.0	81.05
19,000– 20,000	11.7	98.08	228.2	82.10
20,000– 22,000	18.7	98.45	392.7	83.91
22,000– 24,000	13.4	98.72	308.2	85.33
24,000– 26,000	10.5	98.93	262.5	86.54
26,000– 28,000	8.2	99.09	221.4	87.56
28,000– 30,000	6.1	99.21	176.9	88.38
30,000– 40,000	17.5	99.56	612.5	91.21
40,000– 50,000	8.0	99.72	360.0	92.87
50,000– 60,000	4.1	99.80	225.5	93.91
60,000–110,000	6.4	99.93	544.0	96.42
110,000–210,000	2.1	99.97	325.5	97.92
210,000–410,000	0.6	99.98	186.0	98.78
410,000–610,000	0.4	99.99	—	—
610,000–810,000	0.1	—	256.0	99.96
	5,018.4		21,640.6[b]	

Source: Milton C. Taylor et al., Fiscal Survey of Colombia (Baltimore: Johns Hopkins Press, 1965), p. 225.

An earlier (and presumably even cruder) study of income distribution in Colombia by a World Bank Mission found that, in 1947, 3 percent of the labor force received 30 percent of the income, while 88 percent received only 57 percent.[18] In 1961, the corresponding figures were about 22 percent and 54 percent, according to Table 3. Fifteen years of substantial, if unsteady, growth in national income thus resulted in little apparent improvement in the relative income position of the mass of the population. Indeed, the poorest group apparently lost some ground at the expense of those just below the highest income brackets—a group which includes at least some of the self-employed and the salaried, and especially the organized industrial workers, all of whose relative positions considerably improved during this period, if we can believe these crude data. (The relative decline of the very well-off may be only apparent, in part because of the probable increase in income tax evasion over this period.) In general, then, the initial picture is one of considerable inequality in income—a situation which, so far as most of the Colombian people are concerned, has not changed much in recent decades.

Another way of viewing the concentration of income in the upper income groups is to consider the high share of nonlabor income in total personal income in Colombia. Although wage and salary income as a proportion of total personal income apparently rose considerably after 1958 (Table 4), it was still relatively lower in Colombia than in a number of comparable Latin American countries and very much lower than in more advanced countries.[19] Furthermore, the rise which has occurred in Colombia in large part reflects not an increase in the labor

a Adjustments were made for: estimated unemployment of 10 percent of total employees (3,887,000, or the total labor force of 5,018,000 minus self-employed of 1,131,000) subtracted from the first five categories; and 225,400 self-employed persons with incomes of less than 10,000 pesos.

b According to the national accounts, the total income of "natural persons" in 1961 was 23.6 billion pesos, not 21.6 billion. Some of the missing income should likely be allocated to the upper-income group, the taxpaying 10 percent, whose income is measured from tax information and hence does not include undeclared income.

share but a change in the composition of the labor force from self-employed to wage and salary workers.

For the 1950–1965 period as a whole, even allowing for increases in employment in the manufacturing and government

Table 4. Types of personal income, 1950–1966 (millions of pesos).

Year	Wages and salaries	Proprietory income of persons[a]	Total income of persons[b]	Employment income as percentage of total
1950	2,662	3,927	6,589	40.4
1951	3,025	4,317	7,342	41.2
1952	3,194	4,756	7,950	40.2
1953	3,627	5,227	8,854	41.0
1954	4,190	6,302	10,492	40.0
1955	4,560	6,190	10,750	42.4
1956	4,957	7,143	12,100	41.0
1957	5,812	8,279	14,091	41.3
1958	6,808	8,722	15,530	41.2
1959	7,857	9,994	17,851	44.0
1960	9,133	11,148	20,281	45.0
1961	10,764	12,798	23,562	45.7
1962	12,611	14,041	26,652	47.3
1963	16,524	16,883	33,407	49.5
1964	19,178	22,393	41,571	46.1
1965	21,752	24,356	46,108	47.2
1966	26,058	29,545	55,603	46.9

Sources: Banco de la República, Departmento de Investigaciones Económicos, "Cuentas nacionales, 1950–1961" and "Cuentas nacionales, 1960–1966."

a Income of family units from property and from unincorporated enterprises. Some return to labor is included in the income of the self-employed, but it is not possible to estimate with any accuracy how important this component is.

b This figure differs from national income by an amount equal to the retained earnings of legal entities, taxes on such entities, and government property and enterprise income, less interest on the public debt.

sectors and the substantial decrease in agricultural employment, it seems clear that the initially better-off industrial wage earners and salaried personnel gained relative to the agricultural workers (including self-employed), who are still by far the largest employment group in the country. This inference accords with the suggestion above that the relative position of some of the "middle" income class has likely improved with the growth (and inflation) of recent years.[20] The factor-share figures similarly support the inference that the small upper-income class has more or less maintained its relative position, the middle-income class as a whole has become a little better off, and the mass of the population, especially the rural population (but probably also the growing urban unemployed), have become relatively worse off than before. (The average absolute standard of living, as noted earlier in this chapter, increased slightly in the postwar period; however, even this is far from certain for those large sectors of the agricultural labor force which did not benefit from good coffee prices in the early 1950's.)[21]

Crude as the data are, we can probably conclude that the present distribution of income in Colombia is very unequal and may well be growing even more so.[22] Given this situation, it is not surprising that many people both within and outside of Colombia have stressed the need, on social and political grounds, to break the control of the upper classes over income, wealth, and political power if the basis for a popular democracy is to be created and more of the benefits of growth distributed to the masses.[23] The merits of this political judgment are not further discussed here, but what perhaps needs emphasis is the economic argument which leads to a similar conclusion in favor of greater equality. That is, it may be argued that a more equal income distribution is not only a desirable goal in itself—a value judgment—but that more equality would also lead to a pattern of production and consumption more conducive to economic growth.[24] A more equal income distribution should, for example, tend to reduce the balance-of-payments pressure resulting from growth, because the consumption of the well-off has a higher foreign-exchange component, direct and indirect, than that of the poor.

The usual economic argument against the desirability of a more equal income distribution in Colombia, as in other developing countries, is that greater income equality means less private saving, and that private saving and investment is likely to continue to be in the future, as it probably has been in the past, in general more socially productive than public saving and investment. This argument is poorly grounded. The high proportion of nonwage income and the present great inequality in Colombia do not mean that private saving has been an important source of capital formation. Table 5 indicates that

Table 5.   Sources of investment finance, 1950–1966 (as percentage of total saving).[a]

Year	Public saving[b]	Foreign saving[c]	Business saving	Household saving	Depreciation
1950	19.5	5.3	6.5	32.4	36.3
1951	28.4	5.6	6.3	16.3	43.4
1952	28.1	6.0	5.8	16.9	43.3
1953	26.0	3.9	6.7	20.3	43.2
1954	27.4	5.9	8.4	21.2	37.1
1955	26.0	11.6	7.2	16.9	38.3
1956	23.6	−5.4	8.8	33.7	39.3
1957	21.2	−4.0	9.2	27.4	46.2
1958	25.5	−1.5	11.7	1.2	63.1
1959	27.5	−8.4	14.0	9.1	57.8
1960	22.8	5.4	14.1	8.9	48.7
1961	16.6	14.4	12.0	12.7	44.3
1962	9.7	11.9	12.3	17.5	48.5
1963	7.7	16.3	15.4	9.4	51.0
1964	20.0	16.3	14.6	4.9	44.2
1965	20.8	2.6	14.3	15.2	47.0
1966	23.2	23.0	13.5	0.8	39.4

Sources: Banco de la República, Departamento de Investigaciones Económicas, "Cuentas nacionales, 1950–1961" and "Cuentas nacionales, 1960–1966."

a Some rows may not sum to 100 percent because of rounding.

b Surplus of revenues over expenditures on current account.

c Surplus (−) or deficit (+) on current account. (In the national accounts as released the signs are reversed for 1950–1961 inclusive.)

private saving net of depreciation has seldom provided as much as one-third of total saving or one-half of the financing for private investment (which has generally been over 80 percent of total investment). Furthermore, as mentioned earlier, the marginal propensity to save out of private disposable income has been extremely low, especially considering the very high proportion of increases in income which appear to have gone to the relatively better-off sections of the community. The result has been a rise in the share of final supply taken by private consumption (see Table 1). An obvious explanation for the strikingly poor performance of private saving in recent years is the increased rate of inflation. Nevertheless, in every year except 1961 and 1962 the public sector exceeded the private sector in average propensity to save out of current income. The apparent high propensity of the Colombian rich to consume suggests that increased taxes on them would have at most a small depressing effect on private saving.

Even if, for example, all of the net household savings of the private sector out of disposable income (an especially unreliable figure) are attributed to the top 3 percent of the labor-force income distribution in 1961, this group would still be saving only about 12 percent of their estimated income, and their consumption would amount to about 20 percent of total private consumption and 15 percent of the gross domestic product. If factor shares are considered, and all personal saving is allocated to nonlabor income, recipients of nonlabor income in 1961–1964 would have consumed over 98 percent of their income (before tax), or an amount equal to 53 percent of total private consumption in those years.[25]

The implication of these rough calculations is that there is substantial room for increasing total public saving in Colombia by cutting down on the personal income and consumption of the rich without serious effects on private saving (most of which is done through corporations). With regard to total saving, the net effect of increased taxation of the upper-income groups would probably be positive, at least as long as the government's marginal propensity to spend on current consumption is less than that of the taxed groups, as has apparently been true throughout the postwar period.

To return to the 1961 income-distribution data (and continuing to assume arbitrarily that the biases from not allowing for taxes and over-allowing for saving offset each other), the estimated consumption of the top 3 percent of the labor force was 4,500 million pesos.* If it were assumed, for example, that the consumption of the 160,000 people in this group were reduced just to the average level of the next lowest income bracket (15,000–16,000 pesos, all of which is assumed to be consumed after taxes), 2,200 million pesos in real resources could be set free for added capital formation and public spending. In view of the probable underestimation of the actual income of this wealthy class on the one hand and the substantial political difficulties of increasing their taxes on the other, perhaps a billion pesos in 1961 might be a more realistic estimate of the possibility of raising additional tax revenue by cutting "luxury" spending. This amount may be compared to total government current revenue of 3.4 billion in 1961, total public saving (defined as the excess of current revenues over current expenditures) of 1.0 billion, and total investment of 6.2 billion (including 0.8 in inventories). On the other hand, the figure is rather small in comparison to the total private domestic income of over 25 billion in 1961 on which the government could theoretically draw for tax revenue.[26]

The conclusion that emerges from this discussion of income distribution in Colombia is that a good part of the additional revenue needed to finance an adequate growth rate can and should come from progressive taxation of personal income and consumption.[27] Some segments of the middle-income groups, notably workers in organized industry, apparently have had the fastest-growing incomes, but the undesirable political implications of increasing taxes on them and the low absolute level of their incomes argue in favor of concentrating on the richest groups as much as possible.

The traditional argument against redistributive tax policy

---

* The value of the Colombian peso in terms of U.S. dollars has varied considerably during the period covered in this book. In 1961 the official rate of exchange was 6.70 pesos per U.S. dollar; in 1963 it was 9.00 pesos; in 1966 the (intermediate) official rate was 13.50 pesos; and by December 1968 the average selling rate in the certificate market was 16.89 pesos to the dollar. For much of this period the official rate substantially overvalued the peso, and the "free" market rate was substantially higher. Comparisons are further complicated by the existence, at different times, of different official exchange rates for oil, for coffee, for capital transactions, and so on.

in poor countries on the grounds that it reduces saving thus has little merit in Colombia, where the public sector appears to be a more efficient saver than the private sector. Reinterpreted to separate out business enterprises from individuals who receive high personal incomes, the conventional reasoning perhaps makes more sense, however, particularly when one considers investment rather than saving. It may well be true, as many in Colombia would contend, that the public sector is a less efficient investor than the private sector. Even so, increased personal taxation of the richer groups in society should not have a particularly adverse effect on private investment, despite the less clear-cut separation of individual and corporate wealth in Colombia than in industrialized countries. (It is true that favoritism to corporate earnings will be reflected in improved asset positions of wealthy individuals, but the effect of this on consumption is unlikely to be important.) Insofar as tax policy is concerned, the key to achieving both growth and redistribution in Colombia lies in proper treatment of the corporate sector. Funds can be transferred from the public to the private sector through either the fiscal or financial mechanisms —for example, by means of tax incentives for self-finance, or through bank credit, or direct government loans. In a country with as developed a financial system as Colombia, there is, conceptually at least, no need for private saving to match private investment and public saving to match public investment. Increased public saving thus need not preclude increased private investment.[28] This argument is developed further in subsequent chapters.

Up to this point, I have suggested that increased taxation of the wealthy and of luxury consumption will have, on balance, desirable economic effects, if properly done. To complete the argument, the effect on income distribution of present government fiscal operations must be considered. One such estimate of tax incidence was made for the Joint Tax Program study cited earlier and enters into the figures set forth in Table 6. An alternative estimate, based on slightly different assumptions as to the allocation of the different taxes, is presented in the same table. The general picture of a very mildly progressive,

almost proportional tax system resulting from these calculations would not be substantially changed by any reasonable
alternative assumptions of tax incidence.[29] Increased taxation
of the upper-income groups will thus not add to an "already
crushing tax burden," as has sometimes been claimed in
Colombia.

Table 6. The incidence of Colombian taxes, 1961 (millions of
pesos).

Income quartile (percentage)	Income[a]	Taxes[a]	Tax burden[b] (percentage)	Taxes[c]	Tax burden[d] (percentage)
0– 25	1,089	119	10.9	110	10.1
26– 50	2,749	257	9.4	279	10.2
51– 75	3,697	409	11.1	408	11.1
76–100	14,105	1,785	12.7	1,693	12.0

Source: Milton C. Taylor et al., Fiscal Survey of Colombia.
a Taylor Report, p. 226.
b Taxes divided by income.
c Calculated on the basis of an alternative allocation of taxes by income
quartiles suggested in Richard A. Musgrave, "Estimating the Distribution of
the Tax Burden," in Joint Tax Program, Problems of Tax Administration in
Latin America (Baltimore: published for the Joint Tax Program by the Johns
Hopkins Press, 1965), p. 58, and the information in the Taylor Report, pp.
224–227. The principal difference in the allocation formulas is that Musgrave
assumes the entire company tax is paid by the fourth quartile, while Taylor
assumes that 50 percent of it is shifted forward as a consumption tax; in addition, the distribution of consumption taxes in Musgrave is more regressive.
d The alternative allocation of taxes divided by the income figures in the
first column. While avoiding the awkward regressivity of the second quartile
in the Taylor distribution, the allocation formula used to derive this estimate
is probably not as satisfactory in the two respects noted in the previous note,
so the estimate in the third column should be considered more reliable, though
both are inherently arbitrary.

It is true that most present taxes—69 percent in 1963—are
paid by the top income quartile, but in relative terms the
remaining tax capacity, the present tax effort, and the probable
tax "sacrifice" involved in additional measures all point to still
more taxes on the better-off as the preferred source of the

needed additional revenues. Tax effort is indicated by the "burden" calculations in Table 6, and tax capacity by the previous discussion of high "inessential" consumption—the "surplus" that can be taxed away without disadvantage to economic incentives. Tax "sacrifice" is a concept which relates the share of income taken in taxes to the level of per capita income. While this concept depends on certain notions of utility not strictly acceptable in modern welfare economics, if any positive weight is attributed to progressivity at all (that is, to the diminishing marginal utility of money), the upper-income quartile in Colombia is clearly the most "undertaxed" of all, with a sacrifice index of 13 compared to 40, 48, and 140 for the three lower quartiles (in order).[30]

In addition, there does not appear to be any significant redistribution through the expenditure side of the fiscal system either, though it is probably to expenditures rather than taxes that one would have to look if one took increased income equality in itself as a goal of policy—something which I am explicitly not doing.[31]

Recent tax changes—especially the introduction of a general sales tax in 1965—have not moved in the direction indicated by this analysis, in part apparently because of exaggerated fears of the effects that higher direct personal taxes might have on economic incentives and savings.[32] Tax policy, like any government policy, will never satisfy everyone since it must serve conflicting objectives to which different individuals will attach different weights. My contention here is that worries about increased progressive taxation in Colombia reducing savings (and to a lesser extent incentives) are not supported by the available data. Such worries can therefore be largely ignored in selecting the set of tax policies most appropriate for development (although Chapter 3 softens this conclusion so far as business taxation is concerned). It further follows from this analysis that increased personal income inequality serves no useful purpose in promoting growth in Colombia at present and should be properly discouraged so far as possible (which is not very far, judging from experience in other countries) by the fiscal system. If one accepts greater equality as a desirable goal in and of itself, the case for progressive taxation becomes stronger. If, on the other hand, one values income *in*equality for itself, or for some intangible benefits not mentioned in this discussion, the case for progressive taxation made here will no doubt remain unconvincing.

Viewing the 1951–1960 period in retrospect, Colombia's planners in 1962 anticipated a considerably better performance from the public sector in the early 1960's than in the previous decade. Their expectations were disappointed for four interrelated reasons: (1) the economy failed to grow as fast as anticipated; (2) the rate of inflation accelerated; (3) certain tax "reforms" which were carried out reduced government revenues, while other fiscal changes that had been expected failed to materialize; and (4) aid levels were lower than expected, in part because of the shortfall of domestic revenues.

The basic Plan assumption on the public sector was that public saving and investment would increase considerably, with a much faster increase in current revenues than in current expenditures. This assumption was based on projecting historical (1950–1959) growth rates for current expenditures (except education and health), despite the higher projected growth rate of national income in the Plan period. The elasticity of public expenditure with respect to national income changes was thus implicitly assumed to be less than one (0.8 compared to an estimated actual elasticity of 1.2). Similarly, the revenue estimates were inflated by including possible rate increases in the projections.[1] Both parts of this optimistic forecast were quickly disproved. The expected 50 percent real increase in government investment in 1961–1965 and the equally substantial increase in public saving hoped for failed of achievement by about one-third. Instead of rising, investment declined as a share of public expenditures (as shown in Table 7).

This great divergence between plan and reality can be understood in two ways: as a result of the difficult economic circumstances of the early 1960's, or as an example of poor planning. Both interpretations seem correct. What the Plan really assumed was that the rate of change in fiscal policies and administration would remain the same in the future as in the past. Any estimate of the future based primarily on an examination of the past assumes both future and past are in some sense "normal." This assumption is invalid when structural changes are contemplated, as they must be in a development plan. Past data do provide the only available basis for projections, but they must be used correctly—that is, as a guide in specifying structural relationships, not as a basis in themselves

Table 7. Comparison between actual and projected public investment and savings, 1962–1965 (millions of 1961 pesos).[a]

	1962	1963	1964	1965
Savings[b]				
1962 mission recommendations[c]	1668	1932	2151	2432
Actual	872	1226	1311	1157
Difference	−796	−706	−840	−1275
Difference as percent of recommendations	− 48	− 36	− 39	− 52
Investment				
1962 mission recommendations[c]	2327	2863	3330	3454
Actual	2335	2141	1880	1844
Difference	+ 8	−722	−1450	−1610
Difference as percent of recommendations	—	− 25	− 44	− 47

Sources: 1962 projections from International Bank for Reconstruction and Development (IBRD), Economic Report WH-119a (1962), table 14; actual savings and investment from IBRD, Economic Report WH-172a (1967), vol. II, table I-3.

[a] Deflated by official cost-of-living index for employees, adjusted to 1961 base.
[b] Defined as current account surplus net of intra-public-sector transfers.
[c] Slightly different from original Plan estimates but of the same order of magnitude.

for estimating the future. This methodological weakness vitiated virtually all of the painstaking data collection underlying the Plan's public-sector projections.

Since the feasibility of the entire Plan pivoted on the public sector and aid assumptions—and aid turned out to depend in many instances on the availability of complementary public-sector financing for projects—it is perhaps surprising that the

Plan analysis apparently escaped close scrutiny either within Colombia or from the international lending agencies. In part, perhaps, the diffidence of the foreign reviewing groups (the World Bank and the Committee of Nine) arose from the fact that, in 1962, Colombia was considered "the showcase of the Alliance," the first country to come up with a comprehensive national plan as called for in the recently signed Charter of Punta del Este. Whatever the reason, no service was done to Colombia or the Alliance for Progress by this easy acceptance of a plan based on unrealizable expectations.[2] It may be arguable whether or not *any* effort at planning could have been successful in the difficult political and economic conditions of Colombia in the early 1960's; it is beyond dispute that the complete "failure" of the unrealistic 1962 plan either to allocate resources more efficiently or to introduce innovations in ideas and techniques damaged severely the image and potential of planning in Colombia.

The performance of the public sector in Colombia in recent years has thus not been good, judged by the standard set in the Plan or by any other. This conclusion emerges clearly from the data. Since 1960, the government has had a hard time holding its own in real terms in spending on either investment or consumption. Although government consumption has remained around 7 percent of total consumption and government investment has accounted for 15 to 20 percent of total investment in most recent years, this performance hardly accords with what one would expect in a country undertaking a major public development effort. As a saver, too, government has performed erratically. On the average the savings performance of government in the early sixties was markedly worse than in the 1950's (and about the same as before the war). In particular, the severe fiscal crisis of 1961–1963 shows up clearly in Table 8: at the very moment when investment efforts were increased in accordance with the Plan, the ability of the public sector to finance its investment in a noninflationary way fell sharply. The main explanations for this poor performance are, as shown in the next section, the relative unresponsiveness of government revenues to the inflation characterizing the period and the considerable responsiveness of revenues (and invest-ment) to the foreign-trade cycle.

"Government" in the preceding paragraph is used, as in the national accounts, to encompass three levels of government: the nation, the departments, and the municipalities. Impor-

Table 8. Public-sector saving and investment, 1950–1966.

Year	Public saving[a] as percent of total saving	Public saving as percent of gross domestic product	Public saving as percent of public investment	Public investment as percent of total investment
1950	19.5	3.3	174	11.2
1951	28.4	4.3	180	15.7
1952	28.1	4.3	197	14.2
1953	26.0	4.0	147	17.6
1954	27.4	4.6	164	10.7
1955	26.0	4.7	119	21.8
1956	23.6	4.3	115	20.6
1957	21.2	4.2	134	15.8
1958	25.5	4.8	157	16.2
1959	27.5	5.2	163	16.9
1960	22.8	4.7	154	14.8
1961	16.6	3.5	90	18.3
1962	9.7	1.9	48	20.4
1963	7.7	1.4	45	17.4
1964	20.0	3.7	124	16.2
1965	20.8	3.7	118	17.6
1966	23.2	4.8	113	20.5

Sources: Banco de la República, Departmento de Investigaciones Económicas, "Cuentas nacionales, 1950-1961" and "Cuentas nationales, 1960-1966."
[a] Surplus of revenues over expenditures on current account.

tant as the two subnational levels of government are in Colom-bia, however, in some ways they are dwarfed by a fourth "level," the many and various national decentralized agencies. As Table 9 indicates, the national government itself plays in some senses a relatively minor role in total public-sector activi-ties. Although it supplied well over half the tax revenue and saving of the public sector, the central government accounted in 1963 for less than one-third of total "public" spending on either consumption or investment. The decentralized organizations are particularly important in direct investment, much of which is financed by national budget transfers. Even the departments and municipalities (including municipal enterprises) combined spent more in 1963 than the national govern-

Table 9. The structure of the public sector, 1963[a] (millions of current pesos).

	Total public sector	National government	Decentralized agencies	Departments	Municipalities
Current revenues	7,684	3,042	2,478	991	1,173
Taxes	(4,632)	(2,815)	(370)	(969)	(478)
Other	(3,052)	(227)	(2,108)	(22)	(695)
Current expenditures	5,454	1,627	2,187	889	751
Saving[b]	2,230	1,415	291	102	422
Capital expenditures	3,750	1,105	1,495	323	827
Investment	(2,421)	(774)	(930)	(195)	(522)
Other	(1,329)	(331)	(565)	(128)	(305)
Capital income	2,366	953	920	70	423

Sources: Various studies (mostly unpublished) by Dirección Nacional del Presupuesto, Contraloría General, Banco de la República, Planeación, and International Monetary Fund staff.

a Excludes intrasector payments and receipts. See Appendix A for an indication of the problems in this netting operation. Although the data in this table are rather old, there appear to have been no changes in 1964 and 1965 which would substantially affect the text discussion, though in 1966 the relative importance of the central government probably increased owing to the marked rise in national taxes in that year.

b Surplus on current account net of intra-public-sector transfers.

ment. Since 1961 the big cities have been especially important spenders and investors, in large part because of the heavy capital expenditure carried out by public utilities. To sum up, in 1963 the national government raised 7.1 percent of the gross domestic product in current revenues (mostly taxes) but spent only 6.4 percent—out of a total of 21.5 percent of the national income which at some point passed through the hands of some agency labeled here as "public."[3] Nevertheless, either directly through intrasector transfers or indirectly through decisions on utility rates and the like, it is definitely the national government which determines the level and structure of public saving and investment in Colombia for the most part. In view of the importance of the large urban areas in particular and of the subnational governments in general in Colombia, I shall argue in Chapter 5 that they ought to do a lot more to finance their own expenditures than has been true in the past, thus removing some of the pressure from central-government revenues. However, the general conclusion remains that the national government, despite its poor performance in some recent years, will almost certainly continue to be in the future, as it has been in the past, the major source of public saving and hence of tax effort in Colombia. What is done at the lower levels of government affects only the size of the needed tax reform at the central-government level, not its nature.

In real terms transfer payments (outside the public sector), mainly wage supplements and subsidies to public employees, and interest on the public debt constituted the fastest growing sectors of total public expenditure after 1960. Salaries and wages and purchases of goods and services increased less rapidly, and investment expenditures hardly at all. Total real public-sector expenditures increased only slightly after 1961, in large part because of the substantial cutback in investment in 1962 and 1963. Total real central-government investment in all categories, for instance, fell more or less steadily throughout the 1961–1965 period (see Table 10). Although central-government current expenditures in real terms rose substantially in this period, real wages in the public sector may have fallen slightly in recent years.[4]

Both current and investment expenditures show the effect of arbitrary policy cuts in response to downswings of the foreign-trade cycle: across-the-board cuts of current expenditures were attempted in 1957, 1963, and 1965, and the pattern of holding back investment established in 1956–1958 was repeated in 1962–1965. In 1965, total central-government expenditure was barely at its 1961 level in real terms, and as a proportion of gross domestic product it fell from 9.8 percent

Table 10.   Central-government investment expenditures, 1961–
1965 (millions of 1958 pesos).[a]

Year	General services	Economic services	Social services	Communal services	Total investment
1961	24.7	675.6	182.5	114.6	997.4
1962	6.0	559.4	96.3	56.8	718.5
1963	6.3	452.7	70.1	48.5	577.6
1964	4.8	466.2	109.4	49.1	629.5
1965	3.2	470.1	57.2	36.5	567.0

Source: Contraloría General de la República, Informe financiero de 1965,
p. 51.
  [a] Deflated by public-construction index used in the national accounts.

in 1961 to 8.6 percent in 1965. A main cause of the fiscal crisis
of the early 1960's and of the resulting cuts in investment and
the development effort was the fall in national revenues. The
ability of the Colombian public sector to play a more sustained
and constructive role in development in the future thus depends very much on an improved revenue performance in the
face of the continuing difficulties caused by inflation and
external instability.

Public-Sector Performance: Gaps and Cycles

A revenue structure is elastic if its yield increases (or de-
creases) more than proportionately in response to a given increase (or decrease) in national income. For some purposes we
are interested in the "automatic" or "structural" elasticity of
a tax system, the change in tax yield that can be expected from
a change in national income without changing the tax structure. This *ex ante* elasticity measures the change in tax yields
resulting from changes in tax base alone. A major reason for
interest in the elasticity of the tax system in Colombia, however, is to find out the extent to which taxes contribute to
mobilizing resources as the economy develops. For this purpose, it is the "historical" or *ex post* elasticity that is of most
interest, even though this measure includes the effects of
changes in both tax rates and the tax base. The *ex post* elas-

ticity of the tax system shows what actually happened, not what would have happened to tax yields had no changes been made in tax policy. Thus it provides some indication of the extent to which policy changes were feasible in the past and perhaps, if the same degree of policy change can be expected in the future, some guide to probable future yields without special efforts. Similar *ex post* and *ex ante* elasticity calculations may be made for current expenditures, indicating the degree to which the other proximate determinant of public saving responds to national income changes.

It has not proved feasible to calculate the *ex ante* elasticities of central-government current revenues and expenditures for this study. The *ex post* elasticities, however, appear to have been about 1.1 for current revenues and 1.2 for current expenditures in 1951–1964 (in current prices), with a 1 percent increase in the gross domestic product being accompanied by a 1.1 percent rise in current revenues and a 1.2 percent rise in current expenditures on the average. In 1960–1964, when inflation was particularly marked, the *ex post* arc elasticity of total government-sector current revenues with respect to changes in the gross domestic product was only 0.7 in real terms. While there are considerable year-to-year variations in the annual elasticity coefficients for both revenues and expenditures (in part because of the effects of the trade cycle discussed below), the general picture is one of a revenue system barely elastic enough to maintain the share of revenues in national income, with most of the annual coefficients being 1 or less and the average close to 1 at all levels of government. Current expenditures, on the other hand, appear decidedly more responsive to changes in money national income than are current revenues. This difference became especially marked in the early 1960's.[5] One would expect the structural elasticity of public expenditure to be higher than its *ex post* elasticity (which reflects the effects of policy cuts) and the structural elasticity of the revenue system to be lower than its *ex post* value (which reflects tax policy changes), so that the "structural" expenditure-revenue gap would be larger than that revealed in the historic data.[6]

Two factors appear to explain the national fiscal crisis of the early 1960's. The first is the combination of accelerated inflation and sluggish response of the fiscal system to the increase in money national income. The second consists of the behavior of the foreign sector in conjunction with the effects of the fiscal policy measures taken in response to this behavior.

The extent to which the revenue crisis was due to the speedup in the pace of inflation—prices more than doubled from 1960 to 1966—may be seen in Table 11. Although total revenues in real terms fell in only one year (1962), current

Table 11. Real growth of national revenues, 1958–1965 (millions of 1958 pesos).[a]

Year	Total revenues	Current revenues	Income tax[b]	Customs	Percent change in income tax
1958	1782	1637	715	196	—
1959	1821	1676	768	320	7.4
1960	1966	1692	819	454	6.6
1961	2220	1492	709	385	−13.4
1962	1909	1332	652	327	− 8.0
1963	1995	1616	628	289	− 3.7
1964	2318	1893	800	304	27.4
1965	2442	1849	792	279	− 1.0

Source: Contraloría General de la República, Informe financiero de 1965, pp. 8, 10.

a Deflated by a weighted government-expenditure index, the appropriate deflector when we wish to consider what the government can purchase rather than what it takes away from the private sector.

b Excludes special taxes and surcharges (which were especially important in 1963-1965).

revenues declined in three (1961, 1962, and 1965), and income-tax revenues fell in four out of the seven years, as did customs revenues. Initially, income-tax revenues declined in part because of the ill-timed 1960 "reform" in which expensive exemptions were legislated at a cyclical peak in foreign-trade taxes, but more important was the effect of the one-year lag in income-tax collections (1964 income tax, for example, being based on 1963 income). Only when the rate of inflation slowed down in 1964 (and the effects of the 1960 reform had worked themselves out) did income-tax collections again begin to approach their 1960 level in real terms. A one-year lag in assessment means that, so long as the rate of inflation is increasing, the real yield of the income tax will fall, and when the inflation slows down it will rise, other things being equal. The Colombian income tax fulfilled these expectations completely. Colombia's relatively heavy reliance on nominally progressive direct taxes, which should theoretically be elastic, has thus led in practice to an inelastic performance owing to the lagged collection system. (It also appears that there may have been increasing tax avoidance and evasion as people rose up the rate structure with inflation, but there is no firm evidence on this point.)

In a sense the present Colombian fiscal situation is the opposite of that prevailing in countries like the United States or Japan, where the built-in flexibility of the tax system is such that revenues tend automatically to increase as a proportion of national income as output increases. In Colombia, because of the low income-elasticity of the tax system, failure to raise taxes or reduce expenditures means that every year public-sector finances will increase inflationary pressure and, unless offset, lead to an even bigger deficit the following year. The present revenue system therefore seems incapable of financing for a sustained period even a constant share of public expenditures in national income without recourse to deficit financing or new taxes, let alone the increasing share that would almost certainly be called for in any development plan. Colombia is not a country which can afford to have a tax structure with an *ex ante* elasticity less than 1, especially when the structural elasticity of expenditures is greater than 1.

An *ex ante* expenditure-revenue gap is not conducive to the stable long-run growth of the public sector or of the economy. Given the basic import constraint on expanding domestic output, larger budget deficits are almost certain to generate more inflation rather than more employment even in a situation of widely underutilized domestic resources. Is there no way around the problem? Perhaps the deficits can be so structured as to increase the availability of imports. While not impossible conceptually (see the discussion of export subsidization in Chapter 4) this result is unlikely in practice. More probable is a lifting of the import constraint through increased foreign aid received, in part, as a reward for better budget performance, that is, smaller deficits. In addition, my judgment would be that Colombian political tolerance for inflation and government deficits is, despite the experience of recent years, still not great—certainly not of the order characteristic of Chile or Brazil—and that increased inflation would have a costly and undesirable effect on the allocation of resources (especially if exchange-rate adjustments lagged and imported capital goods became relatively cheaper). If continued large deficits are undesirable and real public expenditures are not to decline, then tax revenues must be increased and the new higher level maintained. The most important tax reform needed in Colombia is to improve the *ex ante* elasticity of the national tax system in order to avoid the recurrent strains a constant need for new revenue imposes on the country's limited political capacity and stability.

This basic inelasticity of the tax system has never received the attention it deserves in Colombia, largely because it has been obscured by movements exogenous to the country's economy. The direct dependence of important central-government revenues on movements in the external sector is shown in Table 12. When foreign exchange is available, whether from higher coffee prices or foreign aid, imports are expanded and the yield of import taxes rises. Similarly, after a balance-of-payments crisis has been resolved by a devaluation, as at the end of 1962 and 1965, foreign-trade revenues increase greatly (in part because of the greater foreign exchange made available as a result of the devaluation), only to decline again until the next crisis, brought on as the exchange rate becomes overvalued and the real value of foreign-trade taxes falls.[7]

In addition to the direct dependence of central-government revenues on foreign-trade taxes, many other national taxes depend directly or indirectly on foreign trade. For example, about one-third of the base of the sales tax is imports. About one-half of income taxes are paid by corporations, many of which depend on imports for raw materials and spare parts necessary for operation. Thus, any foreign-exchange crisis that chokes off imports tends directly to reduce the yield of these two major taxes. (The collection lag in the case of the income tax might in theory act to smooth out this cycle; but in prac-

Table 12. Foreign-trade tax receipts, 1960–1966 (millions of pesos).

Year	Import taxes[a]	Export taxes[b]	Total	Index	Index in real terms[c]
1960	616.6	2.4	619.0	100	100
1961	616.8	9.6	626.4	101	96
1962	548.0	1.6	549.6	89	80
1963	599.3	470.1	1,069.4	173	124
1964	693.0	627.4	1,320.4	213	130
1965	701.0	346.0	1,047.0	169	95
1966	1,971.8	347.1	2,318.9	375	180

Sources: Contraloría General, Informes financieros, various dates. (The 1966 data are provisional.)

a Customs duties and some small import taxes.

b After 1963, mainly exchange differential and, in 1966, exchange profits, arising from the treatment of coffee exports. See also Appendix B on coffee tax policy.

c Deflated by the average annual cost-of-living index for employers. (It does not make much difference which index is used since they all moved similarly.)

tice it appears the inflation effect and the backlash effects of credit squeezes on tax collections—discussed later—prevent it from fulfilling this role.) Furthermore, since domestic income and expenditure in Colombia still depend on the external sector to a large extent, almost all taxes are affected indirectly by external movements. The yield of most central-government taxes is also affected (unfavorably) by inflation, and the rate of inflation in Colombia appears to be closely related to the country's foreign-exchange situation, with large devaluations, such as those in 1962 and 1965, being considered by some observers to be important causes of inflation, given the Colombian wage-bargaining and price-setting structure.

The marked influence of this foreign-trade cycle on revenues has led to a great many tax-policy changes in recent years, but few of these changes have done much to improve the long-run elasticity of the tax system, on the one hand, or to insulate government activity or the economy from the temporary aberrations of coffee prices, on the other. With the notable exception of the general sales tax introduced in 1965, most revenue crises have been met by temporary resources such as income-tax surcharges (in 1963–1965) and the compulsory placement of government debt.

A look into the history of the latter type of measure suggests that such expedients are inadequate. Forced debt placement goes back at least to 1940 and was employed in 1941, 1943, 1952, 1961, and 1965. All forced loans—even with (true) interest of 10–15 percent, as in Colombia—contain a tax element, which may be defined as the difference between the interest paid and that which would have to be paid to float a loan with the same effect on consumption spending. The size of this tax element will depend on time preference and the expectation of inflation. While it may occasionally be politically expedient to resort to forced loans rather than taxes, experience in most countries indicates that people are well aware of the tax element. If the idea behind the loan is that it will somehow have less adverse incentive effects (for example, because the taxpayer, suffering from a debt illusion, considers it to be not a diminution in his wealth but only a change in form), it is hard to see why the failure of a loan to deter spending as much as a tax should be considered an argument for the loan in Colombia. My assumption throughout this book is that there is no real possibility of substantial voluntary debt placement in Colombia—unless perhaps some form of indexing is introduced—and that even if the government could borrow instead of tax, there is still a strong case in favor of taxing, in part because of the likelihood (given the narrow Colombian capital market) that increased public borrowing will cut private investment instead of private consumption. The tendency to resort so often to borrowing in Colombia appears to reflect not only political weakness but also the fact that far too much weight is given to the alleged adverse incentive effects of outright taxes.

Temporary relief from fiscal pressure afforded by devaluation and an upswing of the foreign trade cycle—as in 1966–67, for example—has usually meant not better decisions on long-term fiscal planning but fewer decisions. Sometimes these decisions have even complicated the long-run task, notably in 1960 when the extensive exemptions and reductions in effective rates granted at the peak of the import cycle made the fiscal situation worse than it would have been in subsequent years. More generally, the effect of the cycle is to loosen temporarily the revenue constraint on expenditure while avoiding any need to alter fundamental views on the tolerable level of taxation. If real expenditure levels are permitted to rise in these circumstances, as is all too likely, the long-run fiscal problem is accentuated. Since the same external movements that loosen the revenue constraint loosen the import constraint on public investment, investment is especially likely to move to higher levels at cyclical peaks and to have to be cut back sharply later because of limitations on both revenues and imports.

If this analysis is correct, the only way to hold public investment at a high, steady level, as would presumably be needed in a sustained development effort is (given the limited scope for noninflationary deficit financing and the assumed undesirability of inflation) by holding real revenues (and saving) steady in the face of the trade cycle.[8] This conclusion is not in contradiction to the recommendation that the money-income elasticity of the revenue system should be increased; both are facets of the same problem.

The Colombian revenue system has in the past managed to generate a substantial surplus in the years of cyclical import peaks (1954, 1960, and 1966). While it would be undesirable to further accentuate the direct dependence of revenues on the trade cycle, this in itself was probably a good result, particularly since the increased imports accompanying the revenue surplus were on balance expansionary (permitting the complementary utilization of unemployed domestic resources) rather than deflationary in impact. The undesirable feature of past experience which should be avoided in the future was the overexpansion of public expenditure (including investment) in these peak years beyond levels that could be sustained in bad years. Related to this overexpansion was a tendency to cut taxes in the peak years. Although it is often a nice question whether the country benefits more from immediate use of foreign-exchange reserves or from a more stable flow of imports over time, on balance more stability appears better, given the drastic domestic effects on employment and output of fits and starts in the flow of imported inputs. The windfall increases in income from upswings in the trade cycle should continue to be sopped up to a large extent through the revenue system (see Appendix B), but these revenues should not automatically lead to increased expenditures on import-intensive investment as has been true in the past; nor should they be, in effect, given to the private sector through tax concessions which adversely affect the long-run structural elasticity of the revenue system in the face of inflation.

The degree of restraint and control demanded of the Colombian government in the face of its apparent cyclical and long-term problems is considerable. Nevertheless, more can be done on all these fronts, once the problems are more clearly understood, than has yet been done. Certainly, the recent shift in the national tax structure away from the income tax toward taxes on foreign trade—up from 32 percent of national government revenues in 1961 to 36 percent in 1966—is neither a long-term solution to any problem nor a particularly desirable move in itself. In a longer perspective the most noticeable change in the tax structure over the 1951–1966 period is the increase in the importance of internal indirect taxes, but the continued importance of foreign trade taxes and the *decline* in the share of taxes on income and wealth are also striking (see Table 13). In part the large proportion of taxes coming from foreign trade in 1966 reflects a high point of the devaluation-inflation-import cycle. But 1956 was also a "good" year in these respects, and the 1956–1966 change is even more marked than that from 1951 to 1966. The implication of Table 13 is that tax policy has, if anything, been moving away from the stress on effective progressive personal taxes suggested earlier in this study and toward greater dependence on taxes more directly responsive to swings in the foreign-trade cycle.

In 1957, the Economic Commission for Latin America, basing itself on an examination of fiscal data up to 1953, concluded that "in Colombia the government budget has constituted a very effective means of channelling part of gross income towards savings."[9] This optimism, which influenced the General Plan, appears to have been unfounded. It is now clear that the great expansion of government revenues in 1950–1956, the stabilization of 1957–1958, and the cautious ex-

Table 13. Evolution of the Colombian national tax structure, selected years, 1951–1966 (percentages).

	1951[a]	1956	1961	1966
Taxes on income and wealth	43.3	53.1	51.8	41.7
Taxes on foreign trade	34.7	32.6	31.6	35.9
Internal indirect taxes	9.6	7.4	6.9	17.8
Other current revenues (nontax)	12.3	6.9	9.7	4.6
Total current revenue as percent of GDP	7.5	7.6	7.3	8.3

Sources: Fiscal data from *Boletín de la dirección nacional del presupuesto*, no. 53 (1966), and Contraloría General, *Informe financiero de 1966* (provisional); GDP from Banco de la República, "Cuentas nacionales," various dates.
[a] Because of rounding, column does not total to 100 percent.

pansion of 1959–1960 (in part financed by higher tariffs) all closely followed movements in the external sector. The fact that these movements roughly coincided with important political changes in Colombia was, according to my interpretation, purely accidental, although this coincidence undoubtedly obscured perception of the cycle in Colombia itself. The essential difference between the early 1960's and the early 1950's was that the attempt to expand government spending in the later period—planned public investment increased 50 percent in one year (1962), for example—was not sustained by an increase in coffee prices. Since the fiscal system remained basically the same, the attempt to increase investment in fact resulted in a decline in real investment and in the continual fiscal and payments crises which have marked recent years.

Although the relationships between the various layers of public activity are complex, and no accurate statistical picture of their total operations exists, it is safe to conclude that in recent years the savings of the national government have been shrinking at the same time as they have been drawn on to an increasing extent for expenditures elsewhere in the public sector (owing to the markedly greater elasticity of expenditures than of revenues at the departmental and municipal levels of government). Financial and political tensions at the center have greatly increased as a result of this process. The low income elasticity of the tax system has made it necessary again and again to search in an *ad hoc* fashion for new revenue sources simply to maintain the present low levels of public saving and investment. Even so, both current and capital expenditures have had to be held down in order to prevent even worse fiscal problems in the face of political resistance to additional taxation. When new taxes could be obtained they were usually only temporary; the constant fiscal strife between 1961 and 1963, for example, barely managed to reverse the decline in real revenues. Similar problems recurred in 1965 and 1966. The basic problem of low revenue elasticity was obscured, and at times accentuated, by the effects of the marked trade cycle on government revenues and expenditures. Without improved elasticity and some sort of stabilization policy to cope with the external problem, there is little hope of the government's fulfilling its important role as saver or of carrying out a sustained public-sector development effort.

Growth, Stability, and the Budget

The principal subject of this book is the reform of tax structure. Few changes in tax structure are so desirable in and for themselves, however, that they can be recommended for any country without careful attention to that country's peculiar economic, political, and administrative setting.

Traditionally, the main contribution that aggregate tax

policy can make to economic growth in any country is to provide savings sufficient to pay in a noninflationary way for the level of investment needed to achieve the desired rate of growth. The appropriate level of taxation will therefore be higher, the higher the needed investment (which in turn depends on the target growth rate and the realized incremental capital-output ratio), the higher government consumption spending, and the lower private (household and business) and foreign saving. This simple national-accounts formulation is employed here to make a useful first approximation of the appropriate aggregate task for the Colombian revenue system in future years.

Government revenues must equal total planned investment *plus* government consumption, *minus* planned private savings *minus* net imports (foreign savings), if the level of investment needed to maintain some rate of growth of income is to be achieved without inflation.[10] To estimate the revenue required to attain a given growth rate without inflation, information on the following variables is needed: the assumed growth rate, the aggregate marginal capital-output ratio, the level of government consumption and of net imports, and the marginal propensity within the private sector to consume out of disposable income.

Although the act is heroic, to say the least, one may make assumptions about the values of these variables—for example, that the marginal capital-output ratio is 4.8, that the marginal propensity to consume is 1.0, that government consumption is 8.0 percent of gross domestic product, and that net imports in 1970 will be the same absolute amount as in 1964. Then one can estimate that the "required" level of revenues in 1970, if the GDP grows at 4.5 percent per annum from 1964, will be 11.6 percent of GDP. At a growth rate of 5.5 percent, the "required" level of noninflationary revenues will be 14.2 percent.[11] If the net imports that Colombia can finance (mainly through foreign aid), instead of remaining constant in absolute terms as assumed in these calculations, declined to its average 1960–1964 level, the "required" level of revenues would rise slightly. The greater the ability of Colombia to obtain foreign savings, the less the need in this model for public savings to avoid inflation. If the 1962 Plan's optimistic expectations of a considerable net export surplus by 1970 were to be realized —which is most unlikely—the required revenues would need to be much higher. Similarly, if the target growth rate were 6 percent, as has been announced by the government which took office in 1966, or 7 to 8 percent, as might be needed to prevent increasing open urban unemployment, the required revenues would also be higher. The results are equally sensitive to changes in other assumptions, particularly to changes in the marginal propensity to consume. Nevertheless, the substantial aggregate task before the Colombian revenue system seems clear from any reasonable calculations. This conclusion stands even if we relax the strict no-inflation requirement and permit prices to rise 5 or 6 percent a year (still substantially below recent experience).

Judging from the experience of the early 1960's, however, Colombia would be fortunate if revenues managed to stay over a sustained period at their recent average level of around 9 to 10 per cent of GDP, let alone increase to the estimated requirements. Admittedly, these were years of considerable economic difficulties, but they were also years of constant attempts to increase taxes and of numerous substantial new levies. Despite these efforts, the arc elasticity of government current revenues with respect to changes in GDP in 1960–1964 was only 0.7 in real terms, largely because of the marked inflation characterizing these years. If this poor performance were projected to 1970, revenues would be only 8.7 percent and 9.3 percent of GDP at growth rates of 4.5 percent and 5.5 percent respectively, compared with the "required" ratios of 11.6 percent and 14.2 percent.

These same estimates may be viewed in a slightly different way in terms of the propensity to tax. To satisfy the revenue requirements estimated above—an average tax level in 1970 of, say, 11 percent to 14 percent of GDP—a 16 to 27 percent marginal propensity to tax away increases in income would be needed. In terms of actual Colombian experience, this may be contrasted to an estimated 7.5 percent marginal propensity to tax increases in real GDP in 1960–1964.[12] The fact that the (aggregate) marginal tax rate was less than the average rate simply reflects the fall in revenue as a share of national income in this period.

These particular numbers should not be taken too seriously in view of the numerous debatable assumptions and guesses underlying them. Any other reasonable set of assumptions on private savings and foreign-aid possibilities, however, also indicates a strong need for a long-run increase in the level of taxes in Colombia. Otherwise inflation will increase substantially and, perhaps, choke off economic growth (especially if the exchange rate proves as slow to adjust to new domestic price levels as has been true in the past).

In the short run, given the abundance of unemployed resources characterizing the Colombian economy, one might think the standard Keynesian remedy of less, rather than more, taxes would lead to increased output rather than inflation (ignoring the probability that much inflation in Colombia is cost-push in nature). This desirable result is unlikely, however, in view of the import constraint on full utilization of industrial capacity. This same constraint operates on capacity expansion and growth, of course, so increased public saving cannot be readily converted to increased investment without additional foreign resources. This fact does not controvert the necessity for increased revenues to finance rising government expenditures—to close the "public saving gap" which I am here assuming will generate undesired and undesirable additional inflation—but the importance of getting foreign exchange should greatly influence the way in which the revenues are raised.

The need for an increasing level of taxes, given reasonable assumptions about the pattern of private consumption and foreign aid as the economy grows, both indicates the single most important task of the fiscal system and provides strong reinforcement to the central theme of this book for more attention to the sources (and uses) of these funds. Once it is accepted that desirable tax reform in Colombia for a long time to come is almost certainly going to mean more taxes, it becomes especially important to be sure that the way in which this growing tax bill is attached to the private sector (and the way in which the additional revenues are spent) does not itself hamper and distort the achievement of development objectives. In particular, every encouragement must be given to changes in the structure of production that will help provide the basis for a more sustainable pattern of growth in the future, that is, one less dependent on the vagaries of coffee prices and American foreign aid.

This conventional development finance conclusion, that more taxes are needed for growth, thus really rests in Colombia on the traditional chain of reasoning: growth requires investment, investment requires saving, and taxes are needed to provide the saving. I am aware that in Colombia at the present time and at least for the next few years one must insert imports as a requirement for investment (and that some, perhaps substantial, growth could take place without new investment if imports permitted full operation of existing capacity). I argued in Chapter 1 that properly structured tax increases would not reduce private saving significantly. My argument now is that properly structured taxes (and expenditures) can help loosen both the immediate and the long-term import constraint on Colombia's growth and that more taxes will in any case be needed over time to transfer increasing real resources to the public sector (or through the public sector to private investment), always supposing the policy aim is to avoid excessive inflation with its attendant economic distortions and political costs. In a sense, given the accepted view of the foreign-exchange problem, the structure of revenues is perhaps more important than their level.

This already complex picture of the requirements of a growth-oriented revenue system in Colombia is further complicated when the important foreign-trade cycle and the short-run stabilization problem are taken into account. Something has already been said about this in the last section. To conclude the discussion of the instability problem, I should first say something about the budget system in Colombia.

Most countries in the world have a government budget.

Most underdeveloped countries also have development plans. In theory, the annual budget should be closely related to the annual development plan, since it is almost always the major instrument of plan implementation. The budget should also serve as a means by which the progress of the plan is appraised and future modifications developed. The fact is, however, that in Colombia, as in many other countries, neither in formulation nor in execution has great success been achieved in tying together budget and plan. The major technical reason for this failure has been the inadequate phasing and specificity of planning efforts. Outwardly the form of the central-government budget, especially since the budget law of 1964, presents no such obstacles, being framed in terms of programs and classified economically and functionally as well. But in reality there remain considerable difficulties in relating the "real" plan figures to current budget figures in a country with inflation, as well as in reconciling the activities of the decentralized agencies with the plan.

A major link between budget and plan is the estimation of resources available for development expenditures. Without good revenue forecasts, plan and budget cannot be integrated, and the need for new tax effort cannot be forecast. Table 14 specifies the forecasting errors in the Colombian national budget since 1954. The considerable errors, often in the direction of overestimating revenues (and underestimating expenditures), shown in this table have been attributed by some to political motives.[13] These critics apparently prefer the pre-1964 system of limiting revenue estimates to a maximum of 10 percent above the previous year rather than the present system of permitting explained increases over this limit, perhaps on the ground that the temptation to government to overestimate revenues under the new system is too great and leads to unjustified expenditure increases. As Table 14 indicates, however, revenue estimates in recent years have been better than they were before the 1964 law. Both before and since 1964 the gravest errors have been caused by the use of primitive extrapolation techniques, based on previous yields, adjusted only by crude guesses, and the fact that substantial unanticipated changes took place between estimate and realization. The 1964 budget law, which permits direct evaluation, is a clear improvement, particularly if more explicit account is taken of the foreign-trade cycle, the overlooking of which in the past has made the estimates of customs revenues so unreliable (see Table 14).[14]

What now needs to be done is to improve evaluation tech-

Table 14. Gross estimating error of central-government revenue forecasts, 1954–1966[a] (percentages).

Year	Total current revenues	Income tax	Customs	Stamp tax	Death tax
1954	14.8	4.1	28.1	32.6	38.9
1955	11.7	15.0	−11.8	15.6	40.5
1956	− 8.4	0.6	−36.2	23.4	51.2
1957	−11.2	8.1	1.8	15.8	− 4.1
1958	5.6	21.3	− 3.7	20.5	− 8.8
1959	12.5	30.2	−20.0	18.1	−32.5
1960	10.8	14.1	12.9	27.6	47.8
1961	−15.6	− 3.9	−23.4	7.2	19.2
1962	−33.2	−28.2	−57.1	− 3.0	−31.3
1963	11.2	− 6.8	−42.6	11.8	1.6
1964	−15.2	−33.4	4.3	− 3.3	1.1
1965	3.3	8.7	− 1.0	− 6.5	69.5
1966[b]	− 6.0	5.2	−19.7	− 4.0	− 5.5
Mean[c]	12.3	13.8	20.1	14.6	27.1
Median[c]	11.2	8.7	19.7	15.6	31.3

Sources: Contraloría General, Informes financieros, various dates.

a Calculated as estimate less actual, divided by actual, times 100.

b Provisional.

c Calculated without attention to sign.

niques and to relate the assumptions underlying the budget more closely to those underlying the development plan (when there is one). More executive control over the budget—Colombia's Congress tends to increase it every year and thus in a way to force initial revenue underestimates—and possibly explicit use of cash budgeting would also help the goal of using the government budget as an efficient major tool of planning and policy.[15] Better initial revenue estimates would, for example, facilitate better planning by avoiding the present pernicious practice of having one or even two "additional budgets" during the fiscal year. Under the present system, even if the initial budget is properly integrated with the plan, the priorities in the additional budget are most unlikely to be similarly linked to planning aims.

Even if all these improvements in the central budget are achieved numerous problems will remain in coordinating the activities of the very large part of the public sector outside the national government. The national public autonomous agencies are notable in Colombia for size, diversity, and the traditional difficulty of knowing what they are doing, let alone controlling them (see Appendix B on the Coffee Fund for one of the worst examples). In part they are hard to handle because so many (37 out of 86, according to one recent list) public agencies and enterprises receive at least some funds from earmarked tax revenues.[16]

Although earmarking in theory makes effective coordination and comparison between sectors more difficult, it has traditionally been viewed in Colombia as a necessary price for administrative stability in the face of general political instability and the uncertainty of reliance on the central-government budget for operating and investment funds. In the light of recent Colombian history this argument is powerful; in fact, I argue in Chapter 5 that more rather than less earmarking of the right kind is what is needed in Colombia. Nevertheless, the current efforts of the National Planning Department to find out more about what the decentralized agencies are doing and to assess their plans by some national development criteria are praiseworthy. Insofar as the agencies depend on the budget, some success may well be achieved in reallocating funds to areas of higher national priority rather than to areas with more access to foreign funds or better technical capacity for preparing and executing projects, as was true in the past. However, the basic reasons for setting up agencies relatively independent of government control—the innovative as opposed to allocative purpose and the stability argument—have not lost their validity in Colombia, and so the present centralizing efforts perhaps should not go as far as some would like. More open and centralized information is, on the whole, desirable and necessary, but it is not so clear that more centralized control of administration is desirable.

The above discussion is moderately optimistic about the possibility of relating budget and plan more explicitly and of making budgeting more realistic in this sense. Steps are, in fact, being taken in this direction. Nothing has been said, however, about the real chances of improving the allocation of public expenditures within this budget-plan framework. The problem here is not, as is so often thought, an organizational one. It will not be resolved by subordinating the budget office to the planning office, or by merging the two, or by putting both in the presidential office. The problem is basically that there are real conflicts in any society, in any government, and that the budget to a great extent is formed by these conflicting forces.[17]

The function of politics is to manage these conflicts, which are particularly acute in societies undergoing transition such as Colombia, and to prevent breakdown of the system. This end is usually achieved by compromise at the price of some inefficiency and inconsistency. Since the budget is the most potent instrument of public policy, it is useless to try to "keep politics out." Thus, for example, organizational changes are sometimes promoted in hopes of changing the decisions being made on expenditure allocations. Yet, unless the distribution of political influence is also somehow changed, much the same decisions will probably emerge from the new system. Recognition of this fact is both an explanation of and a justification for the prevalence of autonomous decentralized public agencies in Colombia and even, to some extent, of their independent financing by earmarked taxes.

What this argument amounts to in the context of budgeting for development in a country like Colombia in which there is a severe total budget constraint is that the pressure on the budget process from all sides is tremendous and that expenditure allocations inevitably accord to a large extent with political strength, not national need, though the two may sometimes coincide. This does not mean that nothing can be done to improve matters. At least some of the issues can be more clearly defined through realistic budget estimates and through closer explicit relations to a development plan which has presidential support. Moreover, through introduction of a budget form that recognizes the apparently inherent instabilities of development in a country as dependent on external forces as Colombia, much improvement can perhaps be brought about without insuperable political opposition.

This suggestion points again to the importance of the short-run stabilization problem in Colombia and its implications for planning, budgeting, and the tax system. Unless the cyclical dependence of public finances on externally induced fluctuations can be diminished, it will be very difficult to institute any sort of consistent public-sector budgeting related to the needs of national economic growth.[18] The previous section discussed briefly the need to reduce the cyclical impact on national-government revenues. A promising approach to the instability problem on the expenditure side is "contingency budgeting."[19]

First, a core budget of projects absolutely essential to the success of the development effort should be prepared. These projects must be tightly scheduled (particularly with regard to the need for foreign exchange) so that they can be closely related to the over-all budget estimating and execution process. The total investment to be carried out with this core budget should not exceed a conservative estimate of public saving and foreign exchange available for noninflationary financing, including some investment in reserves necessary to ensure the timely completion of core projects even in the face of an adverse move in coffee prices. That is, expenditure plans should be related to revenue trends rather than cycles. Second, other projects to be undertaken if funds, domestic and/or foreign, become available should be ranked in some rational order of priority. This variant of the "shelf" of public-works projects familiar from discussion in the industrial countries in the 1930's will require much better project preparation and phasing than has been true up till now both from the central government and from most agencies, and it is perhaps doubtful if it could be carried very far in present Colombian circumstances. More careful project preparation and scheduling will, in any case, be the key element in any successful planning effort, however, and as the prospects of implementing contingency budgeting improve, it should be attempted.

An approach along these lines would give the government more leverage to require better project planning and performance from autonomous executing agencies. The particular virtue of contingency budgeting in Colombia, however, is that it would better enable the government to cope with the budgeting difficulties inherent in the dependence of national revenues on often unpredictable movements in external trade, assuming it has the political fortitude not to spend every peso (or dollar) as soon as received. The system will, of course, be biased against projects with long gestation periods, but this is a healthy bias in a capital-short country. Only through some such contingency device, once accepted, might budgeting for development in Colombia play an active role in establishing the conditions for its own success and not simply constitute the summation of the current resolution of opposing political forces.

The stress laid on this particular reform also reflects my view that effective growth policy in Colombia will require more effective stabilization policy than has been achieved in recent years.[20] For this purpose a more coherent mix of monetary and fiscal policies is necessary. There can be no doubt that much of the monetary expansion of recent years has been due to ill-advised government fiscal policy which, either directly through borrowing from the central bank (under a total permissible credit limit set by the international lending agencies) or indirectly through increased taxation, has resulted in a consequent liquidity squeeze on the private sector. On a number of occasions this has led to offsetting increases, sometimes quite illegal, in private credit facilities. When, as in early 1965, private credit was not expanded adequately to offset a tax increase, tax payments were delayed.[21] Once again the government was forced to borrow from the central bank, even though it too postponed its payments (again accentuating the private liquidity squeeze).

Since liquidity is important in private production and investment decisions, successful attempts to hold down inflation in the private part of the economy may well add to inflation by cutting down the available supply of goods. It is therefore advisable to concentrate on reducing budget deficits in the first place and to avoid adding to inflation. In Colombia, this brings us once again to improving the money-income elasticity of the tax system. The budgetary-planning reform suggested above might improve the allocation and timing of public investment, but in itself it will do nothing to relieve the total budget constraint. This can be done only by raising taxes.

A related question concerns the implicit assumption made earlier that the revenue "requirement" for growth and stability is unrelated to which sector, public or private, carries out the investment "needed" to maintain a certain rate of growth. Given the imperfect capital markets in Colombia, it may not appear reasonable to assume that government saving can flow easily and quickly to those investing in the private sector, as it would probably have to do, given the assumed weak saving in the private sector and the fact that most investment in Colombia will probably continue to be carried out by the private sector. If, for example, only 18 percent (the 1961– 1964 average) of the gross investment required in 1970 (5.5 percent growth rate, capital-output ratio of 4.8) were to be carried out by the government proper (excluding some important decentralized agencies), public investment would amount to 1,786 million pesos (in 1958 prices). The required government over-all budget surplus (assuming government consumption of 3,164 million pesos and a private marginal propensity to consume of 0.95) would then be 378 million pesos, and this amount of resources would have to be transferred to private sector investors. However, since most of the relevant investment would be carried out by industrial corporations and since the banking system in Colombia is highly developed, it does not appear as though there would be much problem in expanding the credit available to the private sector through tax relief to corporations and bank credit to permit this transfer of real resources (amounting to about 1 percent of estimated GDP). If the need were to transfer savings from the private to the public sector, the banking system could similarly expand lending to the government without an inflationary effect, so there does not appear to be any theoretical problem with this assumption.

Guidelines for Tax Structure Policy

The basic assumptions underlying the proposals for tax structure reform in the remainder of this book may now be brought together. In the first place, continuing pressure for increased real revenues to finance an expanding public sector (and perhaps some private investment also) can be expected. This pressure will be felt at all levels of government, particularly the municipal and national. Insofar as the larger urban areas and municipal utilities can finance their own expenditures, they should do so on both theoretical and practical grounds, as outlined in Chapter 5. The main fiscal pressure, however, will continue to be on the national tax system, which must therefore be made much more responsive to increases in money incomes than has been true in the recent past. The need to improve revenue elasticity is especially important because of the limited capacity of the Colombian political and administrative structure to cope with the recurrent fiscal crises that would otherwise arise. This task is a necessary one for development, if development is indeed a goal of the government, for the only alternative is increasing recourse to inflationary financing. The effects of inflation, both in political strain and in distortions of the pattern of growth, have been found in Colombia in recent years to be at least as hard, if not harder, to live with than those of more taxes.

In the second place, the way in which these increasing revenues should be obtained is itself heavily conditioned by the economic situation of Colombia today. The foreign-resources gap is a crucial factor in the country's development, and all tax reforms, no matter how minor their immediate impact, should be designed in the light of the urgent need to alleviate this problem. The misallocation of resources in Colombia owing in large part to the distorted incentives of the price system is not merely wasteful in itself; it constitutes a major obstacle to productivity growth. Whatever helps to solve the allocation problem is thus a crucial element in development policy.[22] Tax policy should be deliberately designed so far as possible to correct major distortions in the Colombian price system.[23] Prices in a country like Colombia are not autonomous regulators of production, investment, and consumption; rather, they are the result of countless distortions introduced by market imperfections and government policies and should be viewed as instruments to be manipulated, within reason, to achieve planning goals. In particular, Chapter 4 outlines how tax-incentive policy and the design of the indirect tax structure (including tariffs) may attempt to correct some of the distortions in the choice of technology with regard to the use of capital and labor and of imports, import-competing goods, and exportables.

Finally, I have argued that the Colombian tax system should move in the direction of greater effective progressivity, both in a static and dynamic sense. Statically, because the apparent high import-intensity of the consumption of the well-to-do and their low propensity to save makes their incomes (and expenditures) a most suitable tax target. Dynamically, because the tax system needs to tap those sectors where incomes increase most rapidly if it is to be elastic, as I have argued it must be.[24] These considerations shape the discussion of income tax policy in Chapter 3, as does the assumption that corporations constitute a key modernizing sector in the Colombian economy and that their growth should be fostered as much as possible within the general guidelines suggested.

The other side of tapping corporate incomes as lightly as possible (consistent with the need for greater revenue elasticity and the severe limits on administrative capability) is the desirability of pushing the lagging sectors of the economy—in particular, most agriculture and small business—toward greater efficiency, thus freeing resources for more productive employment elsewhere in the economy. Although what can be done in this field is severely constrained by the quantity and quality of the tax administration, as well as by obvious political problems, what can be done should be done.

The three great external objectives of a tax system—growth, stability, and redistribution—have been discussed in some detail. The traditional internal public-finance criteria for appraising a tax system and new taxes deserve at least brief mention. The importance of these criteria in a poor country with a weak administration need not be stressed.

Tax changes are both politically and administratively costly; as stable and certain a tax system as possible should therefore be established. The administrative machine with its limited capacity is always in danger of strain brought on by too complex or costly special tax gimmicks.[25] Collection and compliance costs should be kept as low as possible, given the social need for increased public revenue, and, subject to the same constraint, those who are equal in significant respects should be treated equally.[26]

The appropriate developmental task of the Colombian tax system may be summed up as follows: (1) to provide adequate public revenues to reach the growth target and to prevent inflation; (2) to prevent the inequality of income from growing and, so far as feasible, to reduce its present extent; (3) to provide proper incentives to efficient resource allocation within the private sector; and (4) to make as effective use as possible of the country's actual administrative and political system. The reasons for choosing these objectives, and for the priority assigned to them, have been spelled out earlier so far as possible. There are many potential conflicts in this list, but, as the previous discussion should indicate, many are more apparent than real and can be resolved through proper design of tax structure. One of the most important things that can be said about most of these matters in general, however, is that not much *can* be said about them *in general*. It is the details that matter, and it is precisely these details of tax reform which occupy most of the rest of this book, for it is in their resolution that the necessary conflicts and compromises must be worked out between saving and consumption, between imports and domestic production, between labor and capital, between inflation and stability, and between the rich and the poor.

Two | Tax Structure Reform

3 | Growth, Equity, and the Income Tax

The conflict between the revenue needs of the state, the need to create economic incentives favorable to growth, and the desire to have a redistributive fiscal system appears most clearly with regard to income tax. The scanty statistical evidence available for Colombia suggests that considerable reliance should be placed on progressive income taxation on all three of these counts. The traditional case against heavy, progressive income taxes in a country relying primarily on private enterprise for investment cannot be simply ignored, but the equity-growth conflict can be resolved through proper use of the set of policy instruments available in the design of income-tax structure.

An income tax was first introduced in Colombia in 1821. The current tax was established in 1935 and modified in 1960. The present income tax consists of a basic progressive income tax on individuals with 56 rates from 0.5 percent up to a top marginal rate of 51 percent. Corporations are taxed at rates ranging from 12 to 36 percent, limited liability companies at rates from 4 to 12 percent. In addition to the basic income tax, individuals are subject to a net-wealth tax with rates from 0.1 percent to 1.5 percent, and there is also an excess-profits tax to which corporations and taxpayers in the upper brackets are subject, with rates (on a specially computed smaller base) ranging from 20 to 56 percent. These three taxes are always considered in Colombia as integral parts of the income tax system.[1]

The exceedingly complex and sophisticated Colombian income tax system has been an important revenue producer since its early days, yielding, for example, 41.7 percent of total central-government current revenues in 1966. The last year for which an estimated breakdown of income-tax yield by source (excluding surcharges and special taxes) is available is 1964, when 71.5 percent came from the basic income tax, 26.7 percent from the net-wealth tax, and 1.8 percent from the excess-profits tax.

In 1962, about 10 percent of the labor force filed income tax returns, although only about half of those filing had to pay anything. The number of taxpayers increased fivefold from 1952 to 1965, in part because, despite inflation, the personal exemptions have been unchanged since 1953.[2] So, although the hundred largest business taxpayers probably pay about one-third of the total income tax, Colombia already has a broadly-based personal income tax which is potentially capable of producing much of the revenue needed for public expenditure.

There were 1.2 million income tax returns in 1965. The high proportion of nontaxable returns (almost 50 percent) results primarily from low filing requirements. The income level at which a tax return is supposed to be filed (2,500 pesos, the same as the basic personal exemption) is so low that probably another 2 or 3 million people should have filed in 1965. It is just as well that the "evaders" evaded, for the cost of processing so many additional nontaxable returns would have broken the already overladen administrative machine. A rational solution would be to raise the filing requirement to an income level at which the revenue yield from the marginal tax return at least equals the cost of processing it. This simplification, combined with the consolidation of the special income taxes (estimated to require 90 percent of processing time on higher income returns) into the basic income tax, would free substantial administrative resources for more urgent tasks, such as improving the elasticity of the income tax system.

The inelasticity of tax revenues with respect to money income in Colombia is explained in large part by the time lag between the earning of income and the receipt by the government of the corresponding tax revenue. When money income rises with inflation, so do government expenditures, but revenues lag behind, thus increasing the size of the current deficit. The collection of revenue one or two years in arrears in inflationary conditions means that the real value of tax payments is lower than their nominal value, so that the incentive to delay payment is particularly strong in the face of inadequate real penalties and inefficient administration.[3] If the government cuts private credit to hold back demand inflation, tax payments may be even further reduced as taxpayers "borrow" from the government by not paying their taxes on time. A lagged tax system costs the government real revenue both directly, by the lower real value of taxes when received, and indirectly, by encouraging delay and evasion.

One solution to this problem is to put the income tax on a current-payment basis. This change in the payment basis is needed to insulate, at least in part, government revenues from the effects of a general price rise. Other groups protect their interests in inflation; so should government. Tax liabilities ought to be met in the year in which they accrue. A substantial gain in the real yield of the income tax will result from such a shift (temporarily if the rate of inflation is constant, permanently if it accelerates indefinitely), and the tendency to chronic fiscal deficits will be curbed.

In principle, current payment should apply to all types of income. Withholding on wages and salaries alone would account for at most one-third of total tax liabilities, though opportunities for evasion would be reduced substantially for this third.[4] Both withholding and current payment, if properly set up, would make tax payment more convenient for the honest taxpayer. Withholding alone, however, would put recipients of wage and salary income in an even less advantageous position relative to recipients of other types of income than is now the case. This increased real discrimination would be undesirable and presumably undesired.[5]

Given the limits on administrative capacity in Colombia, however, some sacrifice will have to be made with regard to fair treatment of different taxpayers in order to make a current-payment system workable. In general, it is not advisable to attempt to set up an ideal, comprehensive withholding system that cannot possibly be administered effectively. Apart from wages and salaries, the only withholding worthy of consideration is the withholding of tax on dividends and interest. Withholding on dividends paid by corporations is administratively feasible, particularly because a relatively

62 | Tax Structure Reform

high proportion of total shares are owned by a small number of shareholders. There is, however, a 12,000-peso exclusion from taxable income for dividend income received by individuals. Coupled with the nontaxation of intercorporate dividends (60 percent of the total), this exclusion may make withholding on dividends hardly worthwhile. Most other incomes—including corporate profits, which make up almost half the total tax base—cannot, by their nature, have income tax withheld at source. To begin with, therefore, efforts should be concentrated on making withholding effective primarily on salaried employees of larger enterprises (including government), and only on those who are almost certain to have to pay some taxes. The aim must be practicality, not perfection.[6]

Nevertheless, equity, political feasibility, and the need for improved elasticity all dictate that any withholding system should be accompanied by compulsory self-declaration of estimated income currently derived from sources other than those subject to withholding—for example, from professional services and business. For persons and enterprises not already subject to withholding on most of their income, the filing of an estimated quarterly return ought to be required. Taxpayers on the estimated basis would estimate total annual net taxable income, compute their estimated tax liability, and pay it in four quarterly installments. Corporations (and other business entities) should also pay on an estimated basis. There must be severe penalties for underestimates and noncompliance. It would not be advisable (in view of inflation) to forego any penalty for underpayment where the taxpayer's estimated income equals the final income assessed the previous year, as is the practice in the United States. In Colombia the minimum permissible estimate should be adjusted by the current year's price index. That is, the estimated income on which tax is paid currently could not be less than the previous year's actual income adjusted by some index without any resulting underpayment being severely penalized in the final end-year reconciliation.

Adoption of a full-fledged current-payment and withholding system would require substantial simplification of the rate and base of the Colombian income tax in order to be feasible. Unless rate brackets are consolidated, special additional taxes eliminated, and various simplifications made in the tax base, the system would result either in a large amount of over-withholding or in the withholding of ridiculously small amounts of tax. In either case, the resulting strain on the administrative (and political) base of the system would be insupportable. Structural reforms are therefore a necessary condition for a successful shift to a full current-payment basis. Viewed another way, this shift might be used as an occasion to obtain many highly desirable structural reforms.[7]

Tax on payments to some nonresidents and on interest from bearer securities has been withheld at source in Colombia since 1953. More important, a modest and practical beginning at a withholding cum current-payment system was made in 1967 and extended in 1968. Tax is now withheld from wage and salary incomes of over 2,000 pesos a month at graduated rates up to 10 percent. In addition, recipients of substantial nonwage income must add 10 percent to their regular quarterly tax payments (based on the previous year's income). This system apparently accounted for 6 percent of tax yields in 1967. It provides a good basis for a more thoroughgoing reform along the lines I suggest, but is no substitute, partly because of the lack of base adjustment for estimated tax and the fact that the present 10 percent addition is the maximum permitted by law. The withholding system, on the other hand, can theoretically be extended above the present percentage limit, but it too cannot do the job satisfactorily since it is based not on tax liability but on an arbitrary percentage of income received.

A good penalty system is a necessary aid to enforcement. It is imperative that sanctions be stiff *and* enforced, for only thus can a high degree of compliance be attained. Penalties ought to vary with the type of infraction, being moderate when the infraction is merely a technical or arithmetic error, more severe when there is some noncompliance by the withholding employer, self-declaring taxpayer, or depository bank, and most rigorous when there is actual fraud. Fines might be related to the degree of under-reporting. All penalties as well as interest on delayed tax and on refunds should also be adjusted by an index. Particularly close attention should be paid to taxpayers with income not subject to withholding; their returns should be promptly analyzed to see that payments have been made currently and in the proper amount. The modern data-processing equipment now available in Colombia makes all this perfectly feasible even without substantial improvements in the quantity and quality of auditing staff.

For withholding "agents" (enterprises) which fail either to collect or turn over their employees' taxes, a substantial interest penalty ought to be levied. A similar penalty should be imposed on those who fail to file their self-declarations properly. In the case of depository banks, the sanctions for delay might be harsher, since one of the main advantages of withholding and current payment is to produce a steady flow of revenue to the national government—a flow which could be impeded by delays in transmitting funds by the banks (as happened with the sales tax in 1965). The success or failure of a current-payment system in improving elasticity can turn on details like this.

A low money rate of interest, low and much delayed penalties, the failure to initiate criminal prosecution in tax cases, and a past history of general amnesties (forgiveness of tax due) work against voluntary payment of income tax on time. These factors are particularly strong when inflation is accelerating and the credit extended to the private sector by banks is being reduced in an effort to hold back demand. Even the gradual transformation of the payment basis proposed here will be very difficult and will not bring about the expected benefits unless enforcement procedures and penalties are made more meaningful to taxpayers. The greatest problems raised by the implementation of current payment and withholding are thus administrative. The importance of this system is not that it makes tax administration easier, but that, if effectively administered, it will ensure the government of Colombia larger amounts of tax revenue with less delay.

In summary, the adoption of a full-fledged system of withholding and current payment for income tax should help maintain the real yield of the income tax in the face of inflation. If, for example, inflation continues at the average rate of the last decade, the move to a current-payment basis should improve income tax elasticity by about 25 percent. Such a system promises also to improve the enforcement, real progressivity, and fairness of the income tax and to serve as a lever to bring about a highly desirable simplification of the present complex base and rate structure. The severe administrative demands of the system might also help bring about improvements in the vital area of administration. Adoption of a scheme like that outlined here would make Colombia's income tax a much more useful instrument of development policy. Important as some of the reforms discussed in the remainder of this chapter are, none is more important than "inflation-proofing" the income tax.

The Taxation of Capital Gains

One area of income-tax design that deserves special attention is the taxation of capital gains. The treatment of capital gains is important because of the need for more effective progression and improved elasticity if the tax system is to be a useful instrument of development policy in Colombia.[8] Furthermore, the arguments for and against inclusion of gains on the sale of capital assets in taxable income reveal as clearly as anything in the literature on financing development the apparent conflict between income redistribution and economic growth as aims of taxation.

The concept of income as equal to "enrichment" is well entrenched in Colombian law. Nevertheless, many of the arguments commonly put forward against full taxation of capital gains in Colombia as in other countries seem to rest on some other concept of income, such as the notion that income is not "income" unless it is recurrent (that is, comes from a regular source such as wages or dividends) or unless it is intentionally earned rather than an "unexpected" windfall gain. These tests of recurrence and intention, though not without influence in some tax systems, have no logical basis in the framework of an income tax and certainly not in the Colombian income tax. Anything which adds to the wealth and spending capacity of the taxpayer is properly "income" for tax purposes, and capital gains fall within this category. In fact, however, until 1961 no tax was levied on any nonbusiness capital gains in Colombia. Since that year certain gains on real property have theoretically been subjected to tax at the basic rate. This provision has apparently had little impact, however, because the taxable capital gain is reduced 10 percent for each year from the date of acquisition to the date of sale. Gains from the sale of real estate held for over two years, where the net wealth of the owner is less than 100,000 pesos, are also free from tax.[9] In 1964, the tax on capital gains paid by companies was only 5 million pesos; it is unlikely that the tax on individuals was any more significant.

If capital gains are not treated as income for tax purposes, those who own capital (and may increase their spending power from this source) are treated favorably in relation to those who do not. Furthermore, since wealth tends to be correlated with income, a high proportion of the income of the richer groups in society tends to be made up of capital gains, so that failure to tax gains reduces greatly the apparent progressivity of income taxes.[10] The existence of a net-wealth tax mitigates the relative favoritism to property income in the Colombian tax system but does not remove the regressive effect of nontaxation of capital gains. Nor does it discriminate adequately between those property owners who make gains (that is, whose property appreciates in value) and those who do not. If, as suggested earlier, the better-off groups in Colombia have gained relatively in the inflation of recent years, a good deal of this increase in income must have accrued in the form of capital gains. The failure to tap these increases adequately explains in part both the low income elasticity of the system and its very mild effective progressivity. Heavier taxation of capital gains would make the system dynamically and statically more progressive; thus, it is doubly desirable.

The only real equity problem with treating capital gains like any other income arises from administrative limitations which, it is thought, restrict the government to taxing gains when they are realized rather than as they accrue.[11] Taxation on a realization basis means that income which may have accrued over ten years is all brought into taxable income at once. When, as is the case in Colombia, income is subject to a progressive rate structure, this "bunching" of realized gains means that the tax to be paid on the gain is generally higher than if it had been paid in installments over the period during which the income actually accrued. To alleviate the apparent unfairness of this result, special systems of taxing capital gains have been developed in different parts of the world. Yet even this unfairness is more apparent than real. For instance, the owner of a capital asset usually has the option, open to few other taxpayers—including those whose income receipts are equally irregular—of deciding when he wants to realize his accrued income. By means of this "do-it-yourself averaging" he can usually realize gains in years when his other income (hence his marginal tax rate) is low. Furthermore, by postponing the payment of income tax until he actually sells the asset he makes an imputed gain equal to the interest on the postponed tax.

There are always, of course, some special circumstances which make for hardship under any law, but there can be no doubt that, on the average, those who make capital gains are more, rather than less, able to pay tax on their income than are other income recipients. Many of the alleged ills resulting from capital-gains taxation are found in other parts of the income tax system as well, and there is little reason for favorable treatment of gains recipients alone.

It is sometimes argued that this is not true when the "gain" occurs not as the result of a voluntary sale or other equivalent transaction but by gift or, especially, inheritance. The gift case is straightforward. Since the owner has voluntarily chosen to dispose of some of his wealth, any accrued gain on the transferred asset should be treated as realized by the donor. The transfer of assets at death is less likely to be an exercise of the transferor's free will. Furthermore, a special tax is already levied in Colombia on the transfer of assets at death.

Nevertheless, any accrued gain on the asset thus transferred should be taxed like any other gain. There is no reason why bequests made out of untaxed gains should be treated more favorably than wealth bequeathed out of previously taxed income. There is no element of "double taxation" in taxing accured gains at death with both a capital-gains tax and a death tax. To be sure, the heavier financial burden on the transfer is often called undesirable, especially since heirs might have to sell assets to pay the combined tax. For a cynic, the weight customarily given to this point indicates something about the sincerity of any supposed desire for redistribution of wealth, since it is clear that nontaxation of gains at death significantly reduces the progressivity of a tax system.

The two most common economic arguments against the taxation of capital gains concern the effect of inflation on asset values and the effect of the gains tax on saving and investment. In a country where some degree of inflation is a normal expectation, as is by now probably the case in Colombia, certain people will always argue that it is "unfair" to tax "mere" increases in monetary values of assets. A basic flaw in this argument is that the basis of the entire income tax system is the treatment of money values as an *index* of real gain in market power and hence in taxpaying capacity. Increases in money wages or dividends or other sources of enrichment are considered to be taxable, and there is no apparent reason why the appreciation in value of capital assets should be treated more favorably. In general, it is true that insofar as the increase in the sales price of an asset reflects a general price rise, the asset owner has no increased command over consumer goods. Nevertheless, he is still better off than fixed-income recipients. Deflation of such gains (or losses) alone would on balance therefore yield more unjust results than no deflation at all.[12]

A more "economic" version of this argument is that capital-gains taxation makes it harder to "maintain capital" and is therefore an undesirable deterrent to investment. From a truly economic point of view, however, the only investment of interest is new investment, and new investment should be considered on its own merits whether or not its designated end is to replace "old" investment.[13] Similarly, any tax, whether on gains or not, obviously reduces net worth and thus the ability to finance investment at the time it is collected. In short, income from whatever source may be viewed as a fund to be allocated between consumption and saving, and the source of the income should, in terms of economic reasoning, have nothing to do with the allocation decision.

The argument that increased taxation of capital gains will adversely affect capital formation is really an argument that such taxation will have a progressive impact in relation to income and will therefore affect saving and investment adversely. The effect of progressive taxation on private saving and the effect of a diminution in private saving on total or even private capital formation are only doubtfully known in Colombia or anywhere else. While it cannot be adequately documented, the savings and income data cited in Chapter 1 indicate that the net adverse effect on private investment and saving of the increased tax pressure on higher incomes would not be large (and is only doubtfully related to Colombia's growth prospects). In any case, increased tax revenues will increase public saving, so that the net effect on the economy as a whole will be even smaller.

Another form of the investment argument against capital-gains taxation concerns corporations. A major agent of private industrial capital formation in Colombia today is the corporation, and a large part of corporate investment is at present financed out of retained earnings. If capital-gains taxation leads to increased pressure from stockholders to pay out dividends, as is perhaps not unlikely since the opportunity to avoid taxes through retentions would be reduced, this source of investment funds will presumably shrink. Furthermore, it may be argued that the imposition of a tax on capital gains will also reduce the possibility of financing expansion by recourse to the capital market, since securities transactions will now make the seller liable to tax and presumably make him want a larger pre-tax gain before selling. The volume of securities transactions would thus tend to be reduced by capital-gains taxation, as would the viability of the weak stock market.[14]

It is sometimes held that capital-gains taxation will also shift investors toward safe, income-yielding investments and away from risky ones, thus discouraging innovation and growth. One may also note that it will shift them away from such speculative investment as urban real estate, which would presumably be an offsetting gain. Given the monopolistic market structure characteristic of Colombia, one may also doubt that real rates of return after taxation will change much in any line of activity as a result of increased capital-gains taxes.

Whatever the facts, concern for the viability of the securities market has been a dominating factor in the tax treatment of capital gains in semideveloped countries like Japan and Israel, so that it may well be thought gains on securities transactions should receive special treatment in Colombia also. (As long as bearer shares exist, many transactions are not really taxable anyway, but since the only conceivable reason for the existence of such shares is tax evasion, they should be abolished as a necessary step in any tax reform.) If a concession is to be given to stock sales, perhaps the most acceptable means would be by a "roll-over" provision, under which no tax is payable at the time of transfer if the gain is reinvested in securities within, say, six months or one year. (The tax liability accrues until the day when the money gain is finally taken out of the relevant market or until death.) This provision is not equitable, or even logical, since there is no reason why investment from capital gains realized in the market should be treated more favorably than investment out of new savings from earned income; but it is an acceptable tactical price to pay if needed to sell full taxation of gains. The inclusion of a roll-over provision might prove the necessary selling point to counteract the politically powerful, if not logically valid, inflation and investment arguments against capital-gains taxes as well.

The major problem with this concession is its administrative complexity. Detailed investment records over a long period would have to be maintained, and it is most unlikely that the tax administrators could prevent serious abuses of any roll-over privilege. Even if the privilege is not abused, it offers yet another easy way in which the recipients of capital gains can avoid taxes by shifting income to low tax years. On the other hand, because the difficulties exist anyway, these objections are not impressive.

Thus far I have argued, first, that in equity capital gains are like other income and should be treated as much like other taxable income as possible, especially since they accrue to the wealthier sectors of the population (whose income is perhaps also faster growing); and, second, that the validity of the usual arguments against full capital-gains taxation is slight, though it may be advisable to make some concessions on securities transactions. The only equity point of which some account needs to be taken concerns the "bunching" in one year of gains in fact realized over a number of years. The major administrative problem in capital-gains taxation is to devise a system to effect the necessary averaging equitably and simply.

At least four systems are possible, each of which is used in some variant in different countries. These systems are (1) some outright averaging, which requires reopening earlier tax years and is the most complex administratively; (2) a special low rate, which takes no account of the recipient's other income and thus violates the basic principle of income taxation; (3) a discount or exclusion of some fraction of the gain from the tax base, which gives more benefit to the wealthy who are in higher tax brackets; and (4) pro-rating.[15] The last is the best system, principally because it suffers from none of the problems of the other systems. The common practice of varying the tax rate in accordance with the length of time the asset was held has little to be said for it, regardless of system. Once again this way of lightening the tax burden favors the wealthy, who can usually hold assets longer.

Under pro-rating, a capital gain is divided by some arbitrary factor (for example, five); this fraction of the gain is then included in taxable income and taxed at the applicable marginal rate and the tax thus computed is multiplied by the division factor in order to yield the total tax on the gain. What pro-rating really does is to widen the tax brackets applicable to capital gains by the factor used. Use of an arbitrary factor instead of the life of the asset seems advisable for administrative reasons. Treating all gains on assets held less than one year as ordinary income would also help the cause of administrative simplicity. The application of such a simple prorating system would be no more complicated than many another item already on the Colombian tax form.

It is clear that *any* special tax treatment of capital gains leads to complications in tax administration and to possible abuses and hardships. But all such arguments are even more true of the most "special" treatment of all: exemption. More effective taxation of capital gains would, on the other hand, reduce the attractiveness of avoiding personal income tax through high retentions of profits, thus transforming otherwise taxable income into untaxed capital gains. The present problems with closely-held corporations would therefore become less serious. On balance, the administrative complications could be overcome if the will to do so exists.

As part of any reform of taxation on capital, fuller provisions should be made for offsetting and carrying forward losses. Generally, increased allowance for loss (covering both ordinary and capital losses) in addition to being equitable will act to restore the neutrality of the tax system toward risky and non-risky investment. These provisions would probably have to be limited (for example, by allowing offset of capital losses only against capital gains), in order to avoid giving too much scope for manipulation of losses and tax avoidance. Similarly, it is in part to reduce the possibility of abuse that all capital gains realized by companies should be treated as ordinary business income. (This is the practice even in countries such as Italy where capital gains are not otherwise subject to tax.) Improved allowances for losses, combined with some changes in depreciation proposed below, should more than offset any adverse effects on the size and nature of private investment arising from increased taxation of capital gains.

In summary, capital gains should be taxed as much like other income as possible both for reasons of equity (horizontal and vertical) and to prevent the money-income elasticity of the personal tax system from eroding away in the upper brackets. The effects of tougher gains taxation on personal saving would be minimal. More serious might be the effects on the development of financial markets and on the allocation of investment resources within the private sector. Since Colombia will no doubt continue to rely heavily on business saving and on corporate investment, it seems advisable to permit some favorable treatment for securities transactions and to provide some inducements within the business tax structure to risky investment.

The Taxation of Personal Income and Wealth

A central argument in this book is that the Colombian tax system should impinge more effectively on higher incomes. Broadening the tax base to include capital gains is one means to this end. Another is more effective taxation of personal income and wealth in general.

Tables 15 and 16 illustrate the nature of the present income tax on individuals in Colombia. As already noted, many (45 percent in 1965) of those who file income declarations are completely exempt. Table 16 shows that numerous others are subjected to very low rates of tax. The importance of the numerous deductions, allowances, and exemptions permitted by Colombian law is indicated by the fact that taxable income is 43 percent of reported gross income—compared, for example, with 58 percent in the United States in 1964.[16] In individual cases, particularly of high-income taxpayers (who can afford better tax advice), the difference is often *very* much greater than this average indicates. Legal tax avoidance is thus a substantial factor in reducing the effectiveness of the income tax. In addition, reported income itself is likely only a fraction of actual income in many cases, especially for incomes derived from agriculture, the professions, and commerce. Also, numerous potential taxpayers do not file declarations in the first place.[17] Unfortunately, the lack of data makes it impossible to estimate the total amount of outright evasion with any security. Although gross income reported for tax purposes in

Table 15. Individual income tax, 1964 (millions of pesos).[a]

	Bogotá[b]	Colombia[c]
Income		
Gross income	5,826.9	17,991.1
Less deductions	1,290.8	4,027.8
Net income	4,536.1	13,963.3
Less exemptions	2,131.8	6,279.8
Taxable income	2,404.2	7,683.5
Income tax	304.2	843.3
Wealth		
Gross wealth	21,832.0	66,132.2
Less liabilities	4,486.3	12,153.7
Net wealth	17,345.6	53,978.5
Taxable wealth	13,626.2	39,368.2
Net-wealth tax	105.7	315.2
Excess profits		
Basic wealth in excess category	433.7	1,041.8
Taxable excess profits	30.6	77.3
Excess-profits tax	9.2	21.6
Total tax[d]	538.0	1,490.4

Source: Oficina de Análisis Económico, Ministerio de Hacienda.

[a] Data on the number of taxpayers, taxes assessed, and taxable income are taken from the tax returns; other information is partly estimated.

[b] 214,696 taxpayers.

[c] 658,413 taxpayers.

[d] Income tax, net-wealth tax, excess-profits tax, plus special taxes, penalties, surcharges, and substitute investments.

1964 amounted to only 41 percent of income received by individuals in that year, my guess—it can be no more—is that outright evasion is substantial for some kinds of income but that it is not in total as large as is often thought, for the larger industries and most salaried employees probably pay most of the tax they should pay, and their income constitutes a substantial portion of the total tax base.

The data presented in Tables 15 and 16, however, do point to two important problems: the complexity and administrative cost of the present income tax, and the high degree of legal avoidance, or "erosion" of the income tax base. Recently it has been estimated that the minimum cost of processing an income tax return in 1965 was 7 pesos, and probably a good deal more in many cases. Perhaps 25 percent of individual income tax returns do not yield enough in tax to pay for their processing—a ridiculous result in a country as short of skilled tax administrators as Colombia.[18] Furthermore, examination of individual returns almost invariably reveals errors by the taxpayers or the official assessors or both. The complex structure of the tax makes effective auditing and investigation unnecessarily difficult. On administrative grounds alone, therefore, a reduction in the numerous exemptions, allowances, and deductions—for example, along the lines urged in the Taylor Report—is highly desirable.[19] The resulting simplification of the tax and reduction of legal tax avoidance would increase both revenue and progressivity and free administrative resources for more effective attempts to control outright evasion. This reform would also fit in very well with the changeover to a full current-payment system proposed above.

Up to this point, I have suggested a considerable tightening up of personal income taxation. The only concession to present taxpayers might be a slightly increased filing requirement (say, 5,000 pesos) on the ground that any intangible benefits from increased tax consciousness as a result of the present low requirement are outweighed by the tangible burden the mass of exempt returns places on the tax administration. In general, the income tax base would be broadened, and the tax rates at lower levels increased. Unpalatable as they might be, these changes would at present affect only a small, though vocal, group of people—the taxpaying income "elite" of Colombia. Without this essential restructuring of the income tax, it will be most difficult to rely on increased revenues from this source in the future, as I have argued is desirable and necessary as part of the strategy of tax reform for development.

Higher-income taxpayers would not be subjected to higher marginal rates under this scheme, but their income tax base

Table 16. Individual income tax by taxable income bracket, Bogotá, 1964[a] (percentages).

	Taxable income brackets (pesos)						Total of all income brackets[b]
	Less than 20,000	20,001 to 40,000	40,001 to 80,000	80,001 to 400,000	400,001 to 1,000,000	1,000,001 and Over	
Income							
Number of taxpayers	87	8	3	2	0	0	100
Gross income	50	14	10	20	4	2	100
Less deductions	41	18	14	24	3	1	100
Net income	52	14	9	19	4	2	100
Less exemptions	67	8	4	17	3	0	100
Taxable income	39	18	14	20	4	4	100
Income tax	7	11	16	42	12	12	100
Wealth							
Gross wealth	44	16	13	21	4	3	100
Less liabilities	42	17	14	21	3	2	100
Net wealth	44	15	13	21	4	3	100
Taxable wealth	36	16	15	25	4	3	100
Net-wealth tax	21	13	16	36	8	5	100
Excess profits							
Basic wealth for excess-profits tax purposes	0	0	5	8	28	29	100
Taxable excess profits	0	1	0	46	28	24	100
Exess-profits tax	0	0	3	40	22	36	100
Total taxes	12	12	16	39	10	10	100

	Taxable income brackets (pesos)						
	Less than 20,000	20,001 to 40,000	40,001 to 80,000	80,001 to 400,000	400,001 to 1,000,000	1,000,001 and Over	Total of all income brackets[b]
Tax ratios[c]							
Income tax as a proportion of gross income	0.8	3.8	8.0	11.0	17.6	33.8	5.2
Income tax as a proportion of taxable income	2.3	7.3	14.5	26.0	35.5	42.0	12.6
Net-wealth tax as a proportion of taxable wealth	0.005	0.007	0.008	0.011	0.013	0.014	0.007
Net-wealth tax as a proportion of gross income	0.8	1.7	2.8	3.3	3.9	5.2	1.8
Excess-profits tax as a proportion of gross income	0	0	0	0.3	1.5	2.1	0.1
Total taxes as a proportion of gross income	2.2	7.8	14.1	18.0	27.4	52.5	2.4

Source: Oficina de Análisis Económico, Ministerio de Hacienda.
a Based on data in Table 15. May not add to totals because of rounding.
b Rows may not actually sum to 100 percent because of rounding.
c These figures are for Colombia as a whole, not just Bogotá.

would be considerably broadened (especially by the inclusion of capital gains) and their effective (average) tax rate would increase considerably as a result. In sum, these proposals should not have particularly adverse incentive effects, since nominal marginal rates will not be increased except at the lower end of the taxable income scale, where the income effect will probably outweigh the substitution effect. The fairness and the revenue responsiveness of the personal tax system in Colombia would be considerably increased.

High-income taxpayers would be more directly affected by more effective net-wealth taxation. Although the present net-wealth tax in Colombia is far from perfect in either concept or practice, it is nevertheless a useful element of the tax structure and one which should be retained and strengthened.[20] The tax on net wealth provides a useful way of offsetting the inevitable discrimination in favor of property income in a country with inadequate tax administration. Furthermore, since wealth is as a rule even more unequally distributed than income, the net-wealth tax adds substantially to the progressivity of the Colombian tax system (see Table 16). Without the net-wealth tax, the contribution of many high-income taxpayers to general revenues would be even smaller than it now is. For this reason the net-wealth tax should be maintained in Colombia even if all the other reforms mentioned in this book were to be fully implemented.

With generally weak tax administration, the main form of wealth effectively taxed in Colombia is probably real estate.[21] The inequities created by the greater susceptibility of real property than of less tangible wealth to discovery and taxation are minor compared to those offset by this taxation. As argued at length in Chapter 5, real property can and should be subjected to heavier taxation on many fronts, including the net-wealth tax. The incentive effects of the tax should be favorable. Wealth taxation should, in principle, induce more effective use of capital. This inducement is especially helpful when there are unemployed complementary resources, as is to some extent true in Colombia (with the usual conspicuous exception of foreign exchange). On the other hand, the effect of net-wealth taxes will tend to be heavier on growing than on declinng firms (assuming that the market capitalizes future expected values), so that their expansion might be somewhat hampered. Any undesirable effect of this sort can, however, be offset at the corporate level by a tax remission related to expansion, such as accelerated depreciation. On balance, the economic effects of the net-wealth tax, like its equity impact, seem highly desirable.

The road to improved net-wealth taxation in Colombia, as with the income tax proper, lies in simplifying the tax base and making it more comprehensive rather than in higher tax rates. The major change that should be made is to remove the present exemption of "unproductive" wealth, which not only cancels much of the incentive to efficient capital use inherent in the tax but also opens a wide channel for evasion.[22] Taxpayers should also be required to report all wealth, whether taxable or not, including wealth held outside Colombia. (This reporting requirement is needed for effective use of the net-worth technique of estimating income discussed below.) Furthermore, wealth held abroad should be taxed, at least in theory, though the practice would be difficult. To prevent abuse, the deduction of fixed obligations from gross wealth should be permitted only when the debts are proved to have been incurred in acquiring taxable assets. Even this tightening of present rules takes no account of the fact that inflation will substantially cut the real burden of fixed debt, but refinements to adjust for this inequity do not seem called for at present rates of inflation.[23]

Any more effective taxation of high incomes and wealth, and property income in particular, will almost certainly lead to increased evasion and hence to greater administrative strain. The pressure on funds to flow out of the loopholes which remain open—and there will always be some—will increase. Legal avoidance will be replaced at least to some extent by presumably even less desirable illegal evasion. Capital flight to other countries may well increase, in illustration of the old saw that nothing is more nervous than money. A few wealthy people and professionals may even accompany their money abroad. Nevertheless, my contention is that in the long run only the development of an effective stable political and economic system can deter such capital (and human) outflows and that an equitable, productive revenue system is a necessary part of this essential framework, even if its short-term effect is to increase capital flight.

Finally, the importance of real political support for better administration in any structural improvement of the tax system is central, if efforts to improve equity are not in fact to worsen it. The realistic possibility of reforms such as those discussed in this section rests squarely on the political will and administrative capability of the country at the time reform is attempted.

The Taxation of Business Income

The criteria for designing an appropriate tax system for business are the same as those for the tax system as a whole. They may be summarized as the securing of revenue, the curbing of income inequality, the provision of incentives to efficiency, and ease of administration. It has sometimes been argued that indirect rather than direct business taxes best satisfy these criteria (except for the second one). Yet the importance I attach to effective progressivity in Colombia, added to the difficulty of achieving it without a substantial tax on business firms to help enforcement of personal taxation on dividends and capital gains, leads me to favor a revised system of income taxation rather than some alternative form of taxation like a value-added tax.[24] In the present Colombian situation, both revenue and equity considerations demand a relatively high absolute profits tax (with no offsetting concession to shareholders on their personal taxes) in order to protect the desirable reforms of the personal tax system. However, it is also at the company level that the necessary incentives to growth and efficiency must be established.

Assuming that a separate tax is to be levied on business profits, at what rate should they be taxed? I believe a single rate of perhaps 45 or even 50 percent should replace the present conglomerate of progressive basic income tax rates which differ with the form of business organization and to which are added special additional taxes and an excess-profits tax (see Table 17). This single rate should ideally also be the

Table 17. Taxation of business income, Bogotá, 1964.

Type of business entity	Total (millions of pesos)	Taxable income (pesos)		
		Less than 100,000	100,001– 1,000,000 (percentages)	1,000,001 and over
Corporations				
Number of companies (1,864)		69	21	10
Taxable income	1,074.5	2	13	85
Income tax	327.2	1	9	90
Total tax	521.3	4	11	85
Limited liability				
Number of companies (5,440)		79	19	2
Taxable income	478.6	21	35	44
Income tax	35.3	14	35	51
Total tax	55.0	10	25	65
Partnerships				
Number of companies (1,010)		84	12	4
Taxable income	91.6	16	28	56
Income tax	4.5	10	25	65
Total tax	8.9	11	22	67

Source: Oficina de Análisis Económico, Ministerio de Hacienda.

top rate of the individual income tax rate schedule (which now goes to 51 percent) in order to avoid providing incentives to tax avoidance by channeling income through closely held corporations. (Some reduction in nominal individual rates is perfectly compatible with an increase in effective progressivity achieved by broadening the tax base through the inclusion of capital gains and the elimination of some exemptions, deductions, and exclusions.)

No increase in taxation at the entity level for the larger corporations, which provide about 75 percent of total business tax revenues, is implied by the suggested rate, but there would be a substantial increase for most smaller corporations and for limited liability companies. The present system imposes the lowest rates on limited liability companies and partnerships—precisely those firms which are probably evading tax the most —and the highest rates on the modern incorporated firms which find it harder to cheat. This arrangement is hardly conducive to development. Because the revenue needs of government preclude much relief for large businesses, the desirable direction of reform is clearly to raise taxes on small businesses. In particular, limited liability companies should be taxed like corporations, with only actual dividends being taxed at the individual level rather than all of their profits as is now (at least in theory) the case.[25] The increased taxation of firms would more than offset any small revenue loss at the personal level. All shareholders would continue to be able to exclude from taxable income a small fixed amount of dividends—say, 12,000 pesos as at present—both as a mild encouragement to channel savings into equities and as a possible stimulus, at least for the few small shareholders (most shares are owned by a relatively few large holders), for increases in saving.[26] Apart from this, I do not see any need for further relief from "double taxation," since, given the oligopolistic nature of most of Colombia's protected industries, one would expect a high degree of forward shifting of corporate taxes so that consumers, not shareholders, really pay them. (Since there is no evidence as to whether the size of a firm affects its capability to shift taxes forward, this possibility is ignored here.)

A uniform profits tax rate is proposed because I see no reason for discriminatory treatment of large corporations and because of the general difficulty in taxing small business fully (as well as the fact that progressive corporate rates stimulate evasion through reorganizations that take place only on paper).

The other side of this coin is that, despite virtually worldwide practice to the contrary, there is no case for favorable treatment of small business as such. Given the substantial financing problems in Colombia and the limited access of new enterprises to capital markets, however, there is a real difficulty for *new* businesses, which of course are usually small. This difficulty can be handled only to a slight extent through the tax system. Its solution lies much more in development finance corporations and credit policy. But what can be done should be done, primarily through accelerated depreciation and fuller provisions for offsetting losses. No special treatment of small business is needed, however, since these measures are recommended for all business income, though they should be of most use precisely to the new, growing business.

Up to this point I have proposed that taxes on large corporations stay about the same while those on other businesses be increased. These increases must be offset to some extent in view of the assumed importance of business saving and investment for Colombia's economic development. Some offsets have already been mentioned. Businesses should be permitted to carry forward operating losses (and unexhausted depreciation allowances) against future income.[27] The special earmarked taxes for housing and steel development should be abolished. Two measures require further discussion: the abolition of the excess-profits tax, and the introduction of accelerated depreciation.

The third member of the triumvirate that constitutes the Colombian income tax is the excess-profits tax. Like the net-wealth tax, the excess-profits tax originated in the desire to tax unearned income more heavily than earned income. But in Colombian conditions no tax which puts a heavier burden on more efficient use of capital (or successful risky investment) is acceptable. The excess-profits tax should therefore be abolished, not only because of its administrative complexities but also because of its adverse incentive effects.[28] The common analogy between development finance and war finance might be thought to support taxes on the "excess income" generated in the development effort, but the sheer difficulty of determining the tax base and the appropriate rate of "normal" profit renders unattainable a sensible excess-profits tax.

A possible defense of the tax is that it takes some of the economic rent accruing from the monopoly position afforded many Colombian businesses by the country's tariff structure. This position is not without merit. However, there is absolutely no reason to expect the excess-profits tax as presently constituted and administered to reach this monopoly rent more effectively than the regular profits tax. As suggested later, the tariff monopoly will soon have to be tackled directly if development is not to be choked off by balance-of-payments problems. As it is, the excess-profits tax—80 percent of which is paid by corporations—has probably been largely shifted forward along with other taxes on profits and is no different, just more capricious, in its effects.

Colombian businessmen and some other observers have long complained that the recent inflation has made it difficult for industrial firms to replace depreciable assets. These complaints led to a partial revaluation in 1960, allegedly to make up for the effects of the 1957 devaluation.[29] But no similar steps were taken after the 1962 and 1965 devaluations, despite the rising volume of arguments for further revaluation or replacement-cost depreciation. The argument for further concessions is simply that depreciation allowances based on the original peso value of a machine do not permit a firm to recover free of tax an amount equal to the real cost of replacement. Also, if depreciation allowances are "too low," taxable profits and hence taxes are "too high." On both counts, it is contended, new investment will be discouraged unless firms are permitted to revalue old assets for tax purposes.

These arguments have a certain plausibility—especially if one looks only at a single-asset firm, assumes no improvement in the quality of capital and no access to outside funds for investment, ignores the need to finance from some other part of the tax system any tax concession to those businesses with old investments, and leaves out of account the fact that tax reductions likely to increase spending feed rather than slow inflation. Besides these points, which already tell against revaluation, industry is usually in a better position to defend itself against inflation than are most sectors of the economy, and any conceivable revaluation scheme is conceptually and administratively very complicated.[30] Without elaborating the argument further, my conclusion is that, judged by all four of the basic criteria—revenue, equity, efficiency, and administration—revaluation is inadvisable.

The case for accelerated depreciation, where at least the benefit goes directly to firms which carry out new investments rather than to those which invested in the past, is much stronger. One of many possible systems would consist in both abolishing the present 10 percent salvage value requirement (that is, allowing the depreciation of 100 percent of original cost), and granting an additional 15 percent deduction in the year of acquisition of machinery or equipment. The present depreciation system permits 90 percent of the cost of a machine to be written off in ten years; the proposed system would permit 115 percent of the cost to be deducted from taxable income in the same period, with 25 percent of the total cost being deductible in the first year.

The new system would, in theory, both improve the after-tax return from a given investment and increase the profits left after tax in the hands of firms which invest, thus providing them with funds for still further investment. In addition, for growing firms (the very ones which it is desirable to encourage for development) the proposed system of accelerated depreciation would in most cases more than compensate for such possible difficulties in the replacement of assets as result from continued moderate inflation. On balance, this system is recommended as the simplest way in which a considerable general stimulus can be given to private industrial investment for a certain cost in lost government revenue. The very generality of the concession—to all new investment in qualifying assets—is itself a virtue (despite the cost in revenue foregone) since it avoids the need to set up cumbersome bureaucratic machinery to process and approve applications.[31]

An additional useful feature of a revised depreciation system would be to relate the rate of depreciation to the degree

of utilization of installed capital equipment. It has been estimated that the average utilization of installed capacity in
Colombian industry has in recent years been as low as 20 to
30 percent of capacity. The country cannot afford the tremendous waste of foreign exchange implied by these figures. As a
small measure in the right direction, firms which employ their
equipment more than one shift a day might be allowed to
increase their annual depreciation write-off proportionately.
Such a system has been used in France with some success, and
there is some precedent for it in present Colombian law.[32]

At least three difficulties may be expected with the system
of accelerated depreciation suggested above: the revenue loss
would be substantial, perhaps as much as 300 million pesos in
1966 (over 10 percent of income taxes); the incentive to further
investment in capital-intensive production is not wholly desirable; and there is some doubt as to whether businessmen
would respond to this incentive anyway (or whether import
availabilities would permit them to respond). Although all
three are valid criticisms, I would nevertheless recommend
that serious consideration be given to accelerated depreciation
in one form or another as a desirable part of the long-run tax
reform strategy for Colombia. The cost could be offset, if necessary, by higher tax rates on business (which would also increase the incentive effect of the tax concession). The present
incentives to employ capital-intensive methods of production
come about mainly through the tariff and exchange systems
on the one hand and labor legislation on the other, and should
be corrected where they originate as far as possible, though tax
policy should not accentuate the resulting distortions in factor
pricing.

To sum up, an acceptable pattern of reform in business
taxation might look something like this: rapid depreciation
(the investment allowance system); generous loss carry-forward;
abolition of the excess-profits tax; and higher rates on limited
liability companies and small corporations. The major incentive to increased business saving and investment would be the
new depreciation system. For maximum efficiency in terms of
investment induced per peso of revenue foregone, an invest-

ment credit system would theoretically be better, but this idea has probably not been sufficiently discussed in Colombia to be accepted; besides, more rapid depreciation has the additional selling point of more obviously dealing with the inflation argument, invalid as I think that argument is (in part because the holders of depreciable assets usually emerge from inflation better than other asset holders, including those whose assets consist in their own capabilities).

In general, the tax treatment of businesses suggested here is intended to favor corporate saving. Business retentions should at least hold their own under this system, and depreciation (by far the most important element in private gross saving) should increase, so that any fall in personal saving as a result of the recommended heavier taxation of high property incomes should be more than offset. Dividend payouts—generally between 60 and 80 percent of total corporate profits in recent years—might even fall as a result of the combined reforms of business and personal taxation.[33]

There is no intrinsic virtue in inducing business saving through government policy rather than increasing public saving as such, but it seems probable that this mixed policy of relying on both the fiscal (public) and self-finance (business) techniques for obtaining and allocating saving would be best for Colombia at the present time, given the relatively high corporate propensity to save and the generally useful investment pattern of corporate retained earnings compared with either dividends or taxes. It is hard to strike a precise balance in this matter, and judgments will differ, but the mixed bag of proposals put forward here would go a long way toward the goal of achieving a more effectively progressive tax system without damaging savings and investment incentives significantly.

The Economics of Presumptive Taxation

This chapter has stressed the importance of taxing the faster-growing sectors of the economy if the income tax is to contribute effectively to the noninflationary financing of expanding public expenditures. Heavy taxation of industry, the most easily taxed of these sectors, will doubtless involve some social cost by reducing industrial investment, but this is a price that must be paid in order to protect the personal tax system from undue avoidance and to raise the necessary revenues. Some ways of shifting the business tax burden onto those firms which contribute less to development were suggested in the previous section. A second line of attack, one common in the literature on taxation for development, is to attempt to tax other sectors of the economy—especially agriculture and commerce—more. The need for other sectors to pay their "fair share" is often stressed in Colombia, and a certain political and psychological appeal is obvious. Economically, too, the tapping of traditional incomes as opposed to modern incomes is attractive.

Even though some progress can be made in taxing agriculture and commerce more effectively, too much should not be expected from this source. There are two good reasons why agricultural and service incomes do not pay many taxes: the very low income of most people engaged in these activities, and the enormous administrative difficulty in any country of taxing the better-off farmers and tradesmen adequately. That is, even if there are no political obstacles at all to increased taxation of agriculture, commerce, and professionals, no really substantial increases in the contribution of these sectors to the public revenues can realistically be expected in the near future. Any nominally "balanced" program of reductions in taxes on industry and increases in taxes on other sectors would probably result in a net reduction in total taxes, owing to the great difficulty of making the increases effective. In my judgment, therefore, the techniques discussed here for increasing taxes on the traditional sectors of the economy complement rather than substitute for the reforms of personal and business income taxes already discussed.

There is by definition no easy way to tax hard-to-tax sectors, but there are some administrative techniques which can help. One such technique is to tax presumed rather than actual income. Presumptive (or notional) assessment of the tax base is an administrative technique used in many countries for collecting income taxes in sectors of the economy where taxpayers do not normally keep adequate enough records for the enforcement of a true net income tax. The essence of the presumptive method is to assume that taxable income is related in relatively fixed ways to some factor (or factors) which can be more easily verified than income itself. In several countries this technique is generally employed both in agriculture and among the self-employed, especially the operators of small firms in commerce, industry, and the professions.

With respect to agriculture, the use of presumptive techniques for more effective income taxation has been proposed for Colombia a number of times in the past. A 1956 report of the World Bank, a National Planning Council recommendation of 1959, a 1963 proposal to the National Agrarian Committee, and the report of the Taylor Mission in 1964 all recommended some form of presumptive income tax for agriculture.[34] None of these proposals became law, however, although the original draft of the 1960 income tax reform went so far as to provide that all rural land over a certain value was to be presumed for tax purposes to yield net income equal to 7 percent (4 percent for tenants) of the value assessed for land-tax purposes (cadastral value).[35] This proposal disappeared completely before Law 81 of 1960 was enacted, however, and the only statutory presumptions of income in the present income tax law concern the rental income of certain owner-occupied luxury urban residences and country estates and (since 1966) a small tax on livestock.

The two main reasons for the popularity of presumptive income taxation in agriculture—at least as a recommendation—are the impossibility of administering the regular income tax in this sector effectively and the allegedly beneficial economic effect of the presumptive method in stimulating agriculture production. The first part of the proposition is sufficient reason for the adoption of some such technique in Colombia at the present time. Less than 4 percent of income tax revenues appear to come from agriculture, according to the inadequate data available, and (except for the coffee taxes discussed in Appendix B) other taxes on agriculture are unimportant.

The second part of the proposition—the beneficial economic effect—is more open to doubt.

The usual argument is that a tax on the presumptive net income of all rural land, regardless of the actual type of production or degree of exploitation, will increase agricultural productivity by inducing owners to bring idle land into use and by increasing the efficiency with which land already in production is utilized.[36] Until the return on the land equals the presumed amount, this system of taxation acts as a penalty to underutilization; and once actual returns are higher than the presumed rate, the marginal rate of tax on the excess is zero, a fact that creates every incentive to earn still more.

All this is true enough, in the short run—at least if we neglect the fact that high returns as a rule already escape tax. This supposed evasion is one of the main reasons for favoring the use of a presumptive system in the first place. But what will the farmer do with the extra income (after tax) he receives from the increased production? Since an effective presumptive system almost certainly must be based in one way or another on assessed property values, improvements to property (new investment) will likely raise the assessed value, and thus the presumptive income and the tax, unless great care is taken to assess only bare land values—the "original productivity of the soil"—a most difficult, complex, and administratively costly task.[37]

In particular, the undesirability of deterring investment in livestock—a potentially great export industry—is a major reason why it is not advisable to include the value of livestock in the tax base, despite the emphasis in Colombia on the need to tax livestock farmers more heavily than at present since they are thought, probably correctly, to be among the largest tax evaders. If, as is admittedly rather unlikely, agricultural land were assessed at its full value, use of this base alone would tend to induce the most efficient use of the land, whether for grazing or for crops. Another reason why it is not very useful to include livestock as such in the tax base is that this form of movable wealth is not at all hard to conceal; again, this very difficulty is one of the factors apparently requiring the use of arbitrary presumptive techniques in this sector of the economy.[38]

Finally, it should be remembered that a presumptive income tax is very likely, under Colombian market conditions, to be shifted forward in a higher price for agricultural products, especially since it is a fixed cost to the producer. The extent to which such forward shifting takes place will, as always, be determined by market conditions rather than by any legal price controls or other regulations. On the other hand, like any heavier charge on land, a tax levied on a presumptive income base may tend to reduce the rate at which the price of land rises and hence deter some of the present speculative investment in rural real estate. Insofar as the tax is thus capitalized, it will not be shifted forward in higher product prices. (Because the extent of any such capitalization will be hidden from view in an inflationary environment, it is unlikely this argument can be put to any empirical test.)

Taxes have traditionally been viewed as a method of altering land-use patterns in the rural areas of Colombia. Land taxation has long been seen, by both Colombians and foreigners, as the key to successful "land reform" (the exact composition of such reform is, as is customary in these discussions, left undefined here). Since the history and outcome of these efforts have recently been expertly reviewed by Albert Hirschman, I shall note here only that the culmination of the various earlier efforts, Decree 290 of 1957, is in some ways a model for this sort of legislation, providing for a classification of agricultural land into four types with detailed requirements for the use of each type if the owner is to avoid severe tax sanctions.[39] Like so many models, however, Decree 290 was never put into effect, nominally because of the tremendous technical difficulty of classifying the land as the law requires. (Nonetheless, certain tax exemptions in the law were put into effect at once, since it was left to the initiative of the taxpayers to claim them!)

Hirschman implies that this law (and its predecessors and successors) was not really a failure, for the continued inability of such tax measures to solve the land "problem" eventually made it quite clear that any desired changes in the land-tenure system would have to be brought about by other, more direct, means—such as INCORA, the Colombian Institute of Agrarian Reform, which was set up a few years later. Hirschman also argues on the basis of Colombian experience that land taxes can never produce substantial land reforms, in part because of the technical difficulties of implementation and the scope for endless arguments on technical points. In general, if direct changes in land tenure are politically unacceptable, it is most unlikely that any miraculous tax gadget designed to achieve the same end can be effectively enforced. Nevertheless, the land-reform objective has usually been one reason behind proposals for the taxation (under the income tax) of presumed income from agricultural land, which amounts to putting heavier taxes on land. Without saying anything about the merits or otherwise of the various changes in land tenure and utilization patterns designed to be brought about by these measures, I think it is fair to comment that most claims for the probable nonfiscal impact of such land-tax changes are naïve, for both technical and political reasons.

The above arguments merely try to moderate the usual enthusiasm about the effects on productivity and other nonfiscal variables that may be expected from the introduction of presumptive income taxation. The administrative impossibility of the national government's getting much revenue from agriculture except by some such arbitrary means is, I think, sufficient argument for some use of presumption in agricultural income taxation in Colombia at present, assuming as usual a real need for increased public revenue.

There are a number of methods by which presumptive techniques may be applied in agriculture. These are not discussed in detail here. I assume that assessed value of agricultural land should be used as the basis, both because this form of presumption has the most beneficial economic effects and because it is the simplest way to administer the tax. The latter consideration is the more important, since, to repeat, the only real reason for using any presumptive technique is the need for an easily enforced administrative procedure.

Most previous attempts to introduce presumptive taxes in Colombia have apparently foundered on the inadequacy and inequity of the assessments on which the levy must be based. Whatever the specific proposal adopted, no reliance should be placed on the availability of thorough land-classification records or potential-value figures, which cannot possibly be available in detail for the whole country for a long time to come. On the whole, therefore, a flat-rate presumptive levy on land values for all agricultural producers is what should be aimed at. Other relevant factors, such as location and land classification, would automatically be taken into account in proper cadastral values, hopefully in a steadily improving and more consistent fashion over time.

Immediate reassessment of large areas is required to make a presumptive tax meaningful, given the present widespread gross undervaluation. The national assessing body, the Geographic Institute, should be given adequate funds for the task and directed to assess first the areas thought to be most undervalued. This rural reassessment program could profitably be closely related to the urgent need for new, up-to-date valuations in urban areas (see Chapter 5). New assessments would also increase the yield of both the national net-wealth tax and the municipal property tax.

The idea sometimes bruited of reviving the self-assessment system used in the early 1950's has little to be said for it as an alternative, although in some circumstances the *option* of altering assessments might be left open to the landowner in order to avoid overburdening the appeal mechanism, particularly if an index adjustment is used to compensate for inflation since the last official valuation. This sort of adjustment was proposed in a recent study of the Geographic Institute. The idea is sound and worth fuller exploration, though the particular procedure outlined in the Institute's study may be unduly complicated.[40] Self-assessment (accompanied by the threat of possible expropriation at the declared value) might perhaps be adopted as a temporary measure to get the system off the ground, but the declared values should be replaced by cadastral values as soon as possible. The use of a self-assessment option in 1963 led to an increase of 10 percent in total taxable rural valuations in 1964, so this device is not completely useless.[41] It seems clear, however, that most reliance will have to be put on the rapid extension of streamlined traditional assessment methods. The index-adjustment alternative, which has been thoroughly worked out in theory and has yielded good results in small-scale trials in Colombia, seems the most promising temporary solution to the serious problem of immediately rectifying the present inadequate and inequitable cadastral values in large parts of the country. The index procedure also has the great advantage of being much easier to maintain current, since each year all the old valuations can be readily adjusted by the chosen coefficient.

Past suggestions as to the rate at which presumptive income might be determined for tax purposes have ranged from 4 to 14 percent of assessed value. An inquiry into the rate of return on some farms which keep records might be useful in indicating what rate is suitable (though it may perhaps be doubted that the return on farms which do not keep records is strictly comparable to the return on those which do).[42] It seems doubtful, however, whether extensive studies of this sort would be a very good use of the scarce data-gathering and analytical resources available: a more advisable procedure might be arbitrarily to choose a rate, such as 10 percent, and observe the results (on tax receipts and agricultural production) over time. The option of appeal by self-assessment and the catastrophe provision mentioned below should take adequate care of any hardship cases arising from this simple procedure.

The presumptive income from agricultural activities determined by the application of the chosen rate to the assessed value adjusted for inflation should be aggregated with income from other sources and taxed at the normal rates of income tax. A minimum exemption roughly equivalent to that enjoyed by families in other sectors of the economy should be granted. To simplify administration, however, this exemption might be based on cadastral value—for example, by exempting all properties of less than 50,000 pesos in value. While this procedure would give undeserved relief to persons who both own agricultural land and have other taxable income—since they would in effect receive double personal exemptions—it would greatly simplify administration by reducing the scope of the tax to only the relatively few large landowners, perhaps 60,000 in total.

The tax should be levied on operators (those in possession), whether landowners or tenants, with landowners being taxed on their rental income as normal income. Alternatively, both landowner and tenant might be taxed, although with the tenant receiving some standard credit for his rent. The first alternative is to be preferred on the grounds of simplicity. That part of the tax which cannot be shifted forward in higher product prices will be divided between landlords and tenants in a manner determined by market forces, no matter what allocation procedures are written into the law.

Provision should also be made to reduce the presumptive income assessed when property is affected by natural catastrophe or civil violence. The determination of these circumstances in specific areas or instances ought to be left to the discretion of the Division of National Taxes. Consideration might be given, however, to the possible use of local committees (including central-government representatives) as a first appeal board on this and some other points (including valuations, if the self-assessment appeal option is not employed). Care would be needed to prevent any such committee from becoming more a hindrance than a help, but the idea is worth further exploration.[43]

Under the proposed system taxpayers would not as a rule be able to offset losses from agriculture and stock-raising against income from other activities. Equally, non-farm losses could not be claimed against farm income. This procedure is completely arbitrary and can only be justified by the need to simplify administration and prevent gross abuse.

Though presumptive taxation by its nature does not require the reporting of income and costs, some provision must be made for taxpayers to switch over from one tax basis to another if the extension of the regular income tax into this sector of the economy is not to be held back. This point is extremely important and indeed is probably the strongest argument against the wide-scale use of presumptive techniques of income taxation. Commercial agricultural enterprises with good records should be treated like advanced enterprises in any sector and not favored (or penalized) by the unwarranted application of the presumptive system. An obvious incentive to changing from the presumptive to the regular tax system would be the application of a relatively high rate of presumption. However, if political pressures alone prevail, an unduly low rate is likely to result.

To sum up, 10 percent of the value of agricultural land ought to be presumed to be taxable income of those engaged in agriculture, with the various exceptions and restrictions noted. Furthermore, an index adjustment should be made to all old cadastral values to take account of inflation, and a full-scale technical revaluation should be undertaken as soon as possible. Increased taxation of real property appears the simplest, perhaps the only way, to get more revenue from the traditional agricultural sector in Colombia today, whether the tax applied is called a property tax, a wealth tax, or an income tax.[44] Provided the system is kept flexible and responsive to inflation, and transitions to a regular income tax are possible and encouraged, I see some virtue in applying this presumptive income tax in addition to increasing the property tax itself, as is later recommended.

Colombians have in the main merely discussed the use of presumptive methods with regard to agriculture. Seldom have they gone even that far with reference to my next topic—taxation of the self-employed outside agriculture. Yet this technique is in common use in many countries, even such relatively advanced ones as France and Israel, to reach incomes in the self-employed sector of the economy, particularly those of small commercial and artisan enterprises and professional persons.[45] The possibilities for evasion in these parts of the economy are at least as great as those in agriculture and probably as widely used. Consideration might therefore be given to the use of presumptive techniques in Colombia for small business enterprises and some professions.

The major technical problem concerns the factors that should form the base of presumption. Among those used in other countries are gross sales, value of property, number of employees, location of business, type of trade, inventory, age and quality of equipment, private style of living, and so on. Variations can be constructed for different trades: for example, in the case of taxi-drivers the year and make of vehicle and estimated mileage might be taken into account. Any such complicated and refined system as this would very likely be as difficult to administer fairly and effectively as the regular income tax. It cannot therefore be recommended for Colombia, since the evasion problem itself arises in large part from the scarcity of trained administrators and the administration's inability to determine the very sorts of norms and standards needed in any complicated presumptive system.[46]

Whatever factors are employed in determining the tax base, it must be remembered that the resulting levy is not really an *income* tax. While an income tax levied on a presumptive basis is in theory an attempt to tax income, it is actually a tax on the factors on which the presumptive income tax is based. The economic effects of a presumptive income tax are therefore quite different from those of a true tax on net income, and it will tend to be shifted like any other tax on factors. If the number of employees is a basis for presuming income, the presumptive income tax has some of the characteristics of a payroll tax and does not seem advisable for a capital-short country with a great deal of open unemployment. If the basis is gross sales, it is like the worst kind of sales tax. Most probably the tax would be a mixture, with an accordingly mixed pattern of shifting and incidence, like the presumptive tax on income from business activities which already exists in Colombia in the form of the municipal tax on industry and commerce. Theoretically this tax is levied on all businesses—sometimes on a basis of gross sales, sometimes on installed horsepower, sometimes on rent paid, sometimes on a mixture of these and other factors, and sometimes (as in the case of most financial institutions) as a flat license tax. Not all municipalities impose this tax, and even in those which do (mostly the larger cities), it is a minor source of revenue— though still one of the larger sources of *tax* revenue. No real effort is, as a rule, made to enforce the industry and commerce tax: perhaps 80 percent of liable firms do not pay the tax at all, and there is every reason to think those who do, pay on a completely arbitrary (and usually low) basis.[47]

Besides the possible drawbacks of a tax on factors rather than true income two other problems might be important in designing a presumptive levy on business. First, if investing more money in one's business changes the presumptive rate of return, such investment will be discouraged. Second, the keeping of books and records will, unless care is taken, also be discouraged by the use of presumptive methods, so that the regular income tax becomes harder to extend throughout the economy. The first of these problems was discussed in connection with agriculture; the second is much graver for business than for agriculture. It would be very difficult indeed to avoid "freezing" many potential regular taxpayers into an inequitable and arbitrary position by the overuse of presumptive methods. Furthermore, even if the initial presumptive factors chosen and the value attributed to them were accurate, they would become much less so over time and would require constant revision, particularly in an inflationary environment, if tax revenues from this source were not to decline steadily over time. Constant political and administrative strife is almost guaranteed by this method. It would probably be as easy, and certainly fairer, to improve the regular administration.

If it is nevertheless decided to put the determination of income for tax purposes in certain types of businesses on a presumptive basis, a few general points on how this might be done can be made. The degree of refinement to be employed in classifying enterprises by type and location must be worked out carefully with respect to tolerable inequities and the cost of taking more details into account. To begin with, only a quite crude system should be considered. On the whole, most weight should probably be given to gross sales, since it would not be wise to discourage employment or investment as much as the other common bases of payrolls or real property tend to do. The resulting levy is equivalent to a crude multiple-stage sales tax. The sales basis is also likely to be more responsive to inflation than the alternatives. The rate of income presumed for different trades might perhaps be determined from the records of those firms which keep records: if all businesses taxed in this system are assumed to have a similar ratio of net incomes to gross receipts, a tax on the gross receipts might be viewed as a form of simplified business income tax. Nevertheless, it is crucial that some provision be made for shifting from a presumptive to a book basis. The greatest incentive to this shift would be presumption at a high rate. A milder alternative would be to grant special concessions and incentives only to those enterprises which maintain adequate records.

Whatever system is used, arbitrary discrimination between firms—for example, by presuming income at a higher rate or, as in a schedular tax system, levying tax at a higher rate on the income presumed—seems undesirable. There is no reason why a particular trade or profession as such should be discriminated against. The unfairness and distortion arising from this sort of discrimination are likely to offset at least in part the beneficial effects resulting from higher taxation on those particularly prone to evasion. Undesirable pressures for administrative favoritism and corruption will also be set in action by arbitrary differentials. The only virtue of a presumptive system is administrative simplicity, and if the system is too complicated, it can easily be worse in all respects than the alternative of trying to apply the regular income tax.

On balance, I would not recommend the widespread use of a system of presumptive determination of income in sectors other than agriculture for Colombia at this time. The advantages of presumption would be few, especially since the initial attractive administrative simplicity would almost certainly soon be lost in an avalanche of petitions for special treatment from every sector of the economy, each with its "unique" circumstances requiring special consideration as soon as the ideal of uniform treatment for all under the general income tax has been explicitly put aside. The disadvantages of arbitrariness, inequity, unresponsiveness to inflation, and retardation of the extension of the income tax are considerable.

A more advisable alternative is to improve the application of the regular income tax in the difficult small business and professional sectors. As always, better staff and simpler procedures are the keys to success, but in addition two particular changes could help considerably. The first would be to require that *all* persons engaged in trade, business, or the professions maintain accounting records in some standard form. This requirement could be enforced by special penalties on the keeping of inadequate records, on the one hand, and by specific inducements (as in the Japanese "Blue Return" system) to keep correct records, on the other.[48] These inducements might include, for example, the right to claim accelerated depreciation on qualifying assets and to carry forward losses.

Those who would not comply with the bookkeeping requirements would probably be either too small to pay tax or too corrupt to keep honest records in any case. The latter group, together with the numerous instances where false or double records would no doubt be maintained, would have to be investigated and the tax due assessed according to certain standard procedures. The factors mentioned in the discussion of presumption—sales, number of employees, and so on—might be taken in part as the basis for this assessment, the minimum tax thus determined being rebuttable only in certain specified circumstances (natural disasters and the like) and by the presentation of documentary evidence. This tax should, if at all possible, presume income on the high side and hence pressure the taxpayer to keep better records in the future. A related alternative would be more effective use of the net-worth technique. Either procedure would require more and better directed administrative effort—which is simply to say that the only sure way to improve tax administration in any sector of the economy is to improve it.

A second change would be to improve the use of the net-worth or "comparison-of-patrimony" method. At present, Colombian law provides that when the increase in a taxpayer's net wealth from one year to the next is greater than the net income reported, the increase in net wealth is taken as his net income for income tax purposes. This procedure is apparently now used in several thousand cases each year, but its effectiveness is considerably reduced by several defects in the existing law. At present, the comparison-of-patrimony method cannot legally be applied if no return was filed in the immediately preceding tax year. Non-filing appears to be quite common, even among professionals. In addition, allowance is made for personal expenditures in the course of the year. A large element of the "enrichment" of the taxpayer, the supposed base of the income tax, is thus left completely out of the account. Finally, some assets do not have to be reported for net-wealth tax purposes (for example, assets held abroad), so that a channel for evasion remains open. It would not be at all difficult to remedy the first two defects. The third could be partially resolved by giving the government authority to take *all* assets into account, though it would never be possible to close all opportunities for evasion by this route. Such relatively simple changes would provide a more effective investigative weapon in dealing with the small business and professional sectors, though they would not help with those who fail to report both income and net wealth. Despite its inherent arbitrariness, the use of indices of external wealth—cars, houses, trips abroad,—seems the most promising way of getting at such hard-core evaders, particularly among professional men, in view of the difficulty of getting very far by any other means. None of these suggestions will "solve" what is essentially an insoluble problem. But more work and thought along these lines seems preferable to the hasty application of a system of presumptive determination of income to important nonagricultural sectors of the economy.

In no conceivable circumstances will it ever be possible to investigate every suspected tax evader in any sector. Some, essentially arbitrary, selection of suspected cases for investigation must be made, and those found guilty of evasion severely penalized. The major purpose of such efforts is not so much to collect the tax in the cases investigated as it is to increase the level of voluntary compliance among the great mass of evaders who cannot be dealt with individually within the limits of available administrative resources. If the lack of discipline in a society renders this selective procedure politically impossible—if, for example, the usual protests of those selected for investigation to the effect that everyone does it and therefore it is "unfair" to pick on them are thought to have any weight at all—then no scheme, plain or fancy, can much improve voluntary compliance, and the increased effectiveness of direct taxation on lightly taxed sectors cannot be considered a very promising source of public revenues.

4 | Taxation and the Allocation of Resources

The introduction of a general sales tax in Colombia in 1965 was, it might be thought, justified by the need to restrain the growth of consumer demand in order to free for public investment and consumption an increasing share of the increase in output resulting from economic growth. The usual economic rationale for general sales taxation in a developing country is that the resources needed for the expanding public sector cannot be obtained simply by increased direct taxation of the wealthy, since their share in aggregate consumption is too small. Mass commodity taxation is therefore needed to check the increase of aggregate consumption, even though the object of tax policy is not to curtail the consumption level of the masses.[1]

The need for additional restraint on consumption seemed obvious to many in Colombia in 1963 (when the sales tax was passed, though it was not put into operation till 1965). According to the 1962 General Plan, increased consumption (including government consumption) was supposed to absorb only 48 percent of the expected increase in final supply (production plus imports) in the 1959–1964 period. In fact, the *absolute* increase in consumption had reached the planned 1964 figure by 1963; but the final supply had increased so much less than expected that this absolute increase in consumption absorbed 87 percent rather than 48 percent of the total increase in available output over the 1959–1963 period.[2] The result was that the investment figures (and growth rates) actually realized in this period were well below those planned.

A rough idea of the magnitude of the problem and of the possible usefulness of the sales tax in solving it can be obtained from a simple illustrative calculation. Suppose the aim of tax policy in 1963 was to divert 52 percent of the increase in total output to the public sector from private spending. About 440 million pesos (in 1958 prices) in additional taxation would have sufficed for this purpose. The sales tax, had it been imposed in 1963, would have yielded perhaps 200 million pesos, or about half the needed amount.[3] The effective rate of taxation on taxable items, which comprise only about one-fifth of total consumption, would have been around 5 percent (a figure slightly above the actual weighted average rate on taxed goods in 1965, owing to apparently greater evasion in the high-rate items). For the sales tax to have held private spending to the assumed target level, this effective rate would have had to be more than doubled, for example, by a combination of more effective administration and higher statutory rates. Nevertheless, if demand restraint was the sole aim of increased taxation, this crude calculation indicates that the sales tax could play a useful purpose in future fiscal policy.

If the scarcity of foreign exchange is the dominant constraint holding back Colombia's development at present, however, a reduction in the investment-savings gap, whether achieved by a sales tax or by any other means, will not permit increased growth and therefore is not in itself a useful aim for a growth-oriented policy. The Colombian sales tax, both through some of its particular structural features and to a lesser extent through its impact on the distribution of private incomes, tends naturally to affect the balance of payments by altering the composition of final demand and the allocation of investment resources between import substitution, exporting, and other activities. The transfer of resources to the public sector by means of the tax also constitutes an important change in the composition of demand, probably resulting in a decreased demand for imports, since much public development spending has a low import content. In addition, whether or not there is a general "savings gap," the greater elasticity of public expenditures than of public revenues with respect to changes in national income insures that there is a *public* savings gap which the sales tax will help close. Other taxes could have done these tasks as well or better, however, and the sales tax as now constituted has no special merit as an instrument of development finance in Colombia.

The most obvious structural feature of the Colombian sales tax is its differential rate scale. The basic rate of tax is 3 percent on the manufacturer's sales price; this rate applies to all products manufactured in Colombia or imported except for items specifically exempted or taxed at one of the higher rates.[4] Table 18 shows the yield of each rate for 1965 and the first half of 1966 and illustrates the great revenue importance of the basic rate.

The administrative argument for a uniform sales-tax rate is strong. For example, a uniform 4 percent rate on the same

Table 18. Sales-tax collections, 1965–1966 (millions of pesos).

Rate (percent)	1965[a]		1966[b]	
	Amount	Percent	Amount	Percent
10	53.90	13.8	76.31	25.3
8	12.52	3.2	15.87	5.3
5	78.13	20.0	47.47	15.7
3	246.62	63.0	162.14	53.7
Total[c]	391.17	100.0	301.79	100.0

Source: Subdivision de Recaudacíon, División de Impuestos Nacionales, Ministerio de Hacienda y Crédito Público.

a These figures include all collections recorded by the Tax Division up to the end of February 1966, covering sales during calendar 1965. Since the potential yield for 1965 was estimated as about 650 million pesos, the actual collection efficiency in the first full year of operation may be put at around 60 percent. (If anything, this estimate is probably a little high, since the base estimate, details of which are not given here, is a conservative one.)

b Includes collections from March through August 1966, covering sales during January–June 1966—that is, up until the rate increases and administrative reforms of mid-1966. The higher yield of the 10 percent bracket apparently reflects mainly importation of automobiles in early 1966.

c Excludes fines and interest.

tax base would yield approximately the same revenue as the 1965 schedule of rates. Rate differentiation increases the possibilities of evasion (as well as the incentive to evade), especially when the higher rates, as to some extent is true in Colombia, affect mainly imported goods of kinds which are already being smuggled in considerable quantities. As a rule, however, the desire to encourage import-substitution industries prevailed over the fear of evasion. The result is that in several instances imported products are taxed under the sales tax at rates two or three times higher than similar goods produced in Colombia.

The differentiated rate structure of the sales tax may be justified either in terms of its effects on resource allocation or in terms of its effects on income distribution. Against the allocative argument, it is often said that specific excise taxes (or differential rates) are inherently less desirable than more general sales taxes (or uniform rates) because the less general a tax is, the more it "distorts" the allocation of resources from that determined by market forces. A general tax, whether on income or sales, which disturbs only the choice between leisure and consumption, is thus preferable to a partial tax which also disturbs the choice between different commodities. If, however, the economy is not in an optimal position before the tax is levied, as was true in Colombia, a set of differential excise taxes with the "right" distorting effects, tending to shift the economy to a better position by correcting existing distortions in the price system, may be superior in its allocative effects to any general tax.[5] It may be argued that increased taxes on leisure activities such as travel, or on leisure complements such as cameras and alcoholic beverages, will induce consumers to work more and thus reduce the loss of "welfare" from the introduction of the sales tax. Much of the rate structure of the Colombian sales tax may be justified on these rather esoteric grounds, although in Colombia as elsewhere, given the vast number of unknowns in any such formulation, there is much to be said for a general tax as providing less scope for worsening rather than offsetting existing distortions.

More important in the actual design of the rate structure was the distributional argument for progressive rates of commodity taxation. Underdeveloped countries such as Colombia, with sharply class-differentiated consumption patterns, often conform closely to the implicit assumption behind progressive indirect taxes that some goods are better indices of taxpaying ability than others.[6] In more advanced countries, where one man's "luxury" is often another man's "necessity," there is no such single-valued scale on which goods can be ranked for tax purposes.

To some extent the items taxed at higher rates can be explained by the desire to tax consumers progressively in relation to income. Given the unequal income distribution and the apparent difficulty of enforcing progressive income taxes, it might seem surprising that really high taxes on domestic luxury goods appear never to have been seriously considered in Colombia. One reason for this may be that the government has never made a good case to its constituents—who are in essence those who buy luxury products—that such taxes are needed. Another might be the desire to foment domestic production, whether of luxury or other goods. In any event, well-off Colombians seem as much concerned as well-off people everywhere with how the anonymous poor spend their money. This conclusion can be drawn from the fact that increased liquor and tobacco taxes—which in terms of income are clearly regressive—figured prominently among the items on which higher rates were levied in the new sales tax. Over one-half of the yield of the 5 percent rate came from beer alone and a large part of the yield of the 10 percent rate from tobacco products (see Table 18), both items being already heavily taxed mass consumption goods, and "luxuries" only in the most moralistic sense.

The other side of the coin is that unconditional exemptions have been granted for a number of "basic necessities." The probable impact of these exemptions is to reduce the regressivity of the sales tax. In addition, however, the complete exemption of food, drugs, and school materials (as well as of all services) had various effects on resource allocation, none of which were discussed in designing the tax, and some of which are not particularly desirable in a developing country.

One such effect might be to shift still more of the demand of the low-income groups to the now relatively cheaper food items. The result of exempting food is likely to be some upward pressure on food prices insofar as consumers are able to substitute untaxed food for taxed nonfood consumption. Unfortunately the available data do not permit the testing of this hypothesis. Since agricultural production is an activity which uses relatively few imported inputs, any minor demand shift induced by the change in relative prices might be of some use in relieving a little pressure from the balance of payments.

The sales tax is also likely to shift more demand (and hence productive resources) to the products of small-scale, often inefficient industries—which are not actually exempted by law but are so difficult to control that there is no doubt considerable exemption in reality—and to the exempted luxury service industries. These nonmodern sectors can, in the shelter of the modern sectors, raise their prices because of the tax, but they are unlikely to turn over all the proceeds to the government.

One might expect a high elasticity of substitution between taxed luxury commodities and such untaxed luxury services as entertainment, travel, and servants, though there is no good evidence in Colombia of the elasticity of substitution in response to tax-induced changes in relative prices. One interesting exception is the apparent rapidity with which smuggling (especially of cigarettes) and illegal domestic production (especially of liquor) appears to expand in response to increases in domestic prices of these goods, although the data are not adequate to permit a satisfactory analysis.[7] Once again the shift in demand induced by the tax is in general toward less import-intensive industries—except for such important luxury items as foreign travel, telephones, and smuggled goods—so that the net effect on the balance of payments is presumably favorable, though at the cost of giving a relative stimulus to some of the less efficient parts of the domestic economy. The exclusion from the base of the sales tax of the sorts of services consumed by the well-to-do also considerably moderates the apparent income-group progressivity of the differential rate scale.

Table 19 contains a partial estimate of the incidence of the sales tax on the incomes of salaried urban employees in Colombia.[8] These figures indicate that the tax base (which is determined by the exemptions) was more or less proportional with respect to expenditures and that the effective tax rate on taxable expenditures (which includes the effect of the differential rates) was therefore mildly progressive with respect to total expenditures, though regressive with respect to income. The basic 1953 consumer budget data used in this table—the only such data available—in all likelihood do not reflect adequately the current consumption patterns of either the politically articulate middle and upper classes or the large

Table 19. Incidence of the 1965 sales tax on 1953 employee income brackets.[a]

Monthly income in pesos	Tax base as percent of total expenditures[b]	Average rate on taxable expenditures (percent)	Tax as percent of total expenditures	Tax as percent of average income[c]
100–199	25.0	2.88	0.72	0.91
200–299	24.7	3.20	0.79	0.96
300–399	24.0	3.21	0.77	0.79
400–499	24.3	3.33	0.81	0.81
500–599	21.9	3.38	0.74	0.69
600–699	23.7	3.33	0.79	0.78
700–799	23.7	3.46	0.82	0.77
800–899	23.7	3.59	0.85	0.75
900–999	22.7	3.48	0.79	0.67
1,000–1,499	23.4	3.55	0.83	0.60
1,500 and over	25.7	3.74	0.96	—

Source: Jonathan Levin, "The Effects of Economic Development on the Base of a Sales Tax: A Case Study of Colombia," International Monetary Fund Staff Papers, XI (March 1968), 72.

a For each of the seven cities, the several hundred consumption items covered in the 1953 survey were first classified according to the sales-tax rate applicable. Since item detail was not available by income brackets, the average tax rate for each of the fifteen major expenditure categories was calculated for each city and applied to the expenditure shown for each income bracket. The resulting tax was then calculated as a percentage of average total expenditures in each income bracket and as a percentage of income at the midpoint of the bracket, and the result for each city was weighted appropriately to obtain the national averages given in the table.

b Percent of total expenditures not excluded by exemptions for food, drugs, and services.

c Excludes tax on domestically produced liquors, which in early 1965 was not being effectively collected by the national government and which was later ceded to the departments.

rural population living close to subsistence level. Even for urban employees, the sales-tax collection data in Table 18 indicate that less has been collected at the highest rates than one would expect on the basis of the consumer budget data, so that the incidence of the tax was more regressive than indicated in Table 19, where it is assumed all taxes decreed in the law are collected.

Also questionable is the assumption of a full shift forward of the tax via higher product prices, particularly of the differentiated rates. Since less than one-quarter of total consumption expenditure is covered by the sales tax, it is clearly a very partial tax and hence unlikely to be shifted forward fully even in the long run, as was indicated in the earlier discussion of the effect on untaxed production. The obvious frictional difficulties of supply adjustments in Colombia would also hinder forward shifting, as may in some instances the import-licensing system if the result of limiting supplies by quantitative restrictions is to make supply, in effect, completely inelastic both before and after tax so that the imposition of the tax simply reduces the economic rent of the importer.[9] That part of the sales tax which is not shifted forward in higher prices will also alter the distribution of income on the sources side, though not in any readily apparent systematic way which can be taken into account here.

One may safely conclude that the Colombian sales tax, while regressive, is not too regressive as general sales taxes go. As noted in Chapter 1, it appears that the highly unequal income distribution before taxes was more or less unchanged by the tax system prior to the introduction of the sales tax. This outcome would not be altered much by the sales tax, except to make the extent of income redistribution through the tax system even less impressive than before. Whether this result is good or bad is in part a matter of personal value judgment and in part depends on one's view of the role played in development by the reduction of income inequalities. Since a key argument in this book is that the aim of tax policy in Colombia should be not so much to cut consumption as such to cut the import-intensive consumption of the well-to-do, I do not think the regressive features of the present sales tax are at all desirable.

It would have been quite feasible to design an alternative system of commodity taxation which would have been easier to administer, the incentive effect of which could have been more consciously designed to be beneficial, and which would have had a more progressive incidence. This alternative of a mixed set of luxury excise taxes—including taxes of various sorts on such services as foreign travel, telephones, and (through heavier property taxes) housing, as well as taxes on income-elastic luxury consumer goods such as gasoline and consumer durables—could have had a markedly greater effect in reducing income inequality, assuming this to be a desirable goal in Colombia on both socio-political and long-run economic grounds.

The sales tax as now established will in part do this job, since it falls on some of the price-inelastic, income-elastic goods (though not the important services such as housing and entertainment) that the better-off groups in Colombia try to buy with increased incomes. The income-elasticity of the sales tax may be estimated at 1.2 to 1.3—about the same as that of the income tax on a full current-payment basis, assuming no other improvements in administration. So in this regard at least it provides a useful addition to Colombia's fiscal arsenal.[10] To hold back inflationary pressure, taxes on income-elastic goods are as necessary as the introduction of a current-payment system for the income tax, though perhaps less effective peso for peso (since the greater the impact of taxes on the price level, the less the marginal revenue yield in real terms). Improved elasticity could, however, have been attained more effectively and with less impact on the general price level by a more markedly progressive set of selective excises.[11] A major component of such a set of excises would be a gasoline tax considerably heavier than that finally introduced in Colombia in 1967—a tax which would be, on balance, progressive in incidence and also a minor aid in rationalizing Colombia's transport structure by increasing the private cost of motor transport. With such a tax, the long-run yield of the suggested selective system, at least for the next decade, should be very similar to that of the more general sales tax, given the administrative difficulties of the latter. Substantially heavier use of the traditional sumptuary taxes (tobacco, beer, liquor, gambling) cannot be equally recommended, because of the proved relative income inelasticity of most of the relevant tax bases and the undesirable regressive incidence of these taxes. Higher taxes on luxury commodities would also work toward a more desirable long-run pattern of industrial development.

Increased use of selective excise taxes, with emphasis on heavy taxes on luxury goods and services, would therefore have been a more advisable policy for Colombia to adopt in 1965 than a general sales tax, especially in view of the considerable administrative difficulties in effectively implementing the latter. The fact that few taxes require as high a degree of cooperation from taxpayers for effective administration as a general sales tax was not fully realized, and it is surprising that even a moderate degree of success was achieved with such a major tax innovation in the conditions of Colombia in 1965.

The form of sales tax introduced was not really adapted to the realities of Colombia's market structure, characterized as it is by an abundance of the small firms and self-employed persons that are so hard to control in all countries. The sales-tax law (like the income-tax law) was couched in such sweeping and unenforceable terms that it inevitably became in large part yet another tax on "honesty" (and bigness). These problems could have been alleviated by such arbitrary, administrative devices as the exemption of small firms in certain lines of business or limited use of a *forfait* system of agreed taxes (as in France), but no consideration was given to such administrative compromises.

The relative success of the sales tax in its first year, given its structural defects and the weakness of the administration, may indicate that there is a larger reservoir of taxpayer honesty and willingness to cooperate in Colombia than is generally believed. If so, this reinforces the importance of improving the degree of certainty with which taxpayers can confront the law, through for instance the provision of much more information to taxpayers and the clarification of the obscure points that remain in the present law.[12] Unfortunately, it seems to be all too easy to forget such mundane matters as these in the excitement of major tax reforms, with the result that the reforms often fail to live up to expectations.

Even if a system of excise taxes had been imposed in 1965, in time, as economic activity and consumption patterns became more diversified, a move to a more uniform-rate general sales tax and a consolidation of the special excises would undoubtedly have become advisable. Since it was decided to impose a general tax instead of excises, a wholesale tax instead of a manufacturers' sales tax would have been a better choice in Colombia because of (1) the importance of imports in the tax base—about 30 percent of total tax yield in 1965 (and a larger share in 1966) came from imports—(2) the importance of small, artisan-type manufacture, and (3) the apparent importance of the forward integration of manufacturers (especially since the sales-tax law defined as "manufacturers" firms such as Sears, Roebuck which have goods made to their specifications) into wholesaling and retailing functions.[13]

Imports probably constituted a large part of the potential sales-tax base, and the problem of achieving neutral (or correctly biased) taxation of imports and competing domestic production is considerably more difficult with a manufacturers' tax than with a wholesale tax, since the former will almost always tax imports on a different price basis than competing domestic manufacturers. Although artisan manufacture accounted for only 13 percent of manufacturing production in the early 1960's, almost two-thirds of the nonartisan manufacturing establishments had less than ten employees and proved—as the sales-tax registration data indicate—almost equally difficult to deal with. A tax collected at the wholesale level (that is, on sales to retail stores by both wholesalers and manufacturers) would have concentrated about 90 percent of the tax base in the much smaller number of regular wholesale establishments (about one-half the number of nonfood manufacturers, not counting artisan-type establishments). The relative distortions introduced by pyramiding (applying fixed markups to taxes) and by differences in the channels of distribution employed by competing firms would also be less with a wholesale tax, simply because the tax is levied one stage later in the production/distribution process. Rather than scrap the potentially powerful fiscal instrument of a general sales tax and start from scratch with a more immediately optimal set of excises of the sort proposed above, it might at present be better to work within this framework toward a wholesale tax.[14]

Indirect Taxes and the Allocation of Resources

The introduction of the sales tax in Colombia in 1965 influenced in several ways the size and composition of the import flow needed to maintain any given growth rate. The change in the composition of final demand owing to the transfer of resources to the public sector and to the allocative effects of the rate and exemption structure discussed above should on balance have reduced the demand for imports and hence increased slightly the potential growth rate at any given capacity to import. Regressivity of the tax would have an opposite effect. The most important impact of the sales tax on the balance of payments, however, at least potentially, is its more direct effect on the allocation of investment resources between domestic, import-substituting, and exporting industries.

It is generally recognized that for allocative efficiency it is better to tax goods, whose consumption is to be discouraged, without regard to national origins than to levy discriminatory taxes on imported goods alone. If luxury consumer goods, for example, are taxed by high import duties, as in Colombia, the inefficient domestic production of these products is encouraged by the height of the tariff wall. An obvious remedy is to place compensating high luxury taxes on domestically produced luxury goods as well, as recommended earlier.[15] Once a country's industrial sector reaches the size of Colombia's, the allocative case for equal taxes on domestic and imported goods becomes strong.

At present the sales tax, by levying higher rates in some instances on imported consumer products than on competing domestic products, no doubt adds only marginally to the pressure for inefficient import substitution exerted through the tariff and licensing system. In the future, however, the government will almost certainly have to rely more heavily on the sales tax for revenues to replace the declining foreign-trade taxes, and the distortions of internal taxation will become more important. Although the persistent public-finance gap in Colombia still leads to the use of tariffs on consumer goods such as automobiles for revenue purposes alone, their importance is bound to disappear in the future as the goose (trade) that laid the golden egg (revenue) is finally killed by its own progeny, the protected import-substituting industries.

Apart from such cyclical peaks as 1966–67, import duties have tended to decline as a source of central-government current revenues in Colombia, in part because of increased exemptions and in part as a result of a shift in the composition of imports toward the more favorably treated raw materials, spare parts, capital goods, and "cost-of-living" or wage goods. In the past the resulting need for increased revenues has been partly satisfied by export taxes and by increased income taxes on the industrial sector.

If the national product grows at 5 percent a year, and the elasticity of government current expenditures is 1.2, then the foreign-trade tax base would have to grow at 6 percent a year in order to provide a constant share of the needed revenues, assuming unchanged commodity and rate structures. Actually, since the commodity structure has changed adversely (from a revenue point of view), and the ratio of total trade to income may well fall over time—though this is not a settled issue— constant tariff rate increases, with all the accompanying increased political difficulties and worsened allocative distortions, would be needed to maintain the importance of taxes on foreign trade. Furthermore, as I have already argued, given the marked instability of exports and imports in Colombia, policies leading to greater reliance on foreign trade taxes are undesirable. The heavy export taxes on coffee which exist, and should continue to exist, are related to the stabilization of the real income of coffee producers and of the economy as a whole and not to the long-run upward pressure for an increased public-sector expenditure (see Appendix B). The only argument for a rise in tariffs would be as one part of a de facto devaluation policy—the other part being increased subsidies for noncoffee exports—if it proved politically impossible under the present ad valorem coffee tax to change the exchange rate without giving coffee growers still more incentives to grow coffee.

Export taxes are thus most important in the context of stabilization rather than growth, and I have already argued against increasing the relative tax burden on the modern sector. Therefore increased personal income taxes and internal commodity taxes appear to be the most promising revenue sources for the next few decades.

The increased use of internal consumption taxation, however, poses a problem with regard to industrialization policy. At present, most import-substituting industries are on the one hand protected by high tariffs on final output and on the other hand subsidized by low tariffs on their raw and intermediate materials and on capital goods (thus putting domestic production of these less protected inputs at a relative disadvantage). If current trends continue and tariff revenues decline further in importance, does it seem reasonable to suppose these protected industries can support sales-tax rates of, say, 40 or 50 percent (tariffs on final products now range from 40 to 300 percent) without great and very likely successful pressure for higher offsetting protective tariff walls and hence more distortion of consumption and investment patterns? Further, would even the captive Colombian market pay such high prices, given the existence of the substantial untaxed service sector and of competition from smuggled goods? At present it is probable that the answer to such questions would be "no," and that there is no politically feasible way in which the declining revenues from imports can be offset by increasing revenues from similar domestic consumption goods.

The same pressures that maintain the distorted tariffs which require the compensating luxury excises thus tend to produce sales taxes with the same distortions. Once artificial fostering has induced the creation of a relatively inefficient (in world terms) industry, its output cannot easily be taxed at rates similar to the protecting tariffs themselves without killing off the industry—an outcome not likely to be politically acceptable. This very argument was discussed in the process of designing the present sales tax. The only reason why even heavier discriminating taxes were not levied on imports competing with domestic production was, as mentioned earlier, the fear of further encouraging illegal imports. The emergence of these relatively powerful (in political terms) and protected domestic industries thus has placed the government on the horns of a small fiscal dilemma as well as adding to the country's balance-of-payments problem by making imports more necessary to maintain employment and production levels and exports more costly owing to the high cost of domestically produced inputs.

Since the same factors that shape tariff policy shape tax policy, it is often impractical to propose tax policies to offset directly the distortions that result from bad tariff policies. The possibility of instituting a system of high luxury commodity taxes in Colombia in the near future is therefore small, though the only real long-run solution remains the reduction of differential tariff protection, with a corresponding increase in taxes on consumption goods regardless of national origin.

In the interval the problem will be to prevent the internal taxes that will have to be imposed to keep government revenues up to the required level from accentuating these problems and making their eventual resolution more difficult. Therefore, all elements in the present sales tax which tend to discriminate against imports (except for imported capital goods) should be removed as soon as possible in order to exert a little pressure in the right direction. The removal of direct controls, as often urged by the international lending agencies, will exacerbate matters, since, while allocatively efficient in a narrow sense, the undesirable distributional effects of import liberalization can be combated only by heavier progressive taxes—and it is the very weakness of these taxes which is often used to justify the controls in the first place.[16]

The foregoing discussion is somewhat misleading insofar as

the way in which sales tax actually is administered offsets some of the bad effects of the sales-tax law. Like most sales taxes nowadays, the Colombian one is levied on the "destination" basis, taxing only products consumed in Colombia and therefore exempting exports and taxing imports. The destination principle is not fully implemented, however, in part because of the difficulty of fully compensating exporters for all sales taxes incurred (for instance, taxes on machinery used in export production) and the allied problem of controlling abuses of the exemption privilege. More important, a number of administrative difficulties on the import side lead to economic effects different from those implied by the formal structure of the sales tax.

Since the sales tax was originally levied on imports only when the importer resold the good, direct imports for own use were favored relative to domestic production, not discriminated against either by higher rates or by being taxed on a higher base price (including the distributor's margin) as implied above. Machinery, for example, is commonly imported directly by the user, so that domestic capital goods were put at a relative disadvantage by the sales tax. Such an obvious means of legal tax avoidance was not long neglected by astute Colombians, who quickly began to change normal trade channels—as in the importation of automobiles, for instance—into apparent direct imports to avoid sales tax. To curb this abuse, the government was empowered in 1966 to impose the tax at the time of import rather than sale.

Administratively, it would probably be advisable to tax all imports, including those for resale, at the time of import. This system would put the tax proceeds into the national treasury sooner and more certainly. On the other hand, this administratively desirable system would restore the relative disadvantage of imports compared to domestic production, especially if the final tax base for imports that are resold continued to be wholesale or even retail price rather than manufacturer's price. (The advance payment of tax at the time of import could be credited against the tax due on resale in this case.) For final consumer products at least, the economic results of this administrative improvement do not appear beneficial in view of the distortions of present tariff structures. Paradoxically, the loophole by which imports can easily avoid all sales tax may even provide a desirable incentive to the rationalization of Colombia's production structure by, in effect, putting relatively higher taxes on competing domestic production. Whether this possible benefit offsets the loss of revenue is questionable, however, and on balance it would be preferable to tighten the administration of the tax on imports. In the case of imported capital goods, however, increased effective taxation is definitely to be recommended for both incentive and revenue reasons.

At present Colombia taxes capital goods at the basic 3 percent rate. Although one might think the taxation of capital goods affects resource allocation adversely from the point of view of development, there has been no discussion of the evil effects of capital-goods taxation alleged in conventional public-finance literature in Colombia: the effect exercised on the choice of productive techniques, the increased justification afforded for raising the price of final goods, and the increased cost of investment. As John Due puts this traditional view in his treatise on sales taxation: "Taxation of such items as capital equipment is particularly objectionable because of its restrictive effect on investment; this result is most objectionable in periods of deflation, in undeveloped countries, and in others in which the modernization of industry is of particular importance."[17] If the basic economic purpose of taxation in a developing country is to raise investment levels, as is often assumed, there would appear to be little point in taxing investment and thus lessening the (minor) substitution effect in favor of saving that would otherwise result from consumption taxation. Conventional public-finance analysis would, therefore, lead to a recommendation for the unconditional exemption of at least machinery designed specifically for production use; exemption conditional on use would be better, but so much more difficult to administer effectively in Colombia that the unconditional approach has more merit.[18]

The actual reasons for taxing capital goods in Colombia,

as in other countries, were the need for revenue—the potential revenue from capital-goods taxation in 1965 was at least 10 percent of total potential yield—and the increased administrative complexities that would arise from still more exemptions. These are valid reasons in the Colombian context. Moreover, even in the limited terms of conventional public finance, precisely because a tax on investment is in a sense equivalent to a tax on saving, it may be argued that the taxation of capital goods makes the final incidence of the sales tax with respect to income less regressive than it would otherwise be.[19] This argument carries more weight if the sales tax is viewed not as a tax on consumption but as an indirect income tax—for example, a way of reaching income that would otherwise escape direct income taxes—as it seems to be considered by some policymakers in Colombia.

The taxation or nontaxation of capital goods is not really a matter to be decided on its own merits within the sales-tax framework alone. Viewed more broadly from the point of view of development policy, there is a strong economic argument for the taxation of capital goods. The existing subsidy granted through the exchange-rate system on the importation of machinery and equipment, combined with the relatively high cost of labor in organized industry (owing at least in part to labor and social-security legislation), means that there is already a considerable tendency to overmechanization in Colombian industry, as in part indicated by the fact that machinery frequently sits idle. If the real cost of labor to the economy (its "shadow price") is below its market price, the resulting bias in the capital intensity of new investment will be redressed, if only in small part, by the taxation of capital goods. Since the exchange rate at which equipment can be imported is probably less than the shadow exchange rate, the small tax on capital goods should also work in the right direction. This appears to be a clear case in which a discriminatory tax will alter the results of the price system in a direction conducive to sounder long-run development. The tax on capital goods should therefore be retained as long as the exchange rate is overvalued.

Actually, three groups of inputs are involved in this problem: imported capital goods, domestic capital goods, and other domestic inputs which may be substituted for capital. The distortion argument for taxing imported capital goods is a strong one; this economic case strengthens the administrative reasons discussed earlier for rectifying the ease with which the tax on imported machinery and equipment may now be evaded. Insofar as the market cost of labor is above its social cost, this amounts to a reason for taxing domestic capital goods. In addition, however, there is also probably a case for levying a discriminatory tax on imported as opposed to domestic capital goods.[20] If the scarcity of foreign resources is holding back Colombia's development, it seems unwise to have a price structure which encourages the adoption of import-intensive, capital-intensive methods of production. The potential role of the sales tax in alleviating this complex of problems is a minor one, but the influence of the present system is exerted in the correct direction and should be maintained and strengthened.

The pattern of investment in Colombia was affected both directly and indirectly by the imposition of a general sales tax —directly by the consequent increase in noninflationary public investment and by the taxation of capital goods, indirectly by the shift in the nature of final demand as a result of the effects of the tax on income distribution and as a result of the differential taxation of different products. On balance, the effects of the sales tax were definitely discriminatory and on the whole discriminatory in the right direction, tending to shift resources to less import-intensive uses.

The probable relation of the sales tax to the pattern and rate of economic growth in Colombia, given the existing set of economic policies and distortions, may now be summed up. The sales tax will enable the government to finance more development expenditure in a noninflationary way (assuming the proceeds to be properly used). It will also restrain aggregate private spending substantially. The more efficiently the tax is administered, the more striking the results. The same transfer of resources and demand restraint could have been achieved at least equally well by other possible tax changes. Earlier I argued that what Colombia needs is not just taxes but more progressive taxes. In this light, only if psychological and political resistance to more direct taxes were so overwhelming as to make expansion of the public sector by this route impossible would the turn to a general sales tax have been desirable. The evidence does not indicate this to be the case.

The incidence of the sales tax on income distribution in the private sector is moderately regressive. This result is not desirable, given the present degree of income inequality and the small amount of redistribution through the pre-existing tax system. A more acceptable pattern of incidence could have been achieved by more selective taxation of certain commodities and services. More selectivity would have also been desirable for providing correct incentives, particularly to offset the distorting effects of high tariffs on luxury imports.

In general, the present sales-tax regulations with respect to imported goods compared with domestic production would definitely add to the distortions imposed by the tariff and license systems on the pattern of investment in Colombia if they were effectively administered. The tax should therefore be altered to apply to consumption of taxed goods without regard to national origin. An exception should be made for the particular imported capital goods against which some discrimination appears desirable at this stage of Colombia's industrial development (and where administration should be tightened to achieve this end). The problem in correcting the distortions in consumer-goods production resulting from the past policy of fostering any and all import-substituting industries is more political than technical. Despite this bias in the present tax and its regressive incidence (which has a similar effect) the import bill needed to maintain any growth rate is probably less than before the imposition of the sales tax because of the change in the composition of final demand toward less import-intensive public investment as well as toward the agricultural and service sectors.

If it was necessary to close the fiscal gap existing in the early 1960's by increased commodity taxation—a debatable proposition—on most counts a more selective system of excise taxes would have been better than a general sales tax even at this stage of Colombia's development. The yield of a properly designed selective system would be comparable to that of the present tax. Since a general sales tax was in fact imposed in 1965, it would now be more advisable to improve it than to attempt a drastic revision. The base of the tax should be changed to a wholesale tax in order to simplify administration, especially with regard to the treatment of imports (which would be put on a more equal footing with domestic production), and taxes on domestic production of luxury consumer goods should be increased as much as possible. The taxation of capital goods should be retained, and every attempt should be made to increase gasoline taxes and to put whatever special taxes are possible on such services as foreign travel and luxury residential housing. Gasoline taxes were in fact substantially increased in 1967. I believe they could be raised still more with generally beneficial effects, although the exact rate cannot be decided without closer consideration of domestic crude oil prices, the taxation of petroleum companies, and the oil exchange rate. Housing could be taxed through heavier property taxes (as urged in Chapter 5) as well as through a more effective net-wealth tax.

The declared goals in imposing a sales tax in Colombia in 1965 were to restrain private demand, to increase government revenues, to discourage luxury consumption, and to reach indirectly incomes now escaping tax (and thus, implicitly, to have a progressive incidence). The first two goals were at least in part achieved by the present sales tax—as they could have been by a number of alternative taxes; the last two were not —though they would be if the suggested changes were made.

Not everyone would consider these goals appropriate for Colombia at this time. Another aim, depending on one's view of the nature of the development problem facing the country, might be to relieve the pressure on the balance of payments and hence reduce the foreign-resources shortage which constrains development. Still another would be to encourage the use of more labor-intensive methods of production, which would also reduce the need for imports as well as increase the present low rate of absorption of additions to the urban labor force. Both of these objectives will be approached a bit more closely as a result of the imposition of the sales tax, but could, if desired, have been more adequately satisfied by alternative taxes.

All the effects mentioned in this summary are undoubtedly small in quantitative terms at present (though probably not so small in the future). But my point is simply that, given the relatively few and limited policy instruments available to the government in most underdeveloped countries, even such minor effects ought not to be neglected. At the very least, gross incompatibilities with the avowed objects of development policy ought to be avoided. Even if an optimal development strategy is too much to hope for on the basis of existing knowledge, an internally consistent one should not be, as indicated by this simple analysis of this particular tax policy. Without a development policy, taxes can hardly be a useful instrument; but with such a policy, and faced by an inefficient market signaling system, they can and should be viewed as instruments to evoke the desired reactions from economic units.

Capital, Labor, and Taxes

Observers from developed countries often deplore the apparent irrational desire in many developing countries to invest in the most up-to-date, capital-intensive, labor-saving technology, disregarding what seems to be a superabundance of labor. The result of this preference for "technology" is often increasing unemployment as population expands and becomes more urbanized while urban industrial employment grows much more slowly. This is the situation in Colombia today.[21]

Some writers imply that the reason for the observed capital-intensive investment pattern is pure and simple emulation of industries in richer countries, combined with a desire not to be thought "backward." Businessmen (and managers of official development enterprises) in poor countries are not, however, noticeably less rational than their counterparts in rich countries, and it seems clear that in most countries firms invest in capital-intensive rather than labor-intensive techniques primarily because it pays to do so. The private cost of capital relative to labor is lower than the social cost, in part owing to government policies.

The importation of capital goods is, for example, often favored by low tariffs and overvalued exchange rates as well as by the relatively greater ease of financing (through supplier credits) the purchase of imported capital equipment than of meeting, say, a larger wage bill. Even in countries where most capital goods are domestically produced, the employment of capital-intensive technology is often favored by tax incentives of one sort or another or by policies holding down nominal interest rates to artificially low levels. On the other hand, the employment of labor in productive pursuits is penalized in many countries by, for example, high minimum-wage laws and extensive compulsory fringe benefits in the modern industrial sector.[22]

An important function of a development-oriented tax system is the producing of price signals to which economic agents will respond by exploiting adequately the available factors and opportunities in the economy. My assumption is that development policy in Colombia must not only accumulate capital but also use it efficiently. Misallocation of scarce foreign exchange in particular is both wasteful in itself and may well handicap productivity growth (and thus development) substantially.[23]

If it is assumed that the supply of all factors is imperfectly elastic to firms, so that relative prices affect the choice of factors, and that labor and capital are to some extent substitutes for each other, then the question I want to consider is the extent to which the present Colombian tax system biases entrepreneurial decisions in favor of capital. Another way of looking at it is: to what extent can the shadow prices of factors—the economy-wide opportunity costs involved in their use—be translated into actual prices through tax policy?

Surprisingly, the effects of alternative taxes on the choice of technology within industries and on the relative growth of sectors with different factor proportions seem to have been almost entirely neglected in the conscious formulation of tax policy in all countries. One would, a priori, think that the establishment of a set of relative prices that would create an incentive to use capital as efficiently as possible should be a main object of tax policy in most capital-scarce developing countries. In fact, however, the underlying concept of developmental tax policy has almost always been that capital investment is the key to growth, so that the more capital investment there is, the better for growth. Very little attention has been paid in the formulation of tax policy to the *kind* of capital investment fostered or to the proportions in which it is combined with other inputs. The result is that many tax policies prevalent in less developed countries widen rather than narrow the divergence between actual and shadow factor prices, making capital less and labor more expensive, thus affecting the development of different sectors of the economy, the technology employed in those sectors, and perhaps even the development of technology in the future. The following sketch of a more nearly neutral tax system—one that does not *favor* the use of capital relative to labor—while it offers no complete program of reform, should serve to indicate some aspects of the present Colombian tax system which could be re-examined from this point of view.

To look first at special tax incentives, it seems clear that there should be no special incentives to invest in capital goods as such in Colombia. If tax incentives are to be granted to new firms (or to industrialization in general) the benefits received might be related to increases in output rather than to increases in fixed capital investment. (Note that this is the opposite to the conclusion one would reach by focusing on the investment-stimulating effect per dollar of revenue lost, as is usually done.) Although the direct stimulus to increase output might turn out in practice to be weak, at least the undesirable effect of increasing capital intensity would be avoided.[24] Even a general tax exemption of new firms would, from this point of view, be better than accelerated depreciation or an investment credit.

The heavier taxation of corporations than of other forms of business organization, which was earlier deplored, does not look so bad from the present point of view, since those sectors in which the corporate form is dominant are also, as a rule, more capital-intensive ("modern"). The same is true of the strictures in Chapter 3 on the difficulty of enforcing income taxes in nonmodern (for which read "less capital-intensive") sectors. Of course, the use of the presumptive method and other administrative techniques suggested above would tend to work in the other direction by increasing tax pressure on traditional sectors. Yet taxing capital (the basis on which income is presumed, at least in part) more heavily in relation to labor within these sectors is an offsetting economic argument in favor of the use of such techniques in Colombia.

The tax structure thus tends to favor one or another sector a little according to prevailing factor proportions; it does not as a rule much affect the choice of technology within a given sector. One feature of the business tax system which may have a strong effect on this choice is the depreciation system. A tax on net income should presumably allow an annual depreciation deduction for wear-and-tear and obsolescence, but there seems no reason to permit any acceleration or other favoritism to capital-intensive methods of production. It has been argued that the use of an original-cost basis for calculating tax depreciation allowances in a country with inflation biases the system *against* capital investment because the value in terms of reduced taxes of an increase in labor cost will exceed that of an increase in capital cost.[25] The exact bias resulting from "inadequate" depreciation allowances depends, however, on the relative rates of increase in wages and capital-goods prices and on the relative rates of growth of inflation and of a firm's assets. This problem admits of no firm over-all answer. My own tentative conclusion is that at present further special incentives to new fixed capital investment are not needed in Colombia. If, however, the exchange rate on capital-goods imports is made more realistic and the labor laws less rigorous—as should be done in any case—there is much to be said for the simple system of accelerated depreciation suggested in Chapter 3 as a stimulus to the expansion of the modern sector and an aid to new firms.

One form of special depreciation incentive which should be used immediately is to relate the depreciation allowed to the utilization of existing productive capacity. An incentive to use capital more than one shift a day is obviously a good policy when capital is scarce and underutilization of existing capital is common, as in Colombia. The present income-tax law contains a provision to this effect already; it should be implemented at once and strengthened if possible, although its effectiveness will be limited so long as imports for industrial operation remain scarce.

As noted, there should definitely not be an excess-profits tax in a capital-saving tax system, since this tax as employed in Colombia in effect penalizes more efficient use of a given capital stock. On the other hand, there is much to be said for a tax on net wealth as an integral part of the tax system. A tax on wealth is a tax on capital and has to be paid out of income (if capital is not to be reduced). Thus, its income effect would appear to provide a stimulus to use capital to produce as much income as possible, while the marginal wealth tax rate on increases in income is close to zero. In addition, a wealth tax falls more heavily on capital-intensive firms and so reduces the attractiveness of those activities relative to others. A tax on real property has similar discriminatory—but in present-day Colombia probably desirable—effects.

The effects of a nominally general sales tax on the employment of factors are not unlike those of a nominally general income tax (irrespective of whether the income tax is shifted forward in product prices or not). Since in practice these taxes will impinge most on the prices of organized industry (or on its profits), factors will tend to shift to other, usually less capital-intensive, sectors of the economy. Within sectors, the factor-choice decision can, as already noted, be affected by the exemption or taxation of investment goods.

Payroll taxes would not exist in a tax system designed to fit the resource pattern of an economy richly endowed with labor relative to capital. Many of these economies nonetheless now have such taxes; and in Colombia they yielded almost 600 million pesos in 1965—equal to about 30 percent of income-tax collections—and amounted to about 10 percent of industrial payrolls. The distributional intent of these taxes (and the benefits they finance) is usually laudable, though perhaps misconceived, given Colombia's economic structure. As in the case of minimum-wage laws, the main effect of social security systems financed through payroll taxes is often to prevent economically beneficial employment decisions. Since most real income improvement in Colombia will come about from expanded productive employment, the social security system will thus to some extent fail of its avowed object of bettering income security and redistribution, except in the narrow sense that the fewer who are employed after the tax is imposed are perhaps better off than they would otherwise be.

To reiterate, the purpose of modifying the tax system in the light of the considerations discussed here is not the employment of more labor as such; it is simply to remove the existing bias against employing labor and capital in proportions reflecting their real costs to the economy. No special subsidies to labor (like those so commonly given to capital) are proposed.[26] On the other hand, more recognition could be given to some expenses of employers (and employees) that are really costs of earning income. Expenditures for education, on-the-job training, and changing residence might, for example, be more leniently treated than at present. They might be viewed as investments in improving the quality of labor and at least as worthy of government support as investments in reseach and development (that is, in improving the quality of capital).[27]

If the use of labor is not taxed, and the use of capital is not subsidized, entrepreneurs are freed from at least some of the present artificial inducements to use more of the scarce and less of the plentiful factor than economic realities would indicate. If a country has more "labor" than "capital," the proper choice presumably involves the use of more labor. This choice would not, perhaps, be too relevant in many industries now— or in some industries ever—because of the relative lack of labor-surplus technology. This is one instance in which there is no advantage in being backward, for the countries in which the technology in most industries was developed were never in the same labor-abundant situation as the presently developing countries. There seems to be a clear case for subsidizing research and development in this field—if not (capital-intensive) basic research, then certainly adaptive research. If relative factor prices reflected true scarcities and the incentives were great enough, one might expect more effort in this field than has been true in the past from either indigenous or foreign business. State and private nonprofit organizations might also play a notable role, just as they have in developing new technology for tropical and highland agriculture (notably through the efforts of the Rockefeller Foundation). These efforts would take a long time to pay off, but no doubt the problem will exist for many years, especially in view of the prospects of continued population expansion in most poor areas. (The possibility of tax measures to restrain population growth is not considered here and is probably not too realistic in most countries.)

The foregoing should give some idea of the sorts of tax policies one might expect to see in a country like Colombia in which capital is scarce and labor plentiful, particularly when most capital goods must be imported. With minor exceptions, none of the methods suggested here for moving actual factor prices closer to shadow prices involves any subsidization. Hence the usual financing problems are avoided.[28]

For Colombia in particular, while no attempt has been made to estimate the quantitative importance of any of the measures discussed above, the conclusion in the previous section on the appropriate treatment of capital goods under the sales tax appears to be reinforced, some suggestions on appropriate tax incentive policy (discussed further in the next section) emerge, and the conclusions reached elsewhere and on other grounds about the appropriate role of excess-profits, net-wealth, presumptive income, and property taxes are again supported. The only important new conclusion is that proposals for increased payroll taxes should be viewed with skepticism, except perhaps insofar as the revenues are used to improve the quality (and hence employability) of labor.[29] Incidentally, the distributive effect of the suggested labor-favoring policies should not be neglected: in general, measures favoring the employment of labor will redistribute income progressively, with the favorable allocation effects discussed earlier, though with less favorable effects on savings and incentives. Any problems can, however, be handled as suggested elsewhere in this book. On balance, therefore, the distributive case strengthens the general allocative argument of the present section.

Current tax policy in Colombia in a number of ways compounds rather than corrects the failure of the market to reflect true factor scarcities. Changes along the lines suggested, while they might not be always politically easy, would tend to mold the structure of production more closely to the real factor mix and thus induce more efficient use of scarce capital and foreign exchange. The capital-output ratio would be reduced, and the rate of growth at which the foreign-resources constraint enters into play would be raised. These would seem to be desirable results, not only in Colombia but in many other developing countries. It is therefore curious that policies favoring the use of labor are found almost nowhere, those favoring the use of capital, everywhere. Admittedly the discussion here in the treatment of "labor" and "capital" as homogenous factors (and the ignoring of the difficult management problems in using more labor) is highly simplified. Nevertheless, it appears relevant in the light of this discussion to ask: is it not in the tax treatment of capital and labor in many developing countries that the real instance of inappropriate emulation of techniques developed for other economies and other times occurs?

A Tax Incentive Policy for Colombia

Up to this point this book has been primarily concerned with the effects, usually unintended, of the basic tax structure on economic development. In Colombia, as in most countries these days, however, a number of special "incentives" have been explicitly introduced into the tax system in order to achieve some stated goal. Now is the time to examine briefly the existing fiscal incentives in Colombia and offer some guidelines for a revised tax-incentive policy.

It is always difficult to object in principle to most proposals for special tax incentives to encourage this or that activity, since the stated objectives are generally desirable ones. Nevertheless, it is astonishing how little examination has been made of how well tax incentives have achieved their objectives in any country. Owing to the usual scarcity of hard data, my analysis necessarily relies as much on general theoretical considerations and on experience elsewhere as it does on specifically Colombian information. Nevertheless, most available evidence on Colombia, impressionistic or factual, supports my generally negative appraisal of the usefulness of the present incentive system as an instrument of development policy.[30]

Appraisal of tax-incentive policy is rendered especially difficult by the lack of any well-articulated development policy in Colombia in recent years. Like most countries, Colombia has made extensive use of tax incentives in an effort both to increase the level of private saving, investment, and exporting and to channel investment and saving activities into lines considered more useful for development. While the effects of the particular tax incentives employed may appear small in the context of the ambitious Plan goals cited earlier, it is fair to say that the various incentives introduced in the last decade were intended to fit into Plan strategy—for example, by increasing exports and stimulating import-substituting investment, and by encouraging increases in total saving, and by channeling more investment to low-income housing and to industry. There appears, however, to have been no conscious evaluation of the cost in terms of revenue foregone (as well as increased inequity) or of the efficiency of the particular incentives chosen in achieving the desired aims, that is, their benefit-cost ratios.

The role, intended and realized, of tax incentives in shaping development can be analyzed only by, first, divining the intended objectives of the incentive provisions; second, appraising their efficiency in attaining the objectives; and third, appraising the consistency of the objectives (and the results) with the development strategy appropriate for Colombia. Obviously, this enormous task can be accomplished here only in small part. The formulation of a coherent, meaningful set of development policies is a necessary precondition for the development of a useful set of special tax incentives that will be worth the effort and cost of designing and implementing them. Until such a strategy is elaborated, the most that can be done to improve the present system is to revise it so that the cost-benefit ratio of all measures is at least positive, and they appear to work toward the general ends of aiding the balance of payments and increasing "productive" investment in the modern sector of the economy (preferably without unduly distorting factor choice).

The upshot of applying these apparently undemanding criteria to the present Colombian tax system is that most existing special tax incentives should be abolished (or, if they are kept, changed considerably in form), since other methods can achieve better results for the same cost in terms of revenue foregone and with less uncertainty and waste of time by both government and taxpayer. The more refined the development strategy and the more competent the revenue and development administrations, the more useful special incentives can be; when, as in present-day Colombia, these conditions are not well satisfied, it should not be surprising that less detailed incentive measures, if properly designed, work out better.[31]

The main purpose of most tax-incentive legislation in Colombia traditionally has been to encourage investment, particularly in certain "basic" industries. For example, corporations formed prior to the end of 1965 whose sole purpose is to turn out a product or products considered necessary for the development of the country receive beneficial treatment. The chief condition is that they purchase at least 60 percent of their raw materials domestically. If so, they are usually entitled to complete exemption from the income and excess-profits taxes from 1960 through 1969. The Ministry of Development determines whether or not an enterprise is eligible for the exemption and is supposed to make one on-site inspection of each enterprise every year to verify that it is fulfilling the dual requirements of "sole purpose" and percentage of raw materials purchased domestically.

In the case of companies which are not only "basic" but also "new" the exemption extends to shareholders with respect to both the income tax on dividends and the net-wealth tax on shares. "New" industries are those which produce articles not produced in Colombia before 1960, or produced in quantity "notably inferior to that required by domestic consumption," or which use methods of production "technically superior in an important way" to methods used previously.

The number of industries considered "basic" for purposes of the tax exemption is quite large, including the extraction and refining of asbestos, sulfur, and coal, a number of chemical products, paper, pulp, fertilizers, artificial fibers, iron and steel, nonferrous metals, and machinery and machine tools. There appears to have been no real study behind these essentially arbitrary choices, which were made by the National Planning Department. Table 20 shows the surprisingly small number of companies that received the "basic" industry exemption in 1963 and the small cost of this concession. The reason for the relative unimportance of this exemption appears to be the difficulty firms have in complying with the requirement that they purchase 60 percent of their materials from domestic sources.

Since 1960 companies "complementary to the production of steel"—that is, those which utilize products of the national steel mill, Acerías Paz del Río, S.A., or elements imported in exchange for such products, in proportion greater than 50 percent of the total value of raw materials employed during the tax year—have also had up to a 100 percent exemption from both the income and excess-profits taxes, an advantage scheduled to continue through 1969. Shareholders of companies which are both "new" and "complementary" enjoy the same advantages as those of "new" and "basic" companies. This exemption is thus almost identical to the exemption for "basic" industries, except that the proportion of materials one can import is 50 percent instead of 40 percent. An important difference, however, is that the incentive stimulates companies to purchase not only domestically but specifically from one enterprise, the state-established steel plant (which has also received substantial government aid in other forms).

Another incentive measure aimed at investment is the provision that firms may, until 1969, deduct 5 percent from net

Table 20. The cost of income-tax incentives in Colombia, 1963.

Incentive	Number of firms benefiting	Estimated cost (millions of pesos)
Basic industries[a]	29	17
Complementary industries[a]	9	4
Exports[b]	—	65
Economic development[c]	161	65
Recuperation of assets[c]	259	

a Based on data from the Ministerio de Fomento and other sources as set forth in an unpublished 1968 study by Richard C. Porter entitled "Basic and Complementary Industry Tax Exemptions."

b A crude calculation assuming that *all* minor exporters could offset presumed export income against a 36 percent tax rate. The figure is probably an overestimate for 1963 (though the value of this incentive was much higher after the 1965 devaluation until, as discussed later in the text, it was abolished in 1967). Most of the benefits probably went to a relatively small number of companies, since only eleven firms accounted for almost half of registered minor exports in 1963 (Banco de la República, *Directorio de exportadores y de exportaciones 1963* [Bogotá, 1964]).

c Based on data obtained from the Superintendencia de Sociedades Anónimas and reported in an unpublished 1966 study by Richard Bilsborrow, "The Structure of Tax Incentives in Colombia," and in Francisco Pineda M., "Aspectos del presupuesto nacional de Colombia" (Thesis, Universidad Nacional de Colombia, Bogotá, 1965). The revenue cost estimate (based on Pineda, p. 69) is as crude as the other figures in the table but is probably of about the right order of magnitude.

taxable income if this amount is used to increase the domestic production of otherwise imported goods, "whose development is convenient for the economy of the country." The scope of this provision includes many of the activities classified as "basic" industries and also extends to a number of currently (or until recently) imported agricultural products, including wheat, hops, malt, cacao, rubber, wool, and tallow, and several manufactured products, including internal-combustion engines, centrifuge pumps, refrigerators, ships, machinery, and metal products.

The administration of this "economic development reserve" is particularly complex. Its scope is determined by the National Planning Department, while the responsibility for verifying that the reserve is actually used to make products which substitute for imports rests with the Superintendency of Corporations, the Ministry of Development, and the Ministry of Finance. Thus one organization defines "import substitutions" for purposes of this law, and several others are supposedly empowered to verify that firms comply with the law. In practice, companies are apparently not usually visited to check that the reserve is used as intended, and there appears to be a great deal of abuse of this incentive.[32]

As a final investment "incentive," firms were allowed to set aside up to 15 percent of their net taxable income in a "reserve for the recuperation of fixed assets," provided the amount set aside did not exceed 15 percent of the historical cost of the assets, until the full cost of assets acquired prior to June 1, 1957, was recovered (which would have been in 1966 for most companies). In most cases the companies receiving the greatest benefits under this provision were the same as those receiving the largest benefits from the reserve for economic development. Not surprisingly, since these deductions were limited to a certain percentage of profits, there was a pronounced tendency for the largest enterprises in Colombia, with the largest profits, to have the greatest reserves: in 1963, for example, a single corporation held 19 percent of total reserves freed from tax for these purposes. The fact that some firms which did not even exist in 1957 were making the deduction for the reserve for the recuperation of fixed assets in 1963 indicates once again the haphazard administration of these exemptions.

The total cost of these four "incentives" to investment in 1963 may be roughly estimated at 86 million pesos, or almost 7 percent of income tax assessments in that year (see Table 20). What benefits were purchased for this price? If the object of the incentives was to induce investment, how much was induced? These are impossible questions to answer in light of both the factual and the theoretical deficiences in our knowledge of the determinants of investment in Colombia.

Very few studies of the determinants of investment exist for any country. Interview studies which focus on taxes are unreliable (in part because of the known tendency of businessmen to overstate the importance of tax factors in their decisions in the hope of getting favorable changes), but the little information we do have indicates that stability and certainty are the most important tax factors affecting business decisions.[33] Even such structural features as the improved loss carryovers recommended earlier, which are usually considered to reduce tax deterrents to risk-taking, appear to be of almost no importance in an environment in which no risky investment is undertaken anyway. In this situation special tax incentives (unless very large and certain) may be perceived more as a handout or a "right" than as an inducement to invest in the favored activities rather than others.

A problem in analyzing any of these incentives is that we really have no adequate theory of investment behavior. In the usual theory, the present value of the tax saving from depreciation deductions is similar to a reduction in the cost of capital assets: the response of investment then depends on the elasticity of investment with respect to changes in the rate of return. Even if investment was profitable and possible (that is, imports were available) so few firms in Colombia use explicit financial criteria in making investment decisions that the small changes in the cost of a project resulting from tax concessions probably would not have any effect. (The larger firms, however, apparently often employ a payback-period criterion, which means they ignore all but the returns of the first few years in making their investment decisions.)

Both direct surveys and some econometric investigations stress not the effect on the rate of return but the liquidity effect of tax concessions on the ability to invest. It is true that many firms either strongly prefer to or must rely on internal financing for investment; nevertheless, it is far from certain that changes in liquidity affect investment directly. Liquidity changes may affect the timing of the execution of investment decisions made on the basis of long-run demand and technical considerations, but if firms do not want to invest, mere availability of money "saved" from taxes will not make them do so. For the liquidity effect of tax incentives to be an important stimulus to investment, a strong desire to invest must be blocked solely by lack of finance. It seems most unlikely that this condition has often held in Colombia, where the weakness of markets and the scarcity of imports have been much more important in determining the pattern of investment. Small, fast-growing firms, it is true, may well have been in this situation at times.

The very fragmentary evidence available in Colombia indicates that the increased liquidity afforded firms receiving the "basic" and "complementary" exemptions permitted some investment expansion, though one cannot say whether it stimulated this expansion or not. The economic development reserve is so hard to administer that it probably serves more as a channel for tax avoidance than anything else. The reserve for the recuperation of assets reduces taxes on large, old firms and can hardly be considered a development-oriented instrument. Retrospective relief contributes little incentive to new investment: this is not a moral issue, as it is so often presented in the inflation discussion, but an economic one.

A simple investment allowance system—15 to 20 percent extra depreciation permitted in the first year an asset is acquired—was earlier suggested as the way to give a stimulus to investment if one is thought necessary. Interview evidence indicates inadequate depreciation is not felt as a great problem in Colombia, but inadequate liquidity is (whatever the facts of the matter are); so one might expect some effect on investment, if the import situation permitted it. It is easy to show that a greater effect per dollar of revenue loss would theoretically be expected from direct investment subsidies, but administrative considerations alone suffice to rule these out in Colombia.

The tax relief from accelerated depreciation improves liquidity immediately. For continuing firms, even those which do not grow, there will always be this free loan so long as the allowance is in force. That is, the typical company does not die once its assets are depreciated. If investment grows, the effective rate of tax is permanently reduced by any form of accelerated depreciation. Accelerated depreciation is thus more beneficial to a firm the faster it grows (in terms of new investment), which is presumably what is wanted. In any event, the immediate effect is always a temporary reduction. If the depreciation acceleration is an addition to full regular depreciation, as suggested here, the "loan" never has to be paid back, even if the concession is later removed—that is, there is no way in which the initial subsidy afforded by faster depreciation may be recouped, so that psychologically at least it is more certain.[34] It would also be much simpler to administer a general incentive of this sort than the four specific incentives to investment now in existence. For all these reasons, I urge that the present incentives be allowed to lapse and that consideration be given to introducing a more general investment-allowance system to encourage saving and investment in the growing modern sector, if any concessions at all are considered necessary in the light of the numerous other policy biases already favoring capital investment in Colombia. As suggested earlier, any increased revenue loss from the more general incentive could be made up by raising the rates on business (unless this were the chosen means of converting public saving into private investment).

Colombia has provided relatively few tax incentives specifically intended to increase and channel private savings. Interest on government bonds and on small savings accounts is tax exempt, but this concession is of minor importance. In 1965, however, a special (and generous) incentive to encourage savings, especially in housing, became law, as usual with little prior consideration.

A tax concession may increase total personal savings either by shifting some of the tax burden to lower income groups with (presumably) lower propensities to save or by a substitution effect which makes saving more attractive relative to consumption (equivalent to an interest-rate change for the selected group of those who get the tax benefit). The extent to which any tax inducement will be a factor tending to increase saving is very uncertain, to say the least. There appears to be little theoretical or statistical basis for even hazarding a guess. The interest-elasticity of savings is usually thought to be low, and I have earlier argued that the propensity to save of the upper-income groups is not very high; so one might guess the effects of tax inducement in increasing personal saving in Colombia would be neglible. Furthermore, tax inducements for saving are not likely to be important in an inflationary environment: if one really wanted to foster personal savings, a substantial increase in real interest rates would seem more direct and at least as efficient as any conceivable tax concession. Higher interest rates would also have the beneficial effects of making the market cost of capital higher and of not depriving the government of any revenue. In short, under Colombian conditions, the use of "incentives" to stimulate savings will incur costs in tax revenues foregone and decreased progressivity. The certainty of these costs outweighs the unknown and unknowable benefits in increased savings. (The only exception to this conclusion is that increased corporate retentions might usefully be encouraged, as argued earlier.)

Many proposals which supposedly favor saving really favor the acquisition of certain assets—for example, housing or industrial shares. This was true with the 1965 Colombian incentive measures and the long-standing exemption of interest on government bonds. The effect of these measures is not primarily one of encouraging more savings as such but of channeling savings that would have been made anyway into "desired" outlets.

An obvious problem with such special savings incentives is that it is difficult to avoid abuse of the privilege by the conversion of assets, with existing savings merely being put into a new, qualifying form. It is also fairly easy to conceal liquid assets in existence when the program gets underway, especially when there are a good many such assets around already as a result of past evasion. This concealment will offer a useful source of future (unearned) tax benefits. For similar reasons, the incentive to conceal capital gains will be increased. Another problem will be to avoid the establishment of patterns of alternate saving and spending, with the frequent reaping of tax benefits by having income accrue in the years in which savings are made and living off the proceeds in alternate years. Some rearrangement of income and spending patterns along these lines is well within the power of, for example, small firms (through inventory manipulation) and professional persons. (Most of these problems would also occur with a direct expenditure tax.) Such arguments, and the obvious tax abuse which quickly resulted, led to the abolition in 1967 of the general savings incentive for housing and industrial shares. No discernible beneficial effects resulted from its year of existence, although at least 100 million pesos in revenue was probably lost.

A final incentive to savings in the Colombian tax system is that all dividends of less than 12,000 pesos are exempt from income tax when received by shareholders whose net income is less than 100,000 pesos; before 1967, the exemption was for dividends up to 5,000 pesos. It seems unlikely that much incentive is provided to shareholding by this exemption (or by the special exemption for shareholders in "new," "basic" or "complementary" industries). Such shareholder exemptions have little to recommend them. Experience elsewhere indicates that they are costly and ineffective measures, which may bring some small increase in saving by making the income distribution even more unequal than before but are unlikely to do much good on balance. Yet, since the dividend exclusion costs relatively little in Colombia and is not worth much to big shareholders, it might nevertheless be kept on, given the long-run goal of broader capital markets and shareholding and the theoretical possibility that the resulting increased rate of return is likely to induce a little new saving from lower-income nonsavers.[35]

Far more important, the effect of other tax measures must be taken into account in evaluating the effect of the tax system on savings. For example, increased depreciation incentives might reduce dividend payouts by making reinvestment more attractive, though Colombian firms apparently view dividends as a fixed charge on profits. Increased retentions are probably desirable in Colombia today, given the low rate of personal saving of dividend recipients. If, in the long run, financing through the capital market becomes equally important, policies which do not unduly favor either retention or distribution might well become more desirable. The net effect of the capital-gains tax (with roll-over), increased personal taxation, the dividend exclusion, and reduced taxation of growing corporations should be to make increased funds available for investment in the modern sector, always assuming that import availability permits the investment to be realized. (The main factor in this conclusion is the suggested system of accelerated depreciation, which should provide over 300 million pesos in increased financial resources to expanding firms in the corporate sector.)

Thus far the argument has been against most of the present special tax incentives designed to encourage investment and savings. The desirability of one type cannot really be in dispute in Colombia today, however: incentives which encourage exports. Given the apparent need for foreign exchange if an adequate rate of growth is to be maintained, and given the desirability of altering the structure of production to favor exporting, it would be worth a considerable sacrifice of government revenue to obtain extra dollars from increased minor exports.

The importance of encouraging exports has been explicitly recognized since 1960 when the first tax exemption for export earnings was introduced. (Other kinds of incentives existed previously.) Under this legislation income originating in "minor" exports—commodities other than unprocessed coffee, petroleum and derivatives, bananas, cowhides, and precious metals—became exempt from income tax. Net income was assumed to equal 40 percent of the gross f.o.b. sales value of exports, subject to the limitation that the taxpayer's total taxable income (on both domestic and export operations) could not be reduced by more than 50 percent as a result of the export exemption. The exemption was not only a monetary stimulus to exports, the intended purpose of the law, but it also both directly and indirectly served as a fiscal incentive for investment. Profitability and liquidity effects on investment decisions ensued quite similar to those of the "basic" and "complementary" industries tax exemptions. Apart from this investment effect (to which the comments made earlier apply), the income tax incentive to exports seems a cumbersome and costly way to achieve the goal of increasing exports, though as is usual with tax incentives its full cost is hidden.

For administrative simplicity, flexiblity, certainty, and proved efficiency, a special subsidy exchange rate for minor exports is much to be preferred.[36] Such a premium rate would provide a more adequate stimulus for exports and one which, unlike the income tax exemption, retains its value whatever happens to the basic exchange rate or the price level. The apparent cost of this form of subsidy would be partly compensated for by abolition of the tax concession (which in 1965 and 1966 cost probably about 100 million pesos a year). Furthermore, one can argue that the net fiscal loss of export subsidies, even very large ones, will be small or nonexistent because of the higher levels of operation and income permitted in Colombia by increased exports (and imports).[37]

The logic of these arguments was apparently partly accepted when the income tax exemption for exports was replaced in 1967 by a system of tax-credit certificates. Under the new system, minor exporters receive from the central bank an amount equal to 15 percent of the total value of foreign-exchange proceeds delivered to the central bank. Apparently this rate was calculated to be equivalent for most exporters to benefits under the income tax scheme. In any event, these certificates, which are bearer documents, freely negotiable and exempt from all taxes, may be used at par to pay taxes after one year from their day of issue. At the end of 1967 tax-credit certificates were selling at about a 30 percent discount in the market; so the present value of the export exemption amounted to about a 10 percent premium on the main exchange rate. Some nuisance taxes and requirements on export transactions were also removed when the tax-credit incentive was introduced in March 1967; all such impediments to trade could usefully be abolished. Considerably larger incentives to nontraditional exports might be considered once experience with the present system can be carefully evaluated, as should soon be done.

The major problem with this suggestion is political. The power of traditional exporters is still such in Colombia that any government would find it hard to implement the recommended policy of increased taxes on coffee (see Appendix B) and increased subsidies on manufactured exports. Nevertheless, until policy provides the "right" incentives, it is unlikely the Colombian economy can grow as it should and must if the present socio-political structure is to survive. Therefore the possibility of substantial political changes being carried out on avowedly technical grounds should not be written off.

To sum up my argument, the objects of most existing incentive legislation are poorly defined. Their administration is complex and appears to be inefficient. The cost of these incentives is never considered and evaluated as an expenditure, as should be done. In any subsequent incentive legislation, it would be highly desirable to include as essential features a clear, well-defined law, a mandatory annual revenue-cost estimate, and a centralized and simple administrative mechanism. All concessions should be granted for a limited time period and should be re-examined periodically. Few rich countries today satisfy these counsels of perfection; but poor countries like Colombia can less afford the waste of resources implied by not satisfying them and must lead the way in devising workable incentives.

The purpose of a tax incentive is presumably to induce someone to do something the government thinks desirable; therefore administrative efforts should be devoted to making the benefits as widely available as possible within the framework of the law, in preference to limiting them to those who fall within a narrow interpretation of the letter of the law. There are two ways of granting special tax concessions: narrowly, by administrative discretion on application, and broadly, to all who fall within the legislative provisions. The first approach has much to be said for it in terms of effectiveness per dollar of revenue foregone *if* three conditions are fulfilled: the administrators know what they are doing; the benefits are substantial; and there is public acceptance of such discretionary concessions or the "need" is urgent, whether acceptable or not. Administrative arbitrariness under such a narrow scheme may be restrained to some extent by giving wide publicity to all the administration's decisions. In Colombia, however, this sort of argument leads me to favor a more general and automatic system like the investment allowance and export bonus suggested above, even at the cost of losing a little more public revenue.

Insofar as tax concessions are granted, they should be as general and as open as possible in order to avoid wasting the scarce human resources of both public and private sectors on needless administrative procedures and delays. A sound tax system with a few general encouragements to investment and exports should give better results in Colombia within a good development program (especially with a good foreign-exchange budget) than any system of special concessions. Without a good development program no tax system, plain or fancy, can be of much help.

Other than increased incentives to exports, possibly a general investment allowance (when conditions are right), and the present small-dividend exclusion, no special tax incentives seem necessary or desirable in Colombia today. A simple scheme of temporary income tax exemptions for defined new activities might have some role to play in industrial policy (once it is worked out in detail), but much greater care than in the past should be taken to reduce the damaging effects of excessive revenue losses because of poor administration— which also results in uncertainty, high cost in other administrative opportunities lost, and unnecessary inequities. At all events, the bad experience of 1960, when new tax giveaways were created at a peak of the import cycle, should be avoided.

In my opinion, a stable and well-run tax system and a sensible public expenditure program would be the best possible fiscal encouragement to sound development of the private sector in Colombia at the present time. Attention might be better devoted to improving the effects on resource allocation of the structural features of the tax system—such as equalizing the treatment of corporations and limited liability companies, improving loss carryovers, shifting the emphasis of tax increases from business to personal taxation, and rationalizing the indirect tax system—than to devising new tax gadgetry in a futile attempt to "solve" the development problem.

5 | Local Government Finance

Many writers on economic development have stressed the need for dynamic local government if development is ever really to take root in a country. Since in a sense national economic development is necessarily a composite of economic activities conducted at the local level, local government is bound to be important either as an obstacle or an aid. Ideally, local leadership and local involvement will help in the adaptation and change that constitute modernization, and a decentralized government structure is one way to obtain this involvement. In reality, however, local dependence, fatalism, and apathy all too often push responsibility up to the central government, whether or not it wants or should have it. As the hopeless state of local governments in most poor countries became apparent, many economists swung over to the other extreme of stressing the necessity of centralized planning and administration on both technical "efficiency" grounds and on the allegedly "practical" grounds of political and administrative incompetence at subnational levels of government. Those public administration and community development specialists, as well as occasional sociologists and political scientists, who continue to emphasize the necessity of community involvement and a functioning local political structure, are often dismissed by economic planners as unrealistic theorists who have been overimpressed by the peculiar history of the United States in these respects.

I have argued that the national government will have to carry the brunt of any expanded development effort in Colombia. This task would be made much more manageable if the extensive local government structure—twenty-one departments, over eight hundred municipalities, several federal territories, and the special capital district—were to cope more successfully with the problem of financing their own expenditures than has been true in recent years. An important factor accentuating the acute national fiscal crisis of the early 1960's, for example, was the assumption by the national government of certain previous departmental responsibilities (police, justice, some education) and the increased national transfer payments to departments and municipalities. Political pressure for further decentralization of revenues continues to be strong. To indicate what can be done to alleviate such problems in the future and because of the considerable present importance and likely potential of local finance in Colombia, I shall examine in some detail the major instruments of urban local finance —taxes on real property. The analysis assumes not only that local government is now important in Colombia and is likely to be important in the future but also that this fact offers as many possibilities as problems for development finance, contrary to the apparent bias of many economic planners against "inefficient" decentralization, the open political influences of regionalism, and the whole messy reality in which planning, budgeting, and taxing is inextricably embedded in any country.

Since the most capable recent student of local government in Colombia, Dick Netzer, apparently has reached the opposite conclusion, however—namely, that there should be no emphasis on local government as a development instrument in Colombia—this assumption is worth some preliminary exploration.[1] Basically Netzer argues that feasible development instruments are available independent of local governments and that increased revenues and expenditures at the subnational level will necessarily replace rather than supplement central-government efforts and will in any case distort resource allocation away from the development optimum. Both arguments are, in my view, mistaken.

There are really no feasible alternatives to reliance on subnational political and administrative structures to perform many tasks essential for development in Colombia today. It is quite true that the great regional diversity in Colombia, the conservativism of local government institutions everywhere, the nature of the local power structure in many areas, and the usual Colombian insistence on applying uniform rules to inherently very different situations all will cause problems in attempting to develop a reasonable regional development strategy. But these problems are not as serious as Netzer (and others) fear. For example, the major problem of local finance in quantitative terms is the financing of urban development. This problem is concentrated in a relatively few cities, and properly designed policies would enable and encourage them to do a great deal to finance their own development, with beneficial effects all around. Putting more responsibility for financing urbanization on the urban areas will add to the total resources that can be mobilized for development and, on the whole, will do so in a manner consistent with the objectives of national tax policy outlined earlier. So long as the key ten or twenty urban areas respond in the right way to centrally decreed policies, it really could not matter less that the landholders who dominate politics in seven hundred rural municipalities will do little or nothing, since they would do nothing anyway. This distinction between the urban fiscal problem— which can and should be resolved mainly at the local level— and the rural problem—which, important as it is to provide basic public services to all citizens, may have to be handled by the national government or regional corporations, if it can be resolved at all—is crucial.[2]

My position is that, given the shortage of administrative talent in Colombia, efforts should be concentrated not on trying to run everything in detail from the center but rather on setting up general policy rules so that people at the local level are induced to make their own decisions as far as possible and to make the right ones from the point of view of national policy. This sort of decentralization may not be so superficially tidy, but in a diverse country like Colombia it is likely to be more economically efficient than further unnecessary centralization.

The virtue of putting the decision closer to the consumers and perhaps calling into being otherwise unutilized enterpreneurial talents is obvious.[3] In addition, establishing a clearer connection between urban services and the taxes to pay for them in this way will both force more revelation of preferences and tend to hold back the demand for these services and increase their supply, in contrast to the almost inevitable result of centralization in ensuring that the demand for expensive urbanization investments exceeds supply.[4] Not only will the total resources for development be increased by encouraging growing urban areas to finance more of their own growth, but the allocation of resources should also be improved by heavier reliance on local taxes where possible—mainly in the larger urban areas.

Subnational governments have traditionally been important in Colombia because of the marked regional differences in the country. There are four distinct major economic zones: the Atlantic Coast, the Cauca Valley, Antioquia, and the Eastern Cordillera. Though at present few of the subnational governmental divisions of the county, except for the departments of Valle and Antioquia, correspond to regional realities, the importance of spatial shifts of activity in a transitional developing economy like Colombia's means that regional organization will tend in fact, if not in form, to become more rather than less important in the next few decades.[5]

In 1963, the combined expenditures of departmental and municipal governments slightly exceeded those of the national government (see Table 9). This situation may be compared with that in neighboring Venezuela, where, in 1958–59, state and local governments were estimated to account for only about 10 percent of total public-sector spending, and 90 percent of even this small amount came from central-government grants.[6] Though state and local finances are more important in federal countries like Brazil, Colombia ranks high among the countries of Latin America in the importance of departmental and municipal finance within the public sector.

The diversity within the general pattern is striking. Per capita expenditures of departmental and municipal governments (including the important public enterprises) in 1962, for example, ranged from a combined low of 60 pesos in Nariño to a high of 234 pesos in Antioquia—with most of the variation being in municipal expenditures. A similar range of variation is found for per capita departmental and municipal revenues (see Table 21). These fiscal differences mainly reflect the vast differences in the real income of the different regions of Colombia, as indicated by the several partial measures of the regional dispersion of income, wealth, and welfare. The "welfare" ranking of departments, for example, and their ranking in terms of per capita local taxes are closely related.[7] Of course, these figures do not include all the levies on the inhabitants of the different departments. The national tax burden is also distributed unevenly among geographic units for the income and complementary taxes, the only ones for which the data were available. While this measure of the geographic incidence of national taxes has some obvious flaws—particularly since businesses often pay tax where their head office is located—the close similarity of the rankings of departments by per capita income taxes and per capita local taxes is striking. While the degree of regional inequality of income, "welfare," and fiscal base (as indicated by the property value figures) is greater in Colombia than in most advanced countries, it appears to be less than in such other Latin American countries as Brazil and Mexico.[8]

Imperfect as the data in Table 21 are, they serve to indicate something useful about fiscal capacity and "tax effort." Most of the more rural departments (except Santander) appear to have above-average tax efforts: their low taxes are not explained by refusal to tax themselves, as is sometimes asserted, but by their meager economic base. But the most striking indication is that three of the four best-off and most urbanized areas—Valle, Atlántico, and Cundinamarca—probably have below-average local tax effort (defined by local taxes levied in relation to per capita income); only Antioquia has above-average effort by this measure. To quote Netzer, "It is only in a few of the largest cities that there seems to be an unwillingness to impose the tax burdens which their economic status would justify."[9]

The principle underlying local government in Colombia is supposed to be "centralized policy and decentralized administration."[10] This sounds like the principle I recommended earlier. In reality, however, local autonomy is legally quite restricted except to a small extent in the capital city, Bogotá.

Table 21. Some indicators of regional differences in Colombia.[a]

Department[b]	Index of per capita income[c]	Index of "welfare"[d]	Index of taxable property values per capita[e]	Per capita local current revenues[f] (pesos)	Per capita income-tax collections[g] (pesos)	Index of tax "effort"[h]	National current transfers[i] (pesos)
Antioquia	101	99	116	195	162	113	20
Atlántico	101	122	86	130	121	74	29
Bolívar	88	109	62	102	26	123	23
Boyacá	71	76	66	61	6	108	27
Caldas	91	94	95	99	44	129	27
Cauca	61	65	52	52	7	121	33
Córdoba	83	118	92	55	17	173	14
Cundinamarca	159[j]	158	159	213	307	81	32
Chocó	32	79	—	24	2	64	65
Guajira	52	—	—	—	—	—	38
Huila	79	86	74	80	16	154	31
Magdalena	99	97	78	55	17	151	20
Meta	119	—	97	106	—	166	51
Nariño	53	68	43	47	7	115	27
Norte de Santander	90	96	65	78	26	117	34
Santander	104	103	84	68	30	77	28
Tolima	105	88	70	94	12	177	34
Valle del Cauca	128	102	128	120	110	81	25

a These data, most of which are subject to many doubts and qualifications, are not fully comparable with each other either in coverage or in time and have been brought together in this table only to give a rough picture of the variations in regional fiscal capacity and effort in Colombia.

b Excludes the three most recently created departments (Sucre, Quindió, Rissaralda) and the relatively unimportant national territories. The major urban centers are in Cundinamarca (Bogotá), Antioquia (Medellín), Valle (Cali), and Atlántico (Barranquilla).

c These are figures for 1964 with the national average equalling 100. From Francesco Marabelli, "Tentativa de distribución del producto bruto interno de Colombia por secciones administrativas del país (1964)," (Bogotá: Naciones Unidas, Programa de Asistencia Técnica, 1966), p. 36. (The national average includes the small national territories, which are not shown in the present table.)

d National average (including national territories and an estimate for Meta) = 100. This index is the arithmetic mean of six "welfare" indexes—deaths per 1,000 inhabitants (1962), mortality from one to four years of age per 1,000 inhabitants (1962), hospital beds per 1,000 inhabitants (1962), elementary school teachers per 1,000 population ages seven to fourteen inclusive (1962), percent of population seven years and over that is literate (1962), and motor vehicles in 1963 per 1,000 population (1962). Data from Departamento Administrativo Nacional de Estadística, *Anuario general de estadística 1962* (Bogotá, 1964) and *Censo automotor 1963* (Bogotá, 1964). The high values for Córdoba and Bolívar are explained mainly by the suspiciously low mortality figures. The value for Meta has been omitted as being completely unreliable.

e In this column the 1964 national average (excluding unreported figures) = 100. Computed in Dick Netzer, "Some Aspects of Local Government Finances," Report no. 51, Economic Development Series, Development Advisory Service, Center for International Affairs, Harvard University (multilith; Cambridge, Mass., 1966), p. 32. See later in the text for further discussion of the property tax.

f The 1963 total departmental and municipal current revenues from own sources (that is, total income less capital income and intergovernmental transfers) have been divided here by 1964 population. Taken from Netzer, "Local Government Finances," p. 37. These revenue figures include the gross receipts of municipal enterprises, which are heavily concentrated in the largest cities, and also the profits of the departmental liquor enterprises.

g Refers to 1962 collections of income (and complementary) taxes by national tax offices in cities in these departments, as reported in Ministerio de Hacienda, División de Impuestos Nacionales, *Impuesto sobre la renta y complementarios año fiscal 1963* (Bogotá, 1964). These figures obviously reflect the concentration of company head offices in Bogotá and Medellín.

h Computed in Netzer, "Local Government Finances," p. 32, by dividing an index of tax revenues (excluding receipts of municipal enterprises but including liquor monopoly profits) by an index reflecting a partial allocation of nonagricultural gross domestic product. A value of more than 100 implies above-average "tax effort." Although obviously imperfect, the general conclusions one might draw from this index—as stated in the text—would not be much affected by more elaborate alternative calculations.

i Sum of 1966 central-government current transfers for health and education (including the "auxilios regionales" granted by Congress) divided by 1964 departmental population. Data from Dirección Nacional del Presupuesto and Departmento Administrativo Nacional de Estadística.

j This is the index for the Distrito Especial, or Bogotá. The Department of Cundinamarca, outside of Bogotá, has an index of 101, according to Marabelli's calculations.

In this the situation in Colombia follows the general pattern in Latin America of legally tight controls—often even tighter in practice—and of a special administrative and fiscal regime for the metropolis.[11] The great regional differences in Colombia have in practice resulted in more local autonomy and variation than the law indicates. But this autonomy has not been put to good use in the fiscal sphere, in part because of the central government's tight control on local revenue-raising authority and in part because present local government structure does not closely reflect regional realities in most cases. In the last few years, however, with the creation of five new departments, departmental governments are perhaps beginning to approach viable regional government units more closely. The views of both Colombian and foreign observers who have taken the local government structure as fixed and consequently concentrated on the "need" for more departmental and/or municipal revenues to meet rising expenditures for fixed functions are thus being partly outmoded by events.[12]

As Netzer has argued, it would make little sense simply to give more revenues and responsibilities to subnational governments which spend, as many Colombian municipalities now do, most of their funds on an elaborate administrative overhead—the product of imposing uniform rules on a diverse reality—and provide no public services for anyone other than municipal employees. Removing some formal decentralization—for example, the municipal level of government outside of the larger cities—might lead to more real decentralization by creating viable units of government which can play the sort of role they should in development and harness local rivalries to more constructive causes. This development is perhaps politically unlikely as a formal matter in the near future, though the current wave of "departmentalization" could provide an opportunity for some needed reform of the present division of functions between the nation, the departments, and the municipalities. Even more important, and much easier to do without constitutional changes, would be to make the growing cities (which now regularly consume a third or more of total public investment) bear more of the fiscal burden of financing their own expansion in order to free scarce resources at the national level for other vital development purposes. This task could best be accomplished not by giving the cities more revenues directly but by giving them more revenue-raising authority and more responsibility for their own expenditures.

To sum up, the frequent suggestions that Bogotá, for example, should get more money from the national government are completely unjustified; what the city needs is more authority to raise its own revenue.[13] This authority could be granted uniformly to all local governments, if political pressures required it, but one would expect it to be used in a variety of ways.

Regional inequality of income, although the focus of much political discussion in Colombia, is not treated separately here because I view it primarily as a facet of the general income-distribution and development problems discussed earlier, rather than a separate problem. Over time, as social cohesion and national integration increase, one would expect the pressure and need for regional redistribution to increase, but this problem should not now rank high among Colombian priorities, however high it appears in political rhetoric. The changed local fiscal policies discussed in this chapter, by equating costs and benefits more closely in urban areas, should, however, act in a small way to weaken the present uneconomic pressures to migrate to the richer areas and should have generally favorable distributive effects.

The Property Tax and Educational Finance

As in most countries, taxes on property are one of the oldest forms of taxation in Colombia. Even at the present time all three major levels of government—the nation, the departments, and the municipalities—levy taxes on property of one sort or another (see Table 22). The major central-government levy falling directly on real property is the net-wealth tax. The real property tax as such (*impuesto predial*) is most important at the municipal level, in 1963 yielding 43 percent of

Table 22.   Taxes on property, 1963.

Type of tax	Millions of pesos
National[a]	
Net wealth	311.1[b]
Surcharge on municipal property	14.6
Valorization	4.0
Departmental[c]	
Property	1.2
Valorization	0.3
Municipal[d]	
Property	202.1
Valorization	81.4
Street lighting and other property	24.5[e]
Regional corporations[f]	
Property	31.1

Sources: National data from Contraloría General, *Informe financiero de 1964*, pp. 10-17; departmental, municipal, and regional corporation data from the Departmento de Investigaciones Económicas of the Banco de la República.

a The national government also received 98.5 million pesos in 1963 from another set of taxes on capital, those on estates, inheritances, and gifts.

b This figure is an estimate, based on the assumption that the net wealth tax in 1963 amounted to the same percentage of total assessments for the income and complementary taxes (including surcharges), as the average percentage in 1959–1961, that is, 21 per cent (calculated from Departamento Administrativo Nacional de Estadística, *Anuario general de estadistica 1962* [Bogotá, 1964], p. 574). As in the case of the estate and gift taxes, not all of the net tax falls on real property, though a large part probably does.

c The departments also got 26.7 million pesos from a "registry and recording tax" which probably falls mainly on real property (see Harvard Law School, International Program in Taxation, *Taxation in Colombia* [Chicago: Commerce Clearing House, 1964], pp. 183–184). Almost all of the property taxes levied by departments were collected by two departments (Boyacá and Meta), and virtually all of the special assessments by one department (Antioquia).

d The municipalities also received 91 million pesos from a tax on industry and commerce in 1963, the burden of which, at least in part, is determined by the value of real property (see Harvard Law School, *Taxation in Colombia*, p. 196).

e This figure does not include some important charges on real property, such as the water rate in Bogotá, which is levied at a basic rate varying progressively with the cadastral value of the property served.

f Only two of the three active regional corporations are included—the CVC in the Cauca Valley and the CAR in the Bogotá area; the third corporation (the CVM, in the north of Colombia) as yet levies no property tax of its own.

total municipal tax revenues and 15 percent of all municipal current revenues (including earnings of public utility enterprises and transfers from other levels of government). When the important valorization tax and other charges on property levied on the same base as the property tax (such as those for street cleaning and lighting) are taken into account, the percentage of municipal tax revenue from taxes on real property rises to 64 percent for 1963. No other tax is even one-half as important in the municipal fiscal picture as the property tax.

Property-tax revenues have in the last decade of substantial price inflation shown themselves to be relatively more income-elastic than most municipal current revenues. The *ex post* income elasticity of the property tax in the 1954–1963 period may be calculated at 1.2, compared with 1.1 both for total municipal current revenues and for all municipal taxes. In other words, for every 1 percent increase in national income, the yield of municipal property taxes increased 1.2 percent, so that real property taxes as a proportion of national income have increased slightly over the last decade.[14] This relatively respectable performance does not mean that the assessment process has kept up with the rise in the general price level; on the contrary, it certainly has not.

The structure and administration of the municipal real property tax are uniform throughout Colombia, along lines dictated from above. Uniform rules applied to different economic structures will yield very different results, however, and this dictum is as true for Colombia as for any other country (see Table 23). The four major cities of Colombia—Bogotá, Medellín, Cali, and Barranquilla—are located in four different departments, the only ones which, on the average, collected more than 30 pesos per capita in municipal taxes in 1963, the over-all range being from 80 pesos in Bogotá to only 4 pesos in the sparsely populated Pacific Coast area of Chocó.

In Colombia, as in most countries, most wealth in the form of real property is concentrated in the larger cities: in 1964, for example, the major urban areas (mainly the departmental capitals) accounted for almost exactly one-half of total assessed valuations. The country is not, however, as dominated by one huge metropolitan capital city as are many Latin Amer-

ican countries. There are at least twenty-four other cities
(and thirty-seven municipalities) of over 50,000 inhabitants
and six of 200,000 or more, according to the 1964 census. The
problem of increasing locally derived fiscal resources to supply

Table 23. Regional differences with regard to property tax.

Department	Per capita municipal taxes[a] (pesos)	Estimated yield of uniform 4-mill property tax[b] (millions of pesos)	Per capita yield of uniform tax[c] (pesos)
Antioquia	45	37.0	15
Atlántico	39	7.9	11
Bolívar	11	8.0	8
Boyacá	8	9.0	9
Caldas	23	17.8	12
Cauca	7	4.1	7
Córdoba	12	7.0	12
Cundinamarca	15	15.4	14
Distrito Especial	80	42.4	25
Chocó	4	—	—
Huila	15	4.0	10
Magdalena	11	8.0	10
Meta	11	2.1	13
Nariño	6	2.9	4
Norte de Santander	21	4.5	8
Santander	20	10.8	11
Tolima	18	7.6	9
Valle del Cauca	31	28.6	16
Colombia[d]	28	218.0	14

Sources: 1963 tax data from Departmento de Investigaciones Económicas,
Banco de la República; 1964 population data from DANE, XIII Censo nacional
de población, p. 2; 1964 assessed valuations from the Instituto Geográfico
Agustín Codazzi, the Departmento de Planeación, Gobernación de Antioquia,
and the Departmento Administrativo de Plantificación Distrital (Bogotá).

a 1963 tax data and 1964 population figures.

b Based on 1964 assessed values.

c 1964 data, assuming 100 percent collection efficiency.

d Excluding the relatively unimportant national territories and the Department of Guajira. The property-tax calculations also exclude the Department
of Chocó.

the needs of these generally rapidly growing urban areas is thus of concern for almost every section of what is becoming an increasingly urbanized country.

Given the relative concentration of property values in urban areas, a uniform rise in the property tax would tend to be relatively more beneficial to the more urbanized areas than to the more rural departments (see Table 23). There are, on the other hand, about a hundred municipalities of over 20,000 inhabitants which have total budgets of less than 1 million pesos. There is little point in treating the city of Cali, for example, with its 600,000 or more inhabitants and municipal budget of about 200 million pesos (or over 300 pesos per inhabitant), the same way as another typical municipality in the department of Valle spending about 20 pesos per capita.[15]

The Colombian property-tax structure in the past has generally recognized the differences in needs and administrative capacities between the larger urban areas and the smaller and usually poorer rural municipalities by permitting the larger cities to levy higher rates on their already larger property-tax base. This trend should continue, in large part because the average small municipality in rural Colombia has no effective local government worth speaking of, and it does not seem likely that matters can be improved much in the near future.

Not only are most rural areas basically poor and often dominated politically by the large landowners who have to pay what few property taxes are paid, but they are also saddled with a cumbersome and costly administrative structure which usually consumes all the scanty available resources merely to keep functioning. Furthermore, the municipal administrators, even if they were potentially capable of taking any effective action to meet the needs of the area, are often prevented from doing so by the equal representation of the two major political parties in the local governing council, where a two-thirds majority vote rule is required as part of Colombia's current "national front" solution to its recent history of political strife. If this constraint were not enough, the conflict between the officials appointed by the departmental governor on the one hand (the mayor or *alcalde*) and by the municipal council on the other hand (the treasurer or *personero*) would usually adequately hamper positive action.

In these circumstances, it is hard to see most of the rural municipalities of Colombia making more effective use of increased property-taxing powers even if they were given them. Most larger cities, however, though they suffer from some of the same structural problems, are in quite a different position as regards the needs and the possibilities of increased local revenues. Suppose that greater autonomy were granted to municipalities and that it were done by a general law satisfying the apparent Colombian need for nominal uniformity. Given the actual situation described above, the fact that such a law would lead to action only in some larger urban areas is to be applauded, not deplored.

Although municipal property taxes supposedly are levied on all real property within the municipal jurisdiction, as is always the case certain classes of property are exempted. In order of importance come government property, including that of most of the numerous decentralized public institutions (58 percent of total exempt property in 1964); church property (14 percent in 1964); and various special exemptions for housing, homesteads, industry, and so on. The magnitude of all these is indicated in Table 24.[16] The fastest growth in exempt property in the last decade has been in the special exemptions, though the variations from department to department in the importance of different classes of exemptions are considerable.

In total, exemptions from property tax are quite important. In 1964, for example, 1.1 million urban properties assessed at 5.9 billion pesos were exempted. That is, about 10 percent of total urban properties were tax exempt in 1964, and, since the average value of these properties was nearly double that of the taxed properties, almost 18 percent of the assessed value in urban areas was tax exempt. Because the exemptions in the rural areas were less important, the picture for the country as a whole shows about 12 percent of the total assessed value being exempted. Assuming the basic tax rate of 4 mills (that is, 4 per thousand) would apply, the total cost of these property-

Table 24. Property-tax exemptions, 1955 and 1964.[a]

Class of exemption	1955[b] (millions of pesos)	1964	1964 as percent of 1965
Government	716.7	2,139.1	298
Ecclesiastical	186.7	507.3	272
Private	120.6	500.5	415
Unspecified[c]	80.7	545.1	675
Total	1,104.7	3,692.0	334

Source: Data from records of the Instituto Geográfico Agustín Codazzi.

a Information for fourteen Departments only, excluding Antioquia, Chocó, the Distrito Especial, and the national territories.

b 1959 for the department of Meta.

c Probably mostly "private": the breakdown between these two items appears to vary from department to department.

tax exemptions in 1964 in terms of municipal revenue foregone may be roughly estimated as at least 29.5 million pesos.[17] It is impossible to say what, if anything, has been the beneficial effect of giving up about 4 percent of total collections through property-tax incentives to stimulate low-cost housing (or, as the case may be, industry), but such uncertainty nowhere appears to act as a deterrent to the granting of new exemptions, and Colombia is no exception, as indicated by the considerably more rapid growth in exempt than in taxed values over the last decade. On the other hand, the country is fortunate in having as good an idea of the tax cost of the various exemptions as it does; other countries might be well advised to imitate the Colombian practice of making a complete census of exempt properties.

The basic rate of the property tax in most of Colombia is only 4 mills. In addition a 10 percent surcharge on this rate is paid to the national government (nominally for financing the work of the Geographic Institute, the central assessing agency for most of the country). Various classes of municipalities have also from time to time been authorized to impose additional rates—a 10 percent surcharge on the basic rate for parks, up to 1 mill extra for street lighting and 2 mills for street cleaning—with the nationally determined limit on the basic real property tax varying from 4 to 10 mills, according to the size of the municipality. Very much higher rates on land values alone have been authorized in some urban areas. The extent to which advantage is taken of the permissable rates varies from municipality to municipality, but the general picture of a basic 4-mill rate for municipal purposes, rising to 10 mills in the national capital district, is not too far from reality.[18] In addition, in some areas (such as Bogotá and Cali) the regional development corporations levy their own 2- or 3-mill rate, and there may well be additional special assessment charges. So theoretically the burden on real property in some of the larger urban areas may be as high as 20 mills (2 percent) or so in some years. Even including all these additional tax rates and charges on property, however, the total statutory rate on real property is much lower in Colombia than in most parts of the United States, where the average nominal rate in 1962 was over 5 percent.[19]

The real burden of these nominal rates depends on how closely the assessed valuations on which the rates are imposed correspond to market values. Despite the generally high technical level of assessment administration in Colombia, the assessed values in most cases are well below the market values. The villain, is, on the whole, not deficient technique but the general rise in prices which the country has experienced in the last decade. Since a great many municipalities were last revalued some years ago, even if all properties were initially assessed at market value, the total assessed value by now would still be much lower than it should be. There is, of course, no justification for assuming initial full-value assessment, and recent studies indicate that a revaluation at market prices would increase total assessments by perhaps 2 to 2½ times: that is, the average ratio of assessed to market value is perhaps between 0.40 and 0.50—even the lower of which is quite respectable by United States standards.[20] Some areas have ratios much lower than this—examples of 1 to 10 proportions are not hard to find and are commonly cited as representative—but this estimate of an average effective rate of about one-half the nominal rate is as good an approximation to the likely total picture as I can make.

For the last decade property-tax assessment throughout most of Colombia has been in the hands of an independent public institution, the Agustín Codazzi Geographic Institute, which maintains sectional offices in most of the departments. (Separate cadastral offices exist in the Special District of Bogotá and in Antioquia, however, and these two areas account for over one-third of the total taxable assessments in Colombia.) On the whole, the level of assessment technique used throughout the country has been considered good by qualified observers, though some think that the techniques employed by the Geographic Institute are too painstakingly exact to cope with the constant problem of keeping property valuations reasonably up-to-date in an inflationary environment. Both observations seem well-taken.

While assessment is relatively centralized and on the whole probably pretty free from illicit influences—though not from inequities—the same happy state of affairs does not prevail in the revenue-producing part of the tax process, collection, which is in the hands of the local authorities. As is only to be expected, the efficiency of the collection process (including enforcement as well as the mechanics of billing, and so on) appears to vary greatly from city to city and rural area to rural area. Scattered evidence seems to indicate that a collection ratio of 70 percent of the tax assessed in any year is very good indeed, and that the proportion collected may fall to as low as 20 or 30 percent in some areas.[21] In general, as might be expected, the larger urban areas appear to have the best collection record, the poorer rural areas the worst. It seems likely that there are as many inequities in collections as in assessments in Colombia at the present time, though one hears very little complaint about any sort of inequity, presumably because of the very low effective rates.

Recognition of the seriousness of the administrative problem in some areas has been growing recently, and interesting steps toward improving the situation have been taken. The regional development corporations in the Bogotá and Valle areas (much of whose own income, being in the form of an additional property tax, depends on the efficiency of the local tax administration) have been providing technical assistance to the local governments within their jurisdiction. In the important and generally progressive department of Antioquia, the recently created Institute for the Development of Antioquia has used its funds almost to double the number of valuers in the department and is considering ways of assisting on the more strictly administrative side as well.

These efforts may be portents of future developments in property taxation in Colombia. Centralized assessment and decentralized administration will probably remain the pattern for years to come, but a speeding-up of the former and a strengthening of the latter are generally agreed to be necessary if the property tax, the principal local tax source, is to remain able to meet the increasing calls that will be made on local finances by the needs of economic development. Local administration might be strengthened by more technical assistance of the type mentioned above as well as by, for example, centralized preparation of tax bills. The possibility of some sort of incentive grant to stimulate local tax effort should also be examined. But whatever may be done to improve administration pales before the importance of improving assessments.

In the last decade assessed valuations have fallen considerably in relation to gross domestic product, as is evident in Table 25. If changes in price levels and in population are allowed for, there was a sizable fall in assessed values per capita from 1956 to 1964 (from 4,150 pesos to 3,180 pesos in 1964 constant prices). The yield of the property *tax*, on the other hand, increased more rapidly than the gross domestic product in this period, largely because of a considerable rise in effective rates. Since statutory rates were not changed, this rise presumably took place because of the relatively more rapid growth in property values in the larger cities where administration is generally better and the applicable statutory rates higher. When population increases and price-level changes are taken into account, however, it appears that this

Table 25. Relative changes in assessed values and municipal property taxes, 1956–1964.

Item	1956	1964 (current pesos)	Percentage change	1956	1964 (constant 1964 pesos)a	Percentage change
Assessed valuationb (billions of pesos)						
Total	20.3c	54.5	168	53.4	54.5	2
Urban areas	9.9	27.8	181	26.0	27.8	7
Rural areas	10.4	26.7	157	27.4	26.7	–3
Assessed valuation as percent of GDP	135	102	–24	141	102	–28
Assessed valuation per capitad (pesos)	1,570	3,180	102	4,150	3,180	–23
Property taxese (millions of pesos)	52.4	202.1	286	160	202	26
As percent of GDP	0.35	0.38	8	0.42	0.38	–10
As percent of assessed valuation	0.26	0.38	46	0.30	0.38	27
Property taxes per capita	4	12	200	12	12	0

Sources: The GDP figures are from the Banco de la República, "Cuentas nacionales." Assessed valuations were supplied by the Instituto Geográfico, the Departmento de Planeación (Antioquia), and the Departmento Administrativo de Planificación Distrital (Bogotá). The tax data came from the Departmento de Investigaciones Económicas, Banco de la República.

a The 1964 constant price calculations for GDP and assessed valuations in 1956 were obtained by the use of an implicit GDP deflator developed by the Departmento Administrativo de Planeación. The tax figures are deflated by a specially constructed index of government expenditures. Obviously, these procedures are rather crude, but in view of the substantial rise in prices over this period some such constant price estimates seem useful and necessary.

b All assessed valuations refer to taxable properties only and exclude the department of Chocó and the national territories. The population figures used in the per capita calculations also exclude these areas. The GDP figures do not.

c 1959 figures are used for the (small) department of Meta.

d The 1956 population is as estimated by DANE; 1964 population from census.

e The tax data refer to 1956 and 1963 collections.

rise in effective rates was barely enough to keep the per capita
yield of the property tax in real terms at the same level in
1964 as in 1956. Given the low basic income elasticity of
assessed valuations, the prospect for future natural growth
of local property tax revenues is not good.[22] Without strengthened assessments, the most that could be hoped for is to
maintain real per capita revenues from property taxation.
Moreover, since other sources of municipal revenues have
been declining in real terms while per capita expenditure
needs have been increasing with expanded urbanization,
either local finances must be strengthened, almost certainly
through higher property-tax rates, or else the burden of
transfer payments to the lower levels of government will
weigh even heavier on the already strained central budget.

On most counts stronger local finances to meet the "need"
for local expenditures seem preferable, and improved property
taxation seems the way to do it. In a country like Colombia,
where so much wealth is still held in the form of real property,
it is probable that increased reliance on property taxes would
not have bad effects so far as distribution goes, though it
would, of course, become much more important to reduce
inequities in assessments. Incidentally, increased local property
taxes per se might tend to reduce central-government income-
tax receipts, since the property tax is a deductible item; but a
revaluation program like that suggested in Chapter 3 and
supported by the immediately preceding argument would
have the offsetting benefit of increasing the yield of the net-
wealth tax.

To sum up the chapter to this point in a few short propositions: local governments are important in Colombia; the
property tax is a mainstay of local government finance; the
likely future pattern of development will require more and
more financing support from urban governments, and the
logical place to look for much of the necessary financing is
the property tax; more rapid assessment, improved collection,
and, possibly, increased rates all offer some hope that the property tax is capable of meeting such new demands. In short,
Colombia in these respects resembles many areas in the United

States, even today. On the other hand, with centralized assessment and a census of exempt properties, Colombian experience may have something to teach North Americans. The generally centralized assessment, in particular, has, I think, been a relatively successful innovation and one worth careful study elsewhere.[23]

The economic case for increased property taxation in Colombia is thus strong. The political possibility of achieving substantial increases in revenues from this source may well turn on how and where the money is used. As noted earlier, budgetary unity is important in a country with as many public enterprises and semiautonomous agencies as Colombia, but the need for public revenues is more important. If this need can be satisfied only by setting up independently-financed autonomous institutions or special districts or by the partial equivalent of earmarking a tax, then earmarking may be justified. In the particular case of the property tax, probably a substantial increase in rates or a general revaluation program would be politically acceptable in Colombia today only if the taxpayers knew the money would be spent on something of tangible benefit to them or their immediate neighbors, such as education.

If the development program in Colombia is to touch the lives of most present-day Colombians significantly, it will be through something like education. If local communities are not interested in sacrificing something to improve their children's lot in life, it is most unlikely that there is much hope for substantial national progress of any sort. One might think this rather middle-class proposition is not too applicable in many poor parts of Colombia, particularly those blighted by the banditry and violence of recent years, since the poor and the displaced look to the future not with anticipation but with fear. On the other hand, it has been argued that those who experienced the *violencia* have come to feel a closer integration with the community and the nation.[24] Whatever the underlying sociological and psychological reasons, in many areas of Colombia the attractiveness of education as a purpose of public expenditure has already led to substantial contributions by many landowners to the community development program (Acción Comunal) for the construction of schools. On balance, these considerations lead me to think that a property tax increase tied to education may be the only way to improve both the financing of education and the general municipal fiscal situation.

The usual arguments against earmarking in underdeveloped countries give too little weight to this all-important factor of political acceptability.[25] The danger of undue distortion of the development program from the particular earmarking suggested here seems remote, especially if the rate of the earmarked tax is kept flexible; in fact, such an assignment of revenues would probably mark a considerable improvement in Colombia's present development program. A major problem with this suggestion would arise, however, because of the complete incapacity of many of the smaller municipalities to take on any responsibility at all for the raising and spending of more money on anything. Some rather fundamental changes in the organization of local government would thus be required if this proposal were to be implemented fully and uniformly throughout the country. As outlined earlier, however, considerable advantage would accrue even if only the larger urban areas took advantage of greater autonomy in this sphere.

Financing Urbanization by Benefit Taxation

One of the most striking phenomena in most developing countries today is the rapid growth and urbanization of their population. Many cities grow continuously at rates seen only in boom periods in developed countries. This rapid urbanization has put a tremendous strain on municipal finances: extremely heavy investments in roads, sewers, aqueducts, street lighting, parks, and schools seem needed if the city is to remain suitable for human existence, but there is no capital market from which funds can be borrowed, and the national governments usually cannot provide adequate assistance to finance capital investments because of their own fiscal problems.

Even though forced by lack of capital markets and government aid to rely on their own resources, theoretically cities should be able to raise considerable revenue from property taxes of more or less orthodox design. In practice, however, in no developing country has the property tax been exploited to anywhere near its potential capacity to provide municipal revenues. In Colombia, shortcomings in administration and rigidities in the legal framework have kept municipal revenues from property taxes low. Even if these hurdles could be overcome and property taxes increased, most of the increase would probably go to finance education. To finance other urban capital improvements, in recent years some Colombian cities have developed an alternative tax on real property.

This tax is known in Colombia as the *impuesto de valorización,* or valorization tax. It is similar to the taxes known as special assessments or betterment taxes in English-speaking countries. This type of tax, which by its nature can be used only to finance capital improvements, was formerly common in the United States and other developed countries, but it has fallen into disuse and has been almost totally ignored in recent taxation literature. Not only is the valorization tax more appropriate for developing than developed countries, but as used in Colombia it is also free of some of the defects that led to its downfall in the United States. Heavier use of the valorization form of benefit taxation would, in Colombia and many other developing countries, be a useful way to finance part of the needs of urbanization.

In Colombia the average rate of urban growth is 5 percent a year, and the three major cities—Bogotá, Medellín, and Cali—grew in the last decade at average annual rates of 7.7, 6.2, and 7.5 percent, respectively.[26] The rapid growth of these cities arises both from their development of dynamic manufacturing and commercial sectors and from the increasing importance of education, health, and other activities which are most efficiently carried on in urban areas.

This urban growth takes place at a time when the public capital requirements for creating efficient cities with "satisfactory" social services are high, but domestic saving is low, and there is a shortage of capital. City growth in developing countries today is usually based on transport by urban buses. For efficient transportation the narrow streets of the central city—in Latin America a heritage from colonial days—must be widened and new streets opened. On the edge of the growing city, streets must be extended rapidly to new factories and new housing (often single-family homes being developed slowly from original squatter settlements by owners lacking the organization, financing, and technical capacities to build more compact multi-family structures even if they wanted to do so). If the city is to be a location of low-cost production, it needs these streets to provide rapid bus transportation. It also needs adequate water and sewerage systems to protect public health, and street lighting, parks and schools for training and social betterment. All these investments require large amounts of capital, and yet they must be provided if the city is to fulfill its potential for economic development. This investment is desirable not only for the benefits which it gives in better living conditions and more efficient production in the city but also because it requires a great deal of unskilled labor, thus helping to ease the always heavy urban unemployment in developing countries. In addition, such public works investment generally uses few imported materials and so puts less pressure on the balance of payments than most other types of investment.

There is no organized capital market in Colombia where domestic funds can be borrowed for long periods at low interest rates to meet heavy capital requirements. At best, some improvements can be financed by borrowing from international lending agencies, but they are usually reluctant to finance local-currency costs of investment, and, as already noted, import requirements for urban investments are low. The city cannot usually call on private enterprises to finance public works through subdivision laws which require the urban developer to provide streets, water, sewerage, and so on at his own expense. Even if such laws exist (as they do in

Colombia), many people purchasing lots do not have the money to pay for complete public improvements; thus the subdivision law must permit new subdivisions lacking street pavement, complete water services, and sewerage connections if the people flocking to the cities are not to be forced into already overcrowded existing housing or else forced to set up shantytowns without any urban controls (or services) at all. Some investment funds may be provided from central-government subsidies, but these are likely to be inadequate, given the usual fiscal difficulties of the central government. Nor do these subsidies to the richest, faster-growing parts of the country seem desirable or necessary in either distributional or allocative terms.

The same factors that lead to the financial difficulties of the rapidly growing city in a developing country—the large influx of population and the rapid growth of the modern industrial, commercial, and service sectors—also lead to a rapid rise in property values, however. This fact can be used to advantage to finance a major part of the needed municipal investment through taxing this increase in value.

The rapidly growing city in a developing country always has many potential capital improvements with such a high social productivity that the benefits to site values greatly exceed the costs of the project. While in theory the valorization tax can recover an amount equal to the entire increase in site values, in practice something less than this should be attempted, given the desirability of securing payment of the tax before the investment is made and the uncertainties of estimating what the ultimate increases in site value will be. Even allowing an ample margin for error in estimating benefits, the tax can usually recover the investment and operating costs of the public agency without exceeding the benefits realizable by any individual landowner from the increased site value of his property. This presumption of increased value in the law—a major reason for the distrust of the textbook writers—has in practice worked out quite well in Colombia.

A valorization tax may be contrasted with a traditional property tax assessed on site value and with a special capital-gains tax on increases in site values. In theory a property tax assessed on site values can collect the entire net rent of the land. It may be viewed as taking away from the landowner the net revenue from all unearned increments in the site value of his property. A capital-gains tax on increments in site value can also recover the total increment in site value, though payment usually takes place only when the increment in value is realized by sale. A crucial point is that neither the site-value tax nor the gains tax on increment in site value is designed to raise the revenues to provide the public investments which will lead to the increment in site value (although if a capital market existed, these taxes could be used to repay loans made to finance these public investments).

Another difference between site-value taxation and valorization taxation is that, in theory, the valorization tax recovers only the benefits from direct public investment which enhances the value of land, while site-value taxation also reaches increases in private site values that may arise in a large, heavily populated urban area from the external economies of face-to-face contact and of the mobilization of an efficient work force. Hence, the present value of maximum valorization taxes in a growing city can never be as high as the present value of the maximum site-value tax.

The valorization tax has the political advantage that it is clearly on a benefit basis. The taxpayer is making no sacrifice, for the value of his property will rise by at least the amount of the tax he must pay. This is an important consideration where political resistance to paying taxes is high, as it is in Colombia and most developing countries. In practice, since the tax is paid before the investment takes place and before site values increase, the estimates of the increase in value must be sufficiently accurate or the upward trend of land values because of urban growth must be so rapid that the forecast of benefit exceeding tax will be true in almost all cases. In effect, the increment in site value from rapid urban growth (and, assuming some money illusion, from inflation) provides a cushion in case the increment arising from the public investment alone turns out to be inferior to the valorization tax paid.

From urban land use and transportation theory, it may be predicted that a valorization tax, justified as it is on a benefit basis, will be successful only if the urban area is growing rapidly and if no drastic changes in transportation technology take place. The main use of valorization taxes in Colombia has been to provide new or improved streets in urban areas, an investment needed to keep production costs low. If benefit taxation is to be successful, there *must* be an obvious connection between the cost and the benefits to the taxpayer. For this reason it would be difficult to use a valorization tax in a static or slow-growing city, for suburban and fringe urban dwellers will not be convinced that the increases in their site values are coming from improved roads located in the older central portions of the city far away. Similarly, theoretical analyses of improved urban transportation providing more rapid access to the central business district show that ordinarily site values in the fringe areas of the city with improved transport will increase, and, *ceteris paribus*, site values in the central areas and other fringe areas will fall as a result.[27] However, if increased transportation efficiency lowers production costs sufficiently in the city to attract new industry and economic activity to central areas at a rapid pace, and urban population increases rapidly, urban land values in central areas also will rise, and values will not fall even in fringe areas which lack improved transport. Thus landowners will be willing to pay valorization taxes. The relation between public investment and site values may be indirect, but the property owner will know from experience that better streets in front of his property or near it will increase the value of his land, and he will be willing to pay a valorization tax even though he cannot distinguish between the increases in site values resulting from particular public investments and those resulting from rapid urban growth in general.

The minor role played by valorization taxes (or special assessments) in the urban areas of developed countries and the consequent neglect of the tax in public-finance literature may thus be accounted for in part by the slower growth of cities in developed countries, with less visible connection between public improvements and increases in site values. Other factors explaining the difference between the potential usefulness of the valorization tax in advanced and less developed countries are the existence of capital markets such that public improvements may be easily financed and paid for out of regular revenues over time and the existence of subdivision laws which force many public improvements to be made at private expense.

From the point of view of stimulating saving and investment, the valorization tax also seems desirable in developing countries. The proceeds from it are used almost exclusively for investment, and the nature of the tax is such that if it is to be successfully used the investment must be highly productive and increase land values. The valorization tax may be considered a forced investment where the taxpayer benefits from the increased site value of his land resulting from the public improvement financed by the tax. Income distribution in Colombia is highly unequal, and much urban land is owned by the wealthy upper classes. While these groups could theoretically be major sources of saving, in fact they consume a surprisingly large fraction of their income. Thus the valorization tax often falls heavily on a group which has the potential to increase its savings considerably and might well do so to pay the tax.

The incentive effects of the valorization tax are also favorable to investment and development. As a tax on pure site values, the valorization tax does not penalize development of unimproved land. The payment of the valorization tax itself is probably an even more important stimulant to investment in practice, however, and perhaps also in theory. It is often stated that in theory a tax on site values should have no incentive effects on land use since it does not affect the most profitable use of the land.[28] This statement, however, implicitly assumes that land is always an investment good. Actually, in developing countries much land is held idle not for speculative purposes but to provide pleasure and prestige to its owners, so that it is in a real sense a consumer good. Under regular site-value taxation, the income effect (there is no substitution effect) can be expected to lower consumption (since the land is probably not an inferior good), so that land formerly used for consumption purposes may be put to productive use as a result of the tax. With the valorization tax the result is different, for payment of the tax is matched by an increase in the site value of the land. The improvements financed by valorization taxes increase the value of the land for productive purposes, not for prestige consumption, however. Hence the valorization tax and public investments combined will increase the opportunity cost of using land for consumption purposes, and the substitution effect will in this case tend to induce more productive use of the land.[29]

In practice, the effect of site-value taxes in forcing more intensive land use may depend most on the lack of liquidity and capital markets facing many landowners and on the common failure of landowners to calculate carefully the most profitable use of their land.[30] Owners may underutilize land when not faced with cash payments, but when the valorization tax must be paid, they may either become aware of the opportunity cost of holding the land idle and hence put it to more profitable use, or else they may have to sell it to someone else who will do so. Since the valorization tax is a relatively large tax assessed over a short period of time, its effect in forcing better land use through the liquidity and attention-to-use effects should be stronger than that of a regular site-value tax, where the rate may be too low to threaten the liquidity or arouse the interest in land use of any but the largest landowners.

From an administrative point of view, the valorization tax may seem attractive to developing countries, for land cannot easily be hidden from taxation. The tax is collected in large sums from a relatively small number of taxpayers, a fact which makes enforcement easier (though it may make compliance more difficult). The crucial factor in administration is that the tax and the public improvements go hand in hand; if poor administration leads to badly planned or executed projects or to projects which are not executed promptly or to poor allocation of taxes among landowners, so that a significant number of people find that the tax they have paid is more than the increase in the value of their property, the tax may easily be discredited and appear only an arbitrary and capricious capital levy.

In summary, the valorization tax in theory seems an attractive one for developing countries. It is suitable only for financing public investments that will be demonstrably productive. It has a clear benefit justification which helps muster political support for the tax. Its effect on saving should be at least neutral and may be positive. Its incentive effects should be favorable. It should be relatively easy to collect. But it will require skilled administration if it is to work in practice as the theory indicates, and skilled people are often the scarcest resource in developing countries. That this administration is not beyond the reach of an underdeveloped country is demonstrated by Colombian experience; whether it is the best use of scarce human resources is another question.

The present valorization tax in Colombia was developed largely in the city of Medellín over the twenty years following World War II, primarily as an indigenous response to the need for financing municipal improvements in a fast-growing manufacturing city.[31] Under Colombian law municipalities have complete autonomy in valorization tax administration. In Medellín, a separate municipal department handles all aspects of the tax from preliminary study of projects, through design, financing, and contracting the public works, to the collection of the tax. The valorization department has in recent years provided Medellín with a large and impressive network of parkways, limited-access highways, improved river and stream channels, and other improvements.

Although formally autonomous, the department is responsive to pressures from taxpayers and other political forces, and it is careful to maintain popular support for its work. Projects are studied carefully to select only those that will produce benefits to property owners greater than their cost. When a project is selected, its cost plus the administrative cost of the agency is charged to the taxpayers in the area benefited. In selecting the area over which the tax will be assessed for a project and setting the relative charges to be levied on each property, the valorization department does not rely at all on formulas (as is done in Mexico, for example); instead, it consults with real estate dealers and other knowledgeable persons to work out a consensus which appears plausible to all on the distribution of the benefits from the project. Despite the theoretical difficulties in determining site values and calculating increases in site values as a result of a public improvement, the Medellín consensus system is reported to work well, and for most projects it has not been difficult to reach agreement on the tax to be charged each property. The valorization tax is payable either before the start of the project or, at the taxpayer's option, in installments over a period of two years or so. This method requires the use of some short-term bank loans or bond financing to carry out projects, and various methods of discounts for cash payment, interest rates on installment balances, and premiums for valorization bonds purchased previously are used in an attempt to limit the short-term financing required from the banks. The valorization tax in Medellín in recent years has produced more revenue than the regular property tax and has contributed about 30 percent of the total current revenues of the city government.

In Bogotá, a larger, more complex, and less homogenous city, the valorization tax has also been used extensively. The system used is generally the same as that developed in Medellín. The tax has been less important in the capital, however, because of greater political interference in the valorization process and noticeably less competent management in the past of the processes of financing and constructing improvements. Still, the tax cannot be called a failure, for it has been used extensively, enjoys good support, and the prospects are for greater use in the future. In Bogotá the valorization tax has provided about half as much revenue as the regular property tax, and contributes about 25 percent of the city's total tax revenue.

In Cali, Colombia's third largest city, the valorization tax has been used very little. The principal reason for this state of affairs is political opposition from large property owners.

Similar opposition was a problem twenty years ago in Medellín, where it was overcome after an epic struggle when the property owners finally recognized that if they wanted improvements which benefited their properties they would have to pay for them through valorization taxes and thus abandoned the hope of getting improvements financed out of taxes paid mostly by others. The process of political education has apparently not progressed this far in Cali.

Yet the day may be coming. Although the municipality of Cali has had little success in financing capital improvements by special charges, the independent municipal utility enterprise has done much better, partly because of its operating success and consequent ability to obtain initial financing from the international lending agencies. Given some initial funding, the municipal utilities have found it quite feasible to recoup capital costs along with consumption charges on a user charge basis. The initiative for requesting the extension of water or power lines has been left largely to the inhabitants of the areas affected, who must get together (under the auspices of the community action groups mentioned earlier) and agree on an acceptable financing plan. Piecemeal provision of services has been avoided, it is claimed, by acceding to the requests of different neighborhoods—all of which are said to want services—only in accordance with the general development plan. The only sanction possible under this system is to cut off the service once the work has been done, but there are said to be few problems since the idea of purchasing water or electricity service on the installment plan is now well understood and accepted. Only community services are charged for on this scheme; thus water pipes more than 12 inches in diameter, electricity substations, and the like are charged to the general funding of the enterprise. This financing system is in many ways an acceptable substitute for valorization and could perhaps be more widely used in financing other utility-type investments. (The even more important question of utility rate policy is not discussed in this book.)

Quite aside from alternatives and supplements, a comparison of revenues for Medellín, Bogotá, and Cali indicates that use of the valorization tax has not just replaced other municipal taxes. As shown in Table 26, on a per capita basis Medellín has both higher property-tax revenues and higher total taxes than the two other cities. Although further study is needed to clarify the relation between the use of the valorization tax and the use of other sources of revenue, the indications are that in Colombia the valorization tax has supplemented rather than replaced other taxes.[32]

Table 26. Municipal tax base and taxes per capita, selected cities, 1963.

	Medellín	Bogotá	Cali
Estimated population (thousands)	675	1,540	600
Assessed value per capita (pesos)	5,750	5,950	4,230
Per capita tax revenues (pesos)			
Total	115	88	50
Property tax	42	40	28
Valorization tax	54	22	3

Sources: Departmento Administrativo Nacional de Estadística, *Cali en cifras* (1965); *Anuario estadístico de Medellín, 1963;* data from Departmento de Valorización and Departmento de Catastro (Medellín), and from the Instituto Geográfico Agustín Codazzi, the Departmento de Planificación Distrital (Bogotá), and the Banco de la República.

The valorization tax appears to have been most successful in Colombia where the greatest efforts have been made to put it on a true benefit basis, as in Medellín. To do this requires eight important measures: (1) freedom from any fixed formulas for distributing the tax among property owners; (2) careful study of projects at the initial stage to determine those which will increase site values at least as much as the cost of the project; (3) participation of property owners in the planning and execution of projects without giving them obstructionist or veto powers; (4) careful costing of projects; (5) prompt construction of projects; (6) prompt and complete collection of all taxes assessed on the property owners while the project is being built; (7) extensive publicity for valorization projects; (8) a general statement of the rules for hardship cases permitting, but not requiring, reduction in tax or delayed payment in certain circumstances. The development of a valorization system is also a matter for careful planning: Medellín's experience indicates the importance of starting with small projects which can be completed quickly and with certainty and thus earn taxpayer trust; at a later stage it might be better to concentrate on large multifaceted projects.

Although there are no empirical studies available to show how closely valorization tax assessments have corresponded to subsequent increases in site value in Medellín, there is a general feeling on the part of officials and other observers that the tax collected has been proportional to benefits. Preserving a popular identification between the tax and the benefits by all possible means is repeatedly emphasized in Medellín. If one believes "you can't fool all of the people all of the time," the valorization tax over the long run must have approached a benefit basis in fact as well as in belief. Some explicit recognition should also be given to the likelihood, especially at later stages of urban growth, that the benefits from public works capitalized in private property values may not always suffice to pay for the project, though its general social productivity may still be very high. It is important for effective functioning of the tax, however, that any such provision be couched in general rather than rigidly specific terms.

There is little reason for exempting any property from the valorization tax. The exemptions of government property common in Colombia have given windfalls to private-interest public groups such as military pension funds.[33] Failure of other government agencies to pay assessments has at times seriously hurt the financial soundness of valorization in Bogotá. Exemption may be justified for small landowners who cannot raise the cash to pay the tax assessed, but this problem usually can be solved by giving small landowners longer periods to pay, in effect requiring them to pay less, especially in inflationary periods, and by making special arrangements in hardship cases. Valorization may force unwanted improvements on some owners, forcing them to sell out and move elsewhere, but in theory at least they can sell out at a profit and suffer no financial harm, although there may be some loss of consumer surplus from valorization, as from any change in supply and demand.

Public-finance textbooks tend to condemn earmarked revenues because they limit the flexibility of budgeting in a government, glutting some activities with too much revenue while other activities starve. This result can be avoided if the rate of the earmarked tax is changed regularly to bring it in line with actual revenue needs, as is the case with the valorization tax. Further, the financing of investments from the earmarked valorization tax gixes an added incentive to examine the prospective benefits of projects more closely than would otherwise be done and hence promotes good budgeting and project appraisal procedures.

Benefit taxation may be made politically popular in the way outlined above. A charge may then be made, however, that those activities which can clearly be financed on a benefit basis will receive too much support, at the expense of other activities which for technical reasons cannot be benefit-financed. Too much emphasis on benefit taxation may also limit the scope for income redistribution from taxation. The force of these charges is lessened to the extent that benefit taxes can be shown to be in addition to other taxes, thus expanding the size of the public sector rather than substituting for other, more general taxes. On the basis of admittedly crude and impressionistic evidence, the valorization tax does seem to be a net addition to public financing in Colombia (see Table 26). The need in Colombia as in many other developing countries is for additional, technically sound benefit taxes to expand the public sector, not less use of those now existing.

The valorization tax is supposed to be applied on the basis of the assumed increase in pure site value, and the continued popularity of the tax when well administered seems to indicate that this aim is achieved.[34] The valorization tax is compatible with a capital-gains tax on increments in site values, provided the valorization tax is included in the original cost of the property when calculating capital gains, as is the practice in Colombia. Assuming that the valorization tax and the capital-gains tax together recoup for the public sector the increment in land values, it may seem unfair to have a regular property tax which taxes both site values and improvements, since valorization projects raise site values and hence property tax on the site. On the other hand, public improvements have maintenance expenditures, and the cost of maintenance should be paid by those who benefit. Also, it will rarely be the case that all increments in land value can be taxed away by the valorization and capital-gains taxes; so some scope will be left for site-value property taxation. Finally, it must be recognized that most property taxes go to finance municipal services for people, who in turn live in and use buildings and other improvements, and if taxes are to be at least in part benefit-based for allocative efficiency, much of the property tax should be on improvements. In the face of ignorance as to the relative weight of these considerations, it would seem a priori best to tax land and improvements at the same rate under the property tax, especially since site value is already reached by the valorization and capital-gains taxes.

In Colombia the increased values resulting from valorization-financed improvements are not automatically included in the assessed values of properties. Owing largely to the continued inflation, the municipalities now are pressing for more regular reassessments anyway. If the target of a four-year (or less) valuation cycle is achieved, the lag between completion of a project and an increase in the assessed value will not be a long one. In any event, if real property is a rational base for taxation in developing countries—as it would seem to be on both benefit and distributional grounds—there is every reason for taxing increases in site value, however caused, under the regular property tax as soon as possible.

In terms of the usual definition the valorization tax is probably a progressive tax through its relation to property, since property ownership is more unequally distributed than income in most countries. Using the more inclusive concept of the "fiscal residuum" the tax is neutral, for all taxpayers would receive benefits equal to or greater than the tax payment. Compared with the probable alternative ways of financing public improvements if this form is not used, the valorization tax probably favors the poor over the wealthy and yields a more equal income distribution. This presumption is somewhat confirmed by the fact that the strongest opposition to valorization taxes in Colombia has come from some of the wealthier groups in the country (who own much of the urban land).

The valorization tax as it exists in Colombia, particularly in Medellín, seems to have a useful but limited role to play in economic development. It is effective in financing some types of public investment at a certain stage in the economic development of a country. For the tax to be useful, the country must have reached a stage where urbanization is proceeding at a rapid rate and large modern cities are emerging. The country must also have developed capable administrators, real estate men, and engineers who can handle the complicated machinery of the valorization tax. City planning must have become feasible. It is essential to relate the works financed by valorization to a coherent city plan if the full benefits of this form of financing are to be realized without the disadvantage of "piecemeal" improvement. The financing and execution of the work should be the responsibility of a single entity. This entity should be as autonomous as possible (except for its relation to the planning department), in order to enable it to hire and retain the capable skilled people success requires, free of the usual fiscal and political constraints of public administration in developing countries.

Yet the country must not have reached the stage of maturity where capital markets have developed which can take over the job from the valorization tax, and where cities have come so large and intricate that the relation between public investment and increases in site value is too complex for valorization financing to work. This stage probably will not be reached in Colombia generally for many years, although there are signs that it may already be approaching in Bogotá.[35]

Many Colombians feel that the experience in Medellín and elsewhere in the last twenty years has established the general principles as well as the specialized methods needed for successful valorization programs. I agree. The success of present attempts to extend the valorization tax will probably depend more on the quality of administration of the new programs than any other factor. It may be safely concluded that the expansion of valorization taxation in Colombia will be favorable for economic development. Certainly, increased use of benefit taxes, together with more adequate public utility charges and better property taxes should suffice to finance most heavy urbanization expenditures for years to come. Through these instruments, properly applied, the larger urban areas can and should look after their own needs, for if the richest and fastest-growing parts of the country cannot do so, there is little hope for the rest. The frequent arguments heard in Colombia that the larger municipalities ought to receive a larger share of the national revenues thus seem to me completely wrong, for most expansions of urban services can and should be financed locally.

Three | Taxing for Development

6 | Taxing for Development

The single most important aim of any tax reform in Colombia today should be to raise more revenue. In particular, tax yields must be made more responsive to changes in money national income in order to avoid feeding the inflationary process through budget deficits. Both more revenue and a more elastic tax system could be best achieved in Colombian conditions if the tax system were more progressive in its incidence. Greater progressivity would also be beneficial in itself by reducing the need for imports without much damaging savings and investment. In addition to the revenue, elasticity, and progressivity goals, this study points out the importance of using the tax structure as an instrument of development policy—for example, to provide some correction for obvious distortions in the market prices of factors. All these objectives of the "ideal" way to tax for development, of course, derive from my perception of the appropriate set of development policies for Colombia at the present time, as elaborated in Part One of this book.

Although no detailed quantification of the task of the revenue system has been attempted in this study, any reasonable set of projections indicates that the public savings needed to finance an increased development effort in a noninflationary way will not be forthcoming from the present Colombian revenue structure.[1] The size of the public savings "gap" (basically, the difference between the surplus on current account of the national government and its investment outlays) will, it appears, be at least 1 to 2 percent of gross domestic product, depending on the growth rate of GDP, the elasticity of government current expenditures, and the extent to which central-government savings are called on to finance investments in other sectors of the economy. Whatever the cause of inflation in Colombia, budgetary deficits of this size, though themselves largely the result of inflation, will certainly make the inflationary spiral worse than it would otherwise be and will probably also lead, as in the past, to investment cuts.[2] This presumably undesirable result is particularly likely to ensue if expenditure expansions are geared to current revenues rather than to the trend of revenues as was suggested earlier in the analysis of the revenue effect of foreign-trade cycles.

Recent tax changes in Colombia—notably the introduction of a partial current-payment system for the income tax, a new general sales tax, and a substantial increase in the gasoline tax —will in some measure alleviate this problem by improving the elasticity of the tax system and hence its ability to mobilize real resources for development. But they are not adequate in themselves to resolve the problem. Furthermore, these changes on balance have probably made the tax system somewhat less progressive than before and have done little if anything to correct market distortions. The need for tax structure reform to achieve developmental goals in Colombia thus remains as pressing as ever.

To achieve these goals the present Colombian tax system must be changed in a number of important ways. In the first place, the income tax should be put on a full current-payment basis (including withholding), with its structure simplified both to make current payment administratively practical and to make effective administration possible. Second, the income tax should be made more progressive by, for example, taxing capital gains more fully, by heavier use of net-wealth taxation, and by more effective enforcement. Third, other taxes, both direct and indirect, should also be made more progressive so far as possible, because of the desirable direct effects of increased progressivity on resource allocation and its indirect effects through changing the composition of demand as a result of altering income distribution. In some instances this aim might be accomplished by altering rates, as with certain indirect taxes and in other cases by administrative means, as in the case of presumptive taxation of agriculture. Fourth, both for their generally desirable distributive effects and, more important, because of their great revenue potential, much heavier reliance should be put on the real property tax and on the valorization tax. Through fuller use of these revenue sources, the larger urban areas could finance a large part of the investment needed to cope with the increasing urbanization of the Colombian population, thus adding to total resources mobilized for development and removing one of the largest unnecessary strains on the national budget.

If fully carried out, this program should raise the *ex ante* elasticity of the revenue structure as well as its long-run ability to close the public savings "gap," thus catching up with current problems and keeping ahead of the new ones that are certain to develop. Furthermore, the suggested reforms would accomplish this task in a way which would make the incidence of the tax system more progressive while realizing much more fully than at present the potential of tax policy to provide useful corrections to distortions of the price system and create a set of developmental incentives.

This program of substantial tax reform would not injure private investment and saving much, even in the short run, provided adequate measures were taken in designing the business income-tax structure (and in credit policy), to provide some offsets. Private investment is a key factor in Colombia's development, but the rate of investment is governed much more by market opportunities and by the availability of imported investment goods than by tax regulations. The major incentive needed in the tax system apart from a little certainty and a few structural features (such as loss carryovers and equal treatment of different forms of business organizations) is therefore not an investment incentive as such but a general incentive to nontraditional exports. Despite the problem created by the present policy-induced tendency to employ too much capital relative to labor, however, some tax incentive to investment is perhaps desirable as part of a comprehensive tax-reform package, both to improve the political chances of the package's acceptability and to avoid adverse incentive effects. On the whole, general tax incentives (for example, allowance of more rapid depreciation) seem advisable on administrative and allocative grounds, despite the greater revenue loss involved, than specific tax incentives—such as the basic industries legislation —which are costly and inefficient in achieving their supposed ends and difficult to administer. Any specific guidance thought appropriate could be exercised more suitably and flexibly through finance and credit policy rather than tax policy.

A great deal thus can and should be done in theory to make the tax system a more responsive and responsible instrument for Colombia's development. But is it possible, politically and administratively, for these changes to be made? How might one go about reforming the tax system in the ways described above as desirable?

The optimal strategy of tax reform might be defined as that which involves the minimum cost in reaching political decisions. Decisions involve scarce resources—in a developing country perhaps the scarcest of all resources, managerial and organizational capacity and political stability. It is clear, for example, that the needs of economic policy are always going to be subordinated to those of political stability. This means that decisions on painful and potentially dangerous matters like tax reform will generally be made only in times of crisis, particularly external crisis as reflected in the balance of payments, when they can be blamed on external forces and when it is obvious to all that some serious consequences will ensue if they are not made.

If this assessment of the probability of tax reform is correct, the implication is that the sorts of changes proposed here cannot realistically be expected to be put into force as a package but must instead be viewed as a set of goals at which, over time, the crisis-induced changes inevitable in any tax system can be aimed. If the long-run strategy of tax reform outlined here is going to be implemented at minimum cost—or perhaps at all —it must proceed by a series of tactical seizures of crisis opportunities for change, with the strategic policy decisions setting the ground rules which constrain and mold the tactical decisions.

In addition to the importance of timing, a further lesson for development taxation (from Colombian experience with the sales tax, for example) is that it is not usually advisable to try to resolve urgent short-run revenue problems before thinking about the long-run implications of tax structure for development.[3] Since to a considerable extent basic tax changes can be made only in times of acute fiscal crisis anyway, there is a real danger that if tax reform is regarded simply as something to be disposed of before going on to the *real* task of long-range planning (and spending), bad economic incentives may inadvertently be established. Once an economic policy is set up in a certain way, to change it becomes much more difficult as a rule than setting it up properly in the first place would have been. Tax policy, like tariff policy, should be constructed so far as possible with an eye not merely to the revenue it will produce but also to its probable effects on the structure of incentives in the economy and on the key variables affecting development possibilities and patterns—the balance of payments, the composition of final demand, the size of the public sector, income distribution, and productive techniques. Since the initial cost of good tax design is generally little higher than that of bad design and the potential long-run benefits are so much greater, more attention to the design of new taxes is a worthwhile investment for developing countries today.

Finally, besides the problems of what to do and when to do it, there is also the delicate question of how to present tax reforms. It is this consideration which underlay the earlier stress on the importance of earmarking and benefit taxation in reforming local government finance. Similarly, at the national level not only might some offsets for business be considered as part of any tax reform, but archaic and complex burdens such as the present stamp tax might be abolished to make the increases a little more politically palatable.[4]

A substantial improvement in Colombia's present tax policy-making machinery is needed if the reform program suggested is to have any chance of success. To meet the needs of Colombia's changing economy, tax reform must be "institutionalized."

Administration, Politics, and the Tax Policy Process

It is not difficult to design on paper a tax system like that here outlined to fit the peculiar circumstances of Colombia. It is much harder to prescribe in detail how to proceed even two steps in the direction of that ideal. Since one of the scarcest resources in Colombia is the capacity to make and implement effective policy decisions, the needed strategy of tax reform is to obtain the desired change for the minimum expenditure of scarce political and administrative capital. Means and ends cannot, of course, be this sharply separated in fact, and no doubt the available choice of means at times determines the choice of ends (progressive indirect taxes), just as some ends can create in part their own means (valorization and earmarking for education). Nevertheless, there can be no doubt that the major problem in Colombia, or in any other country, in implementing a tax reform program like that I have outlined is political and administrative.

The political problem has two dimensions. The first concerns the ability to make effective policy decisions, which depends in part on the administrative machinery available and in part on the autonomous strength and political base of the government. The second is the interest of the government in making such changes, or the will to make effective decisions. Many efforts at tax reform in Colombia in the past have amounted to little or nothing—whether or not they resulted in a new law's appearing on the books—simply because the reforms were not the real policy of those in power but a game performed for the international lending agencies or other interested spectators.

The political autonomy of a government may be defined for present purposes as its ability to make decisions independent of the wishes of other groups and interests in society. Is tax policy the reflection of the pressure of vested interests or of the decisions of relatively autonomous policymakers? Evidence pointing both ways may be found in Colombia's recent tax history.

The most important income-tax reform of the postwar period, for example, occurred in 1953 under the military dictatorship of General Rojas Pinilla, who had recently taken power in a generally welcomed coup.[5] This reform was perhaps the most explicitly political tax change ever made in Colombia. The Rojas government increased tax rates on high incomes and on corporations and, for the first time in Colombia, taxed dividend income received by individuals. Avowedly anticapitalistic (though tax depreciation allowances were somewhat liberalized), these measures were naturally bitterly attacked by the national industrialists' association and by the well-to-do classes. This storm quickly passed, however, and the changes became part of the accepted tax system. This episode suggests the relative autonomy of a strong government in some important aspects of tax policy, despite the publicity and uproar that almost inevitably accompanies any major tax change.

No further important tax changes took place until the National Front government replaced Rojas (and an interim military government). The National Front government, a coalition of the two traditional political parties (Liberal and Conservative), was established by a constitutional reform in 1958. This reform also meant, in effect, that any tax measure required a two-thirds vote in each of the two houses of Congress in order to become law. Given this legislative hurdle, there are perhaps few countries which could have done much better than Colombia in response to the recurrent fiscal feasts and famines resulting from the trade cycle and the greater *ex ante* elasticity of expenditures than of revenues. What was done in the tax field was generally done under either extraordinary executive powers (granted in the 1963 crisis) or state-of-seige powers (imposed in the 1965 crisis). The record of the last decade viewed from the perspective of this study is a dismal one, marked by constant recurrence to flat surcharges on existing income taxes (1963–1966). Heavy reliance has been placed on foreign-trade taxes. (For example, tariffs were raised in 1959 and 1965, and primarily for fiscal reasons import licenses were granted for high-tariff items such as private automobiles. About 10 percent of total central-government current revenues in 1966 came from a few thousand cars.) The government also forced bond placements and made numerous abortive attempts at other tax "reforms."

Amidst all this flurry two events stand out: the income tax reform of 1960 and the introduction of a general sales tax in 1965. The income tax reform of 1960, while a useful consolidation and, to some extent, simplification of the law, was not a major reform. Its main immediate effect was to reduce revenues, primarily because of the introduction of income-splitting (which reduced the progressivity of the tax rates on the "middle-income" brackets of taxpayers) and because of the tax incentives discussed in Chapter 4. The only other innovation of any importance was the introduction of a limited capital-gains tax on gains from the sale of real estate. The 1960 reform cannot be considered a major change in Colombian tax policy and does not compare in importance to the 1953 reform. If anything, the 1960 measure reduced the progressivity and flexibility of the income tax and hence was a backward move.

More important, and more revealing of the direction of most current thinking on taxes in Colombia, was the introduction of the country's first general sales tax. Colombia in late 1963 was in serious fiscal difficulty. Following a substantial devaluation in December 1962 and some unfortunate domestic policies early in 1963, inflation was proceeding at a faster rate than the country had ever before experienced. The public finances were approaching collapse as expenditures grew rapidly, owing chiefly to a substantial statutory wage increase which added 30 percent to labor costs in the public sector, while revenues as usual lagged well behind. It seemed clear that something had to be done at once to close the growing fiscal gap, and a 20 percent surcharge on the income tax due to be paid in 1963 and 1964 was chosen as the best way to increase government revenues quickly. Some more permanent fiscal change seemed necessary, however, to avoid another fiscal crisis as soon as the surcharge lapsed. The desired change was found in the introduction of a general sales tax, legislated in 1963 to go into effect in 1965 when the income tax surcharge was to disappear.

A main reason given for introducing a sales tax was that Colombia's reliance on direct taxes was far too heavy for a country at her stage of economic development and that a sales tax was needed to redress the balance between direct and indirect taxes. This argument—always popular with politically articulate taxpayers in Colombia—is superficially strong in that the income tax in the past has often accounted for as much as 50 percent of central-government current revenues. However, Colombia takes a relatively small proportion of the national income in taxes, even compared to other countries in Latin America, so that income taxes amount only to about 4 percent of national income and personal income taxes to about 2 percent. These figures are by no means out of line for a country at Colombia's level of development. More important, the use of comparative data of this sort as evidence of the need for a change in any particular country is in general neither convincing nor helpful. There is no apparent reason, apart from the hortatory one, why the tax structure of the "average" (or "representative") poor country should be taken as a model for the other poor countries.

The delayed imposition of the sales tax was the cause of considerable confusion and uncertainty both to the public and to the tax administrators themselves. Press criticism of the impending tax grew in volume and strength in the closing months of 1964, most of it focused on the expected disastrous impact of the sales tax on prices and the cost of living. Surprisingly little was said at first about the probable regressive impact of the tax. Though the equity issue was later raised in connection with a general strike (especially by the Communists), it never received the prominence given to the alleged impact of the sales tax on prices.[6]

Great efforts were made within Congress to repeal the sales tax before it could come into effect: a repealing measure actually passed the lower house but was defeated in the Senate. Even some officials of the Ministry of Finance believed until the last moment that the sales tax would never come into force. This belief, together with the lack of staff and of funds and all the other ills common to tax administration in most underdeveloped countries, meant that administrative preparations by the Ministry to issue the necessary regulatory decrees, to process sales-tax registrations, and to make sure that firms obliged to register did so were no more advanced than public acceptance of the tax.

On January 1, 1965, however, sales taxation came to Colombia. Although the effect on prices appears to have been minor (the cost-of-living index rose about 1 percent from December 1964 to February 1965), there were no doubt some abuses in the form of speculative price rises, and considerable resentment developed toward the tax because of its alleged impact on the cost of living. This resentment culminated in the two major trade union groups' scheduling a general strike for the end of January, intended as "a collective demonstration against the sales tax, the high cost of living, and other governmental measures which have brought about confusion and general uneasiness."[7] While the imposition of the sales tax was the occasion for this strike threat, it was hardly the principal cause since an atmosphere of uncertainty and doubt had long been building up in the country.

At the last minute the general strike was called off when the government agreed to convene a high-level study commission representing all major interest groups to discuss its fiscal problems, including the new sales tax. While this commission was sitting, the tax was revised somewhat, particularly by clarifying the scope of the exemptions, so that the commission's final report, presented in March 1965, essentially recommended the retention of the existing tax with some further minor changes in exemptions and rates.[8] Although these proposals were embodied in a draft law presented to the Congress in 1965, interest in the sales tax had by then so much lessened that this draft was never even discussed by Congress. By January 1966, when a new revenue-raising increase in some sales-tax rates was proposed, the earlier controversy appeared forgotten by everybody.

This episode has been recounted at some length both as another example of the apparent ability of a strong national government to exercise its taxing authority against considerable opposition—this time, unlike 1953, from the left—and because it indicates so clearly the trend away from heavier income taxation. This trend has been further manifested in other tax measures since 1965—for example, the increased taxation of automobiles, gasoline, and foreign travel in 1966 and 1967, though these measures, unlike the sales tax, were generally desirable in their distributional and allocative effects. One conclusion of this brief and selective account of recent Colombian tax history is that some of the major issues highlighted in this book have not yet been faced and that, even worse, the system seems to have been moving to some extent in the wrong direction—toward more reliance on relatively regressive taxes and taxes on foreign trade.

More optimistically, both the 1953 income tax reforms and the 1965 sales tax might be taken to indicate the relative independence of the government decision-makers, once they make up their own minds. The role of interest groups—regional and sectional, as well as economic and social—is not inconsiderable, but there is no reason to think a strong, determined government could not overcome these obstacles without serious damage to its political future, if it really wanted to do so. There is more room on the basis of past performance, however, to doubt the ability of the government to tax the traditional agricultural sector very heavily. Appendix B illustrates the power of the coffee interests in determining coffee policy. The cattle interests have been similarly successful in blocking moves to tax them more effectively.[9] The relative impotence of industrial as compared to agricultural interests in determining economic policy has been noted as a general characteristic of Latin American politics by many observers, and Colombia proves no exception to this rule.[10]

No final conclusion on these complex and delicate matters can be reached here. My present interest is simply to point out that the prospects of substantial tax reform can be no more than a reflection of those for real change in the political and social balance. It may be frustrating when advice formulated after careful and objective study is unheeded by policymakers, but their response is not necessarily wrong. The nature of policymaking is to reconcile conflicting interests in order to bring about acceptable and workable solutions. In some instances, technical advice may be too narrowly formulated to be acceptable as it stands. In other instances, private interests, whether those of the decision-makers themselves (elite, oligarchy) or of nongovernmental groups (pressure groups), may conflict with the technician's view of the "public interest." Who is to say who is "right" in such cases? Elements of all these conflicts seem to me to be present in Colombia, as in most countries, and to make the chances of substantial tax reform along the lines argued here uncertain at best.

Whatever the facts, it seems clear that in the past Colombia often has lacked not so much a government free to make changes but a strong government determined to bring about substantial change. In part this reflects the country's relative lack of national solidarity and the consequent lack of an "ideology" of change.[11] Government action in the economic policy field has more often been reactive than directive. The fact that there has been in reality as much tax change as there has been is largely explained by the severe balance-of-payments problems which could not be avoided and which forced decisions on a reluctant government.

Past history and limited personal observation lead me to conclude that, first, a strong government could do a great deal to reform taxes in Colombia even within present administrative, political, and economic limits; second, even a weak government will *have* to do a great deal in the tax field, given the problems it is likely to face; and finally, in both cases, what is done in the future could be better planned and more appropriate than has been true in the past. My final section suggests a way in which the tax analysis and design function might be institutionalized. My major doubt, to reiterate, is whether the direction of reform—in particular, more progressivity—which seems to be indicated on economic grounds will be politically acceptable to any Colombian government in the near future, be it strong or weak. The recent actions to strengthen indirect taxes at the partial expense of direct taxes support this doubt.

Thus, from this point of view, the prospects for immediate substantial tax reform in Colombia are not great since the present form of government was primarily set up not to bring about change but to maintain political stability and the traditional elite. To say this is not to say a mere change of government would permit substantial social change, which, in a small way, is what tax reform is all about. Unless the functional structure of the political system is altered, the values of government are not likely to be much changed in the near future. On the other hand, although the task is hard, it may be that a simple reinterpretation of some social objectives by existing elites may suffice, as is presumably the hope of American foreign-aid policy in countries like Colombia.[12]

Although one might think tax reform has no natural allies and many enemies, some private support for fiscal changes to reduce "tax evasion" is almost always forthcoming, in part on the principle of "proportional sacrifice": loosely, reform the other fellow's taxes. Everyone is against tax evasion. Every tax economist has often been asked: "Why should government penalize honest taxpayers by raising tax rates when so much revenue is foregone by evasion?"[13]

As with all illegal activities, it is hard to get a good idea of the extent of evasion in Colombia. The only survey evidence we have (that cited earlier from the Taylor Report) indicates that income-tax evasion is common among professional men in Bogotá. Other evidence, such as the income-tax tables in Chapter 3, experience with the sales tax, the property tax, gossip, and personal observation, also indicates tax evasion is common in Colombia, as one would expect when the government is considered by most taxpayers to waste what it gets and when the penalties for evasion are low and the probability of being caught very small.[14] On the other hand, I doubt—and this is a personal judgment since data are lacking—whether illegal evasion is as quantitatively significant as many foreigners and Colombians seem to believe, and I am certain it will be hard to do much to improve the situation quickly.[15] Every possible effort should of course be devoted to improving the objectivity of tax information and the mutual respect of taxpayer and administration, since better planning and more equitable and tougher administration are the only answers to tax evasion.[16] It will all take time, however, even with the best will in the world, and thus cannot be counted on to provide much of the revenue needed for development.

J. K. Galbraith once noted of economic administration that

there is no problem for which intimacy breeds such respect.[17] This dictum certainly holds true for tax administration. In the hands of an incompetent administration, good tax policy and bad tax policy may end up looking remarkably alike. Tax-reform proposals that assume good tax administration exists are unlikely to be relevant in most poor countries, except perhaps as an ideal at which, within the severe limits of reality, policy revisions may aim. Similarly, comparisons between an existing, badly designed, badly administered system and a better-designed alternative that assume the new system will be well administered are usually more misleading than helpful. A safer assumption is that the present poor administrative machine, perhaps with some marginal improvements, will continue to function at the same low level no matter what changes are made in tax policy or in tax structure. Indeed, it often seems to be easier to make drastic changes in tax policy than to overcome the inertia of the system and improve the administration of existing taxes. Once a policy change has been made, however, there is usually little reason to expect the new tax to be administered better than the old, for the same people must administer both.

There is perhaps little economic advisers on taxation can do about such problems except to be aware of them and to take them explicitly into account in formulating the strategy and tactics of practical tax reform for developing countries. I have already expressed my belief that it is much more difficult to administer a tax policy effectively than it is to devise the policy in the first place. Whereas internationally minded officials and outside advisers may formulate tax programs, tax administration more closely reflects the society in which it must operate.[18] If the common view of government and of government expenditures is disaffected, as appears to be true in Colombia, tax administration is bound to be a most difficult and unpopular task. Institutional difficulties, such as the greater relative importance of the always hard-to-control farm and small-business sectors, will also make tax administration difficult and inequitable. The social and economic structure of a country thus conditions the feasibility of effectively administering different taxes, just as it determines their desirability from a policy point of view. Furthermore, insofar as the problems of tax administration come about through political forces, their resolution must be political, not technical. To a large extent, improving tax administration, like improving tax structure (the distinction between the two is not in this respect sharp), is an inherently political process, subject to all the general problems of policy decisions in Colombia.[19]

Since the quality of tax administration is such an important constraint on the possibility of tax reform, it would appear logical to suggest tax reforms which can be handled by a poor administrator. Sound tax policy must be premised on a realistic understanding and appraisal of the capabilities of the tax administration, and administrative reform is often most readily accomplished when tied to specific and pressing action programs.[20] One improvement would be to recognize explicitly the need for crude, arbitrary solutions in many instances and to attempt to be consistent in applying them rather than assuming that a perfect law can be perfectly administered. Difficulties will always arise in administering any tax law, but they need not always arise unexpectedly. (The proposal for presumptive income taxation made in Chapter 3 is an example of such a feasibility compromise.) A less-than-ideal tax designed for a poor administration may work better—its effects may be more in line with those desired—than a "good" tax badly administered. It is unfortunate that in tax policy and administration, as in so many other aspects of development in poor countries, it seems less possible and more necessary to do things well. My point is simply that tax reformers are going to have to live with this state of affairs for some time to come and cannot just ignore it.

In short, while improved tax administration should be a high-priority goal, it cannot be expected to come about rapidly or to produce large revenue increases quickly. One useful step might be the appointment of a small corps of elite, highly trained, well-paid officials to tackle some key administrative problems and to show what can and should be done. The experience of those developing countries with such an elite, however, shows that even this improvement, important as it would be in Colombia, is only a small step on the long road to better tax administration. Another bridge to administrative improvement would be structural simplification of the tax laws to facilitate compliance and enforcement. An increased budget for tax administration would also help. Whatever is done, however, no miracles can be expected.

To sum up the general ideas of this section, tax reform, whether in policy or administration, will inevitably be a piecemeal process because of the nature of the problems and the political and human resources available to deal with them (assuming it has been decided as a matter of high national priority that they should be dealt with). Second, tax reform is a continuous process. Not only will no grand once-and-for-all reform scheme be adopted, but even if it were, it would never be sufficient for very long. Circumstances will change, and policies must change with them. Crisis implementation of tax reforms will most likely continue to be the rule in the future as it has been in the past; so the road to an improved tax system lies in constant tinkering with tax design in readiness for the moment when a policy change can be effected. Success in this task requires putting official study of tax policy and tax administration on a regular basis—"institutionalizing" it.

Technical Assistance and the Institutionalization of Tax Reform

The evolution of the Colombian tax structure has been greatly influenced by foreign technical-assistance missions, beginning with the Kemmerer missions in the interwar period (1923 and 1931) and continuing after the war with studies and reports by the United Nations, the Organization of American States, and various other groups. Though most of the reports were pigeonholed, several of them had substantial, and not always beneficial, influences. An important report prepared by the Economic Commission for Latin America in 1957, for example, argued against increased reliance on the income tax as unfavorable to saving and investment, especially in the manufacturing sector. Since the authors of this report also viewed indirect taxes as tending to discourage demand and the growth of domestic markets, they concluded that no stress should be put on income-elastic consumption taxes either. Therefore, their report favored even more use of tax incentives to private investment and saving and of taxes on foreign trade.[21] These recommendations, which were influential in the 1960 tax reform, are completely contrary to my own emphasis on the need for increased revenue elasticity and progressivity in Colombia.

Colombia thus has a long tradition of foreign tax missions, as well as a surprisingly good record of listening to them, not always with desirable results. One reason for the relatively poor success record of foreign tax advisers in the past has been the inadequate consideration of local conditions affecting the international transferability of tax techniques. Advice to a Finance Minister which consists mainly in telling him all the things he should do—once he has all the things he does not have—is not likely to be very helpful. It is no wonder that so many technical-assistance reports are considered useless by those advised, for they do not at all relate to the actual constraints within which the recipients must work. Economists have constructed many rationalizations for working in "institution-free" terms in countries in which they are familiar with the institutional structure anyway; but this attitude cannot be safely carried over to quite different societies.

Whatever the reason so many suggestions of foreign advisers have proved useless, it is perhaps more important for present purposes to note that these suggestions, whether or not sound, have been taken up so readily in Colombia not only because of the usual desire to be "modern" but also because a well-reasoned argument (even one out of touch with actual conditions) is usually listened to with respect. This last point offers some hope for the future of technical assistance in the tax field and for improved tax analysis in general, provided proper use is made of outside consultants. They are most useful either to prepare special reports on particular, limited subjects or to comment on studies, draft laws, and the like prepared locally.

In either case, the essential requirement for effective technical assistance is that there be a functioning local entity willing and able to utilize such assistance.

In addition to having someone to work with, an effective technical-assistance group in the tax field must also be in basic agreement with the real objectives of government policy, since in order to be effective the group needs to appeal to the real interests of those in control, rather than attempt to impose its own conception of social welfare in the sterile pursuit of abstract perfectionism. Sometimes it may be better to posit all-or-nothing alternatives—to plant "bombs" which may explode much later—but this tactic will seldom forward long-term efforts at improving the rationality of decision-making. The ideas may survive and have influence at a more propitious time; but the group is unlikely to survive if it is not seen to be useful.

One can learn much, it has been said, from studying one's failures: if so, the future for development planning and tax reform in Colombia looks bright, since there is such a good record of failures on which to build. Attempts have been made at least three times already, for example, to institutionalize the tax research and analysis function either in the Division of National Taxes (in the late 1940's and again in the late 1950's) or in the Minister of Finance's office (since 1963). What can be said of the prospects of success—defined as improving the rationality (in relation to development objectives) of tax changes—of the present attempt to create an office of tax analysis, and what is the potential role of foreign technical assistance in this task?

Holistic planning is now seldom recommended by non-Marxian economists in connection with general development plans: we are almost all piecemeal planners now. Yet all too often the vital problem of tax reform is approached in a holistic, all-or-nothing manner. Tax reform too should be approached in a piecemeal, incremental way. Though at times a big effort might have a big payoff, the occasion and the payoff will usually arise only after a long, often outwardly unfruitful, preparatory period. Splendid distant objectives can be reached only by successful tactical maneuvering; and if there is no hope of successful tactics, there is little point in plotting grand strategy. Furthermore, tax-reform efforts to be effective must be closely and continuously integrated with the development planning process. The fiscal problem cannot be regarded as something to be disposed of before settling down to the real work of planning. It must be recognized that taxing policies like spending policies need to be continuously adapted to changing economic, political, and administrative reality if the tax system is to realize anything like its full potential as an instrument of development policy.

Successful long-term development policy must be implemented through a series of short-term tactical actions. But concentration on being "effective" in the short run will get one nowhere unless some idea is kept in mind of where one should be going. Short-term crises always abound in developing countries: if this short-run corrective opportunity is not seized, another will be along all too soon. It may be essential for tax advisers in a new technical-assistance group to prove its worth by prompt and on-the-spot assistance during crises. But their most important task must be to attempt to link together these opportunities in some coherent chain related to the long-run goals of tax reform, for if the advisory group does not do this, it is unlikely anyone else will. On the other hand, if they do not rush to the rescue at the first sight of a short-term problem, some evasive action will no doubt be taken anyway. The choice of where efforts should be concentrated seems obvious. Nevertheless, the attractions of "firefighting" have often been such as to damage severely the strategic aim of seizing tactical opportunities (crises) to further longer-term objectives. An essential requisite for effective technical advice in the tax field is thus a planning horizon extending farther than the next crisis. The only way to achieve this goal—and to utilize effectively whatever technical assistance may be available—is to develop in-house tax research. While it is possible to contract with outside agencies for particular pieces of research, this method by itself cannot really be used either to develop basic reform proposals or to embody them in proper legislative form for enactment; nor will pieces of research contracted out be of much value unless a competent in-house staff is built up which can and will utilize any results of the outside studies. In short, without completely discarding the possibility of employing outside researchers, top priority should be given to developing a government's competence and ability to do its own work.

The single most important factor in the development of a tax analysis office is *people*. The quantity and especially the quality of the persons hired provides the only certain evidence of sincere intent to improve economic analysis in the tax field. If enough capable persons are made available, full-time, for this task, a formal organization, while desirable, is not really necessary. In a society where the factors of communication and identification are as crucial as in Colombia, however, any tax analysis agency or advisory group, whatever it may be called, should be located near the top. The appropriate location may shift from time to time, but on balance the Minister of Finance's office is probably the best compromise as a long-term proposition, since an effective tax analysis office must also be located close enough to the operating level to understand the actual administrative system as distinct from the purely formal tax system. Such a tax analysis group, working closely with development planners, could, over time, do as much if not more than any of the substantive suggestions in this book to help Colombia in its task of taxing for development.

The advisory group in the Ministry of Finance should concentrate on tax policy. I would suggest that the group, at least until it has been fully functioning for some time, should focus *only* on tax policy. This recommendation is made for three reasons, which I hope do not reflect my professional bias as much as they do the realities of the Colombian situation: the importance of sound tax policy; the fact that nowhere else in Colombia is tax policy systematically studied; and the need to focus the work on one particular subject if the efforts of the professionals in the office are not to be dissipated in hopeless attempts to keep up with all aspects of economic and financial policy. Since the need is there and no one else is meeting it, the conclusion seems obvious. Tax policy planning is a long-term process and should be formally recognized as such. In a developing country like Colombia, fiscal needs and economic circumstances will always be changing and requiring new tax measures. These needs, added to the fact that in no country is the work of tax reform ever really completed, ensure that there will be more than enough useful and constructive work for a tax policy unit in the Ministry throughout the foreseeable future. This arrangement is quite compatible with substantial work on departmental and municipal as well as national finances.

Organizationally, there should be no conflict or, indeed, very much overlapping, between the suggested tax analysis office and the National Planning Department. (While overlapping economic advice, given the inherent uncertainties of life, is probably a good thing, technically competent people are so few in Colombia that unnecessary overlapping should be avoided.) What Colombia would ideally have is several public-finance planning units, each performing essential tasks and each unable to function effectively without the other. The Planning Department would presumably concentrate on pointing out long-run fiscal needs—the demands that will be made on the revenue system by the expenditure needs of development—and in indicating desirable economic guidelines to be followed in meeting these needs—in relation to industrial incentives, factor proportions, and so on. There should be another group concerned with fiscal and financial planning for stabilization. The Ministry's staff would take the guidelines developed and refined in close consultation with planners and develop tax policies which would implement them. This task cannot be done properly from a central planning agency since it requires close and intimate collaboration with and knowledge of the tax administration, the taxpaying community, and the existing tax system. Both parts of the work are essential to the establishment of a sound, development-oriented tax system for Colombia; neither is now being carried out effectively; and no matter how much the central planning agency is improved, the task of using the tax instrument effectively for development cannot be accomplished without the creation of a competent tax analysis staff in the Ministry itself. Idealistic as the scheme outlined here may appear, it indicates, I think, the direction one must proceed to develop a sound fiscal situation and a useful rather than obstructive tax system for Colombia.

To sum up, the first requirement of a full-fledged tax reform effort in Colombia is real desire on the part of a strong government to carry it out. But inspired leadership alone is not enough, and a second essential requirement is that concern with tax policy and tax administration be institutionalized if the presumed good intentions are to be converted into workable reality. If these two conditions are met—a real desire for change and some continuing group concerned with implementing that desire—then Colombia can carry out successfully the reform program sketched here to make its fiscal system more responsive to the needs of development. Without both desire and concentration on improved technical competence, it is unlikely that any foreign advice will be of much use in improving tax reality in Colombia, however useful it might be to students of development taxation in general.

Appendix A
The Accuracy of Fiscal Data

Fiscal data are probably among the most accurate available in Colombia. Yet there are substantial problems in the use and interpretation of even fiscal figures. This appendix illustrates some of these problems, using intergovernmental transfer payments as an example. The first column of Table 27 shows the percentage differences between transfers recorded as paid to one level of government by the other and those recorded as received. The second column does the same for transfers in the opposite direction, and the third shows how the differences in the recorded sizes of these two flows affect *net* transfers.

The discrepancies quantified by this approach are substantial. Even more disturbing for many purposes, there appears to be no consistent pattern in these differences, so that recorded changes in transfer payments are no more reliable than the base figures.

A number of explanations of these discrepancies are conceivable: errors of transcription; errors of accounting and classification in the basic accounts; discrepancies arising from timing—some transfers recorded as paid by departments in 1960 are recorded as received by municipalities in 1961, for example; differences in classification of receipts and payments at different levels of government. The last appears to be the most important in this instance, since it is apparently common for a department, for example, to record as a transfer to municipalities a payment that does not actually pass through the municipal budget but instead goes directly to some entity within the municipality. On the other hand, the differences even in figures purporting to show the same transfer as recorded at the same level is so great (see the source note to Table 27) that one cannot by any means blame all the discrepancy on classification problems.

While it is not possible to obtain similar quantitative indications of error magnitude for other data, fiscal or otherwise, used in the present study, this example should suffice to indicate the need for considerable caution in interpreting small changes. Almost every figure used in this book can be legitimately challenged on these grounds. Nevertheless, whatever changes may be made in the details, I believe that the broad patterns outlined are sufficiently reliable to serve as a sound basis for discussion.

Table 27. Comparison of departmental and municipal statistics describing transfers to each other.[a]

Year	$\dfrac{T_D - R_M}{T_D}$	$\dfrac{R_D - T_M}{R_D}$	$\dfrac{n_D - n_M}{n_D}$
1950	81.3	31.6	84.7
1951	9.5	57.8	1.1
1952	4.1	72.1	−21.7
1953	17.9	67.4	5.8
1954	−1.4	60.9	−19.1
1955	26.3	66.2	18.7
1956	65.0	55.6	65.4
1957	62.8	− 20.4	67.9
1958	64.7	26.2	67.5
1959	36.3	76.2	34.8
1960	40.4	31.1	40.8
1961	45.8	57.6	45.3
1962	23.0	−776.2	34.6
Unweighted average[b]	36.8	51.9[c]	39.0

Source: Data in the National Accounts Section of the Departmento de Investigaciones Económicas, Banco de la República, except that R_D (receipts from municipalities as recorded by departments) is from *Boletín de la dirección nacional del presupuesto,* no. 51 (November 1964), p. 40. Though the data in both sources are based on Contraloría figures as reported by the Departmento Administrativo Nacional de Estadística, there are nevertheless wide discrepancies between these two sets of figures purporting to show the same item as recorded at the same level of government. This confusion is additional to the discrepancies discussed in the text.

[a] The symbols used in Table 27 are defined as follows: T = transfer paid; R = transfer received; n = net transfers. The subscripts D and M indicate that the data come from the departmental or municipal governments, as the case may be. For example, T_D means transfers recorded by the departments as being made to the municipalities in a particular year. R_M means transfers recorded by the municipaities as being received from the departments in the same year; $T_D - R_M$ (the difference in these two figures) expressed as a percentage of T_D is a measure of the discrepancy in the recorded figures. (This approach is based on Oskar Morgenstern, *On the Accuracy of Economic Observations* [2d ed.; Princeton University Press, 1963].)

[b] Without attention to sign.

[c] Excluding the abnormal value for 1962.

Appendix B
Coffee Tax Policy

The nature, role, and problems of coffee taxation in Colombia, although too complex to admit of ready treatment in the main text of this study, are too important to be left out completely. Coffee taxation is important in Colombia because coffee is important. Although its importance has declined since the early 1950's, coffee production in 1964 still accounted for 38 percent of total agricultural production, 8 percent of the gross domestic product (in real terms), and 72 percent of total exports.[1] Not only is coffee by far Colombia's major foreign-exchange earner, but its fortunes are of vital importance to economic growth and to rural living standards. It is therefore no wonder that the government's coffee policy is a subject of considerable discussion and, at times, owing to the confusing manner in which it is conducted, mystery.

The principal agency concerned with coffee policy in Colombia is not the government itself but the relatively independent Federation of Coffee Growers, which buys and holds surplus stocks, supplies and regulates the domestic market, provides technical assistance to growers, controls export standards, and does a lot of exporting itself (accounting for 32 percent of total coffee exports in 1965–66).[2] Many of these operations are really carried out in the name of the National Coffee Fund, which is managed by the Federation and financed by the national government.

The Federation was established in 1927. The first coffee tax, a small one, was established to finance it at that time. The Coffee Fund was established in 1940 to manage the stocks created under the first international coffee agreement.[3] The active coffee policy of today did not really begin, however, until after the great fall in coffee prices in the mid-1950's (see Table 28). Coffee policy is now largely guided by the International Coffee Agreement, which was signed in 1962 and began to operate in 1964. Under this Agreement, export quotas have been set for each producing country in an effort to stabilize and support world coffee prices, the underlying rationale being that the price elasticity of demand for coffee is low.[4] The 1965–66 quota for Colombia, for example, was set at 5.7 million 60-kilo sacks, compared to estimated production in that period of 7.6 million 60-kilo sacks. Despite the efforts of the Federation in recent years to encourage domestic coffee consumption (in competition with cocoa), even at times to the point of selling coffee within Colombia below its internal support price, production is still so high that perhaps as much as 1 million 60-kilo sacks had to be added to coffee stocks in 1965–66.[5]

There apparently have been three objectives of Colombian coffee policy in recent years: to hold back domestic production (and, secondarily, to increase domestic consumption) in order to reduce the cost of buying

Table 28. Basic data on Colombian coffee policy, 1958–1967.

Year	Export price[a]	Internal support price[b]	Surrender price[c]	Coffee rate[d]
1958	52.3	457	82	6.10
1959	45.2	389	73	6.10
1960	44.8	432	70	6.30
1961	43.6	473	68	6.50
1962	40.6	481	64	6.80
1963	39.5	559	59	7.10
1964	48.8	739	73	7.30
1965	48.5	721	71	7.71
1966	47.4	456	68	9.94
1967	41.7[e]	753[f]	61[f]	11.14[g]

Sources: Calculated from data in *Boletín de información estadística sobre café*, no. 40, pp. 48–49; *Revista del Banco de la República*, various issues; International Monetary Fund, *International Financial Statistics*, and *International Financial News Survey*, various issues.

[a] In U.S. cents per pound. In 1954, the price was 80 cents; in 1956 74 cents; and in 1957 64 cents.

[b] In pesos per load *(carga)* of 125 kilos for *tipo pergamino corriente* (coffee at the processing stage before the last covering—"parchment"—has been removed from the green bean). In many instances the purchase price was changed during the year and the figures given here represent a computed average price (each separate price being weighted by approximately the portion of the year for which it was in force).

[c] The surrender price in U.S. dollars per 70-kilo sack exported (that is, the number of dollars which had to be turned over at the coffee rate). A similar averaging procedure to that described in note b was used when changes took place during the year.

[d] Pesos per dollar. The same averaging procedure was used where the necessary information was available; for some years the rate given is a simple average of those in force during the year.

[e] January–October average.

[f] January–November average.

[g] Since March 1967 there has been no official coffee rate. The 11.14 figure in the table (from *International Financial Statistics*) was obtained by deducting the export tax from the certificate market rate. To avoid double-counting, the original March 1967 certificate rate of 13.50 was actually used to calculate the "tax" in Table 29; since this rate increased somewhat over the relevant period the "tax" thus calculated is overstated.

and holding surplus stocks; to maintain the real income of coffee growers; and to reduce (or eliminate) the Federation's domestic borrowing (from the central bank), which has at times had a substantial inflationary impact, especially in 1963 and 1964. Unfortunately, these objectives are to some extent contradictory. These contradictions explain the numerous changes in coffee policy as well as the failure to achieve any of the apparent objectives very satisfactorily for very long. Table 28 illustrates the complexity of, and the numbers of changes in, coffee policy in recent years.[6] The remainder of this appendix outlines briefly the main "tax" instruments employed in the exercise of this policy and attempts to estimate the net tax burden on the coffee sector.

Coffee taxation has taken four main forms in Colombia in the last decade: a retention tax; an export tax; an exchange differential; and a difference between the surrender price and the actual export price. Since 1958 these taxes have been levied in a confusing pattern, both separately and together.[7] The "retention tax" refers to the requirement that private exporters—who still account for over two-thirds of coffee exports—deliver to the Coffee Fund a certain percentage of the amount exported, either in kind or the equivalent cash value in pesos at the current support price. This tax not only helps finance the Fund's purchases of coffee but also acts to offset the Federation's cost disadvantage relative to other exporters. This disadvantage stems in part from technical-assistance activities and the like that the Federation—but not the private exporter— carries on. The retention tax has been reduced and raised many times throughout the period of controlled marketing, ending up at a high of 19 percent at the end of 1966. It appears to be relatively acceptable to the growers, for it has never completely disappeared.

From 1957 through 1961 an export tax of 15 percent (reduced to 9 percent in 1961) was also imposed on the foreign-exchange proceeds of coffee exports. It was deducted by the central bank from the surrender price in dollars that the exporters had to turn over to the bank for pesos at the official coffee exchange rate. Always unpopular, the export tax was abolished in January 1962, but was revived in a new form early in 1967.

A third tax measure which has been employed is an exchange differential. From 1958 to 1962 there was a small differential, varying from about 10 to 30 centavos per dollar, between the peso rate for a dollar earned in coffee exports and the official (import) rate; the proceeds of this differential went to the Coffee Fund. Beginning with the devaluation at the end of 1962, however, the coffee differential was greatly widened in that the official exchange rate was raised much more than the coffee rate. Similarly, in 1965, after some weakening in the interim, a new devaluation led to a new widening of the differential. Continual grower pressure, however, led in 1966 to an increase in the coffee rate (that is, a narrowing of the differential) and a consequent drop in the noninflationary financing of the policy of supporting internal coffee prices. The differential was replaced by an export tax in the 1967 exchange reforms. The rate of this new tax was set initially at 26 percent (approximately the same as the differential it replaced), but by the end of 1968 it had declined to 21.5 percent.

The final instrument by which the coffee sector has been "taxed" in some recent years is through a difference between the actual dollar export price and the number of dollars the private exporter has to surrender to the central bank (the *reintegro*). When the surrender price is above the actual price, as it was in 1961, for example (see Table 29), the exporter had to purchase enough dollars for pesos on the "free" market, and at the higher free-market exchange rate, to make up the difference. In other years (1963, for example) the surrender price was below the actual price, and so the exporter made an additional profit by selling his excess dollars at the free market rate rather than being taxed by this device. The 1967 reform, however, put a stop to this possibility by making the surrender price a minimum, so that any higher actual price had to be turned over at the certificate rate as well.

The exchange differential and export tax are the major government policy variables as regards the coffee sector. The retention tax and the surrender price devices are primarily related to the problem of the relative shares of the Federation and the private exporters in coffee exports. For this reason (among others) the illustrative "tax" calculations in Table 29 are definitely on the high side.

Until 1965, the National Coffee Fund's operation of the support price policy more or less constantly incurred losses, primarily because its domestic buying price adjusted to the downward changes in the international price only with a long lag (see Table 28). These losses became especially substantial after the retention tax was reduced from 15 to 1 percent early in 1963. The fund obtained about 220 million pesos in finance from the central bank in 1964 (in addition to substantial borrowing abroad), thus adding substantially to inflationary pressure in that year. With the new measures accompanying the 1965 devaluation these losses disappeared as the yield from the exchange differential doubled as a result of devaluation. By the end of 1966, however, pressure from growers to raise the coffee rate, lower the surrender price, and raise the support price had again led to a reduction in the rate of coffee taxation and a fiscal loss, according to one estimate, of about 190 million pesos.[8] The 1967 exchange reform more or less restored the 1965 situation, so that one of the apparent objectives of recent coffee policy, to reduce Federation borrowing, had been partly achieved by the end of the period, though it seemed unlikely it would last.[9]

The other two objectives, however—the cutback of production in order to conform to the quota assigned under the International Coffee Agreement without expensive stockpiling, and the maintenance of grower incomes—have turned out, as in other countries with similar agricultural

Table 29. Estimated rate (in pesos) of coffee "taxation," selected years, 1961–1967.

	1961	1963	1965	1967
Value of 70 kilos at market rate[a]	558.6	610.1	1,231.4	1,046.8
Loss or gain to exporter from purchases or sales needed to make up required surrender price[b]	−7.2	18.4	60.9	0.0
Peso equivalent of retention tax[c]	52.0	4.1	84.5	104.5
Export tax[d]	39.8	—	—	176.7
Peso receipts of exporters[e]	343.0	433.2	523.8	585.8
Estimated "tax" rate[f] (percent)	39	29	57	44

a Export price from Table 28 multiplied by a conversion factor of 154 and by the "free" exchange rate (except in 1967 when the capital market rate was used).

b Since the dollar amount actually received for coffee sold abroad is not necessarily equal to the amount which must be turned over to the central bank at the coffee rate, the exporter is considered to buy or sell the difference at the free market rate (except in 1967 when the surrender price acted merely as a minimum and the entire actual price had to be turned over at the certificate rate).

c A retention tax of 15 percent in 1961, 1 percent in 1963, 16 percent in 1965, and 19 percent in 1967 was assumed. The price per kilo at the internal support price (see Table 28) was then multiplied by this percentage of exports and by a factor of 1.31 to allow for the conversion from the grade of coffee to which the support relates (*pergamino*—explained in note b to Table 28) to the grade of coffee required for the retention tax (*excelso,* or green coffee for export).

d An export tax of 9 percent in 1961 and 26 percent in 1967 was assumed on the foreign-exchange value of the surrender price.

e This figure results from multiplying the surrender price by the coffee rate (see Table 28), then adjusting for the items calculated in the second, third, and fourth rows. For 1967, the certificate rate of 13.50 was used instead of the coffee rate and the actual price instead of the surrender price, since the latter was the lower of the two.

f This "tax" rate is the difference between the peso receipts of exporters and the value of 70 kilos of coffee at the market rate as a proportion of the latter figure. It thus measures not the revenues received by the government but the difference between the pesos exporters actually receive and those they would have received had they sold their coffee at the higher rate used in these calculations. All calculations in this table are illustrative and to some extent arbitrary because of both data and conceptual problems. The notes to this Appendix contain an alternative formulation of this "tax" calculation and even more qualifications.

problems, to be inherently contradictory.[10] In the resulting struggle, the victory has on balance gone to the maintenance of grower incomes, with the result that production has continued to stay well above the amount of permitted exports and internal consumption. As Table 29 indicates, this has happened despite the apparently high average "tax" burden on the coffee sector in recent years. Heavy as it has been at times, the deterrent to increased production has clearly not been high enough to overcome the fact that coffee, which is grown on hilly lands not very suitable for most other crops, still produces by far the largest return of any agricultural activity.

One reason for the surprising failure of these nominally high taxes to deter production is that the illustrative calculations in Table 29 definitely overstate the tax burden on coffee growers. The "tax" rates are inflated by the use of the free-market rate as the "true" equilibrium value (except for 1967 when there was no "free" rate). If all coffee were to be traded at this rate, one would expect the "free" price to be considerably lower. Furthermore, the national government's receipts from coffee are much less than one might gather from this table, since much of the revenue was channeled back to supply the import market at the official rate (always lower than the free rate): in 1965, for example, the coffee differential (the only tax passing through the budget) yielded only 340 million pesos, or about 1 peso per kilo of exports compared to a theoretical tax of over 9 pesos per kilo.[11] Finally, it should be remembered that the retention tax and the "tax" imposed through the surrender price are paid by the private exporter only and are intended primarily to regulate the share of exports traded by him rather than by the Federation. It is therefore questionable whether these taxes should be included as taxes on coffee producers, since much of the "tax" revenue goes right back to the coffee sector through the activities of the Federation. Indeed, as already noted, in some years (1963 and 1964, for example) coffee policy has entailed substantial financing from general funds—usually by inflationary credit from the central bank—so that the coffee sector has not contributed much if anything to general taxation despite its nominally "high" tax burden.

An interesting way in which to view some of the data in this appendix is as a test of the political strength of the traditional coffee export sector in shaping the Colombian fiscal system. One measure of the political power of the coffee sector is revealed in the relation between the internal support price of coffee and the prices of what coffee growers buy. Table 30, which contains a crude "parity" measure of this type, indicates that growers have lost ground since the mid-1950's but that they more or less maintained their relative real income position from about 1959 to 1965 in the face of the considerable internal inflation during those years. This "success" was principally achieved by increasing domestic support prices to match export price changes—at times to the point where, as in 1964,

Table 30.   Coffee-sector parity, 1956–1967.

Year	Index of internal prices[a]	Index of export prices[a]	Nominal "parity"[b]	Cost-of-living index[a]	Real "parity"[c]
1956	100	100	100	100	100
1957	117	86	136	114	103
1958	112	71	158	132	85
1959	93	61	152	141	66
1960	103	61	169	146	70
1961	113	59	192	159	71
1962	115	55	309	163	70
1963	134	54	248	216	62
1964	173	66	262	253	68
1965	172	66	261	253	68
1966	181	65	359	297	61
1967	180[d]	57[e]	317	320[e]	56

Sources: *Revista del Banco de la República* and *International Financial Statistics*, various issues.

a For this column, 1956 = 100 Manizales coffee prices; the Manizales urban workers' price index is used on the assumption that it most nearly reflects the consumption pattern of the coffee sector. It does not make much difference, however, which indexes are used in this calculation.

b Index of export prices divided by index of internal prices.

c Index of internal prices divided by cost-of-living index.

d January–November average.

e January–October average.

export prices (at the official coffee rate) have really been below internal support prices. The results of this relative success is maintaining the real income of the coffee sector were mentioned earlier—no deterrent to coffee production and severe financial problems for the Coffee Fund and the country.

The conclusion which emerges from this brief and inevitably superficial study of Colombian coffee tax policy is that taxation of the coffee sector will have to be maintained at a high level if problems like those of 1963–64 are not to arise again. The present taxes, heavy as they are, are not heavy enough to prevent continued accumulation of stocks.[12] The political power of coffee growers in Colombia, despite their relatively heavy tax burden, is clearly substantial.[13] The argument sometimes heard in Colombia that the burden of "strengthening" coffee, the country's principal export since before World War I, should fall on the economy as a whole perhaps reflects this power. It surely does not reflect economic realities. In the field of coffee tax policy at least, if not with respect to other taxes, the political autonomy of the Colombian government seems relatively small.

The only solution to Colombia's coffee problems appears to be much heavier taxation of the coffee sector itself, combined with increased efforts to reduce the present surplus of coffee growers. While there is no reason to expect that Colombia's version of the American farm problem will be any easier to solve in Colombia than it has been in the United States, a brief consideration of the most efficient way of achieving the needed heavier taxation seems an appropriate conclusion.

Although the case for outright coffee taxes is attractive to the economist, in part because it would be easier to understand than the confusing price, tax, retention, and exchange-rate system that has usually prevailed in Colombia, there is also a strong argument for continuing to maintain a separate coffee exchange rate as an easier way of discouraging production. In view of the great absolute advantage of coffee production, a unified exchange rate which encourages just the permitted production for export (plus domestic consumption) would be so low that the country could export nothing else. Any higher rate for coffee would, unless offset, simply stimulate production. Although exchange differentials stimulate smuggling and under-recording of exports, a careful examination of the import statistics of major countries in 1963 indicated that these illegal coffee exports probably amounted to no more than 4 percent of the total in that year.[14] The case for a differential in preference to an explicit export tax has also been argued as a means of avoiding outright political conflict.[15] To achieve a level of taxation adequate to hold back production without overt political revolt, it may well prove that something like the present confusing system is necessary to obscure and thus soften the issue. Given the political importance of the coffee sector and the economic importance for Colombia of avoiding overvalued exchange rates, it is highly desirable that whatever package of measures constitutes coffee policy be such that coffee growers have incentives to support rather than oppose exchange-rate alterations. The need for this support was apparently one reason for the abolition of the formal exchange differential in 1967.

In view of the relatively low incomes of most coffee growers and the probable impact of higher coffee taxes on their incomes, this conclusion in favor of heavy taxation (however achieved)—a necessary one if the basic elasticity assumptions underlying Colombia's adherence to the International Coffee Agreement are valid—is not particularly attractive. It might be made more palatable if other employment opportunities could be opened up for the numerous small coffee growers, whether in rural or urban areas, as is supposed to be done under the Coffee Agreement's diversification provisions. The likelihood of this occurring appears slim, however, given the great absolute advantage of coffee production and the serious foreign-exchange constraint hampering Colombia's industrial growth.

Appendix C
Report of the Commission on Tax Reform

In February 1969, some months after the completion of this book, the Commission on Tax Reform, headed by Professor Richard A. Musgrave, submitted its report to President Carlos Lleras Restrepo. Its Spanish version, *Bases para una reforma tributaria en Colombia* (Bogotá: Biblioteca Banco Popular, 1969), has since been released. In view of the importance of this report, it seems appropriate to include a brief summary of the Commission's main recommendations for reform of the Colombian tax structure.

This summary cannot do justice to the wealth of informative detail found in the Commission's work, but it should suffice to bring out some of the main similarities and differences between their work and mine. For convenience, I have grouped the Commission recommendations on relevant topics in approximately the order in which the material has been covered in my book. The reference in parentheses beside each heading indicates the chapter in which I treat the subject.

Individual Income Tax (Chapter 3):

(1) There should be fuller withholding at source and an equivalent current-payment system for the self-employed, based on anticipated tax liabilities.

(2) The interest charged on late payments of tax should be increased, and there should be a general review of the penalty system.

(3) All capital gains should be taxed at realization, using the asset value in 1960 as the basis for calculating the gain. Unrealized gains should be taxed at time of death or gift. The present 10 percent reduction for each year an asset was held should be dropped, and a system of prorating the gain by a factor of five or by the number of years the asset was held (with a maximum of five) should be introduced. Gains from assets held less than two years should be taxed as ordinary income. An adjustment should be made for "inflationary" gains either by taxing gains at a rate five percentage points lower than that otherwise applicable under prorating or by adjusting the tax base by one-half (or all) the increase in the cost-of-living index and taxing at the full rate. Capital gains on the sale of assets related to business activity will not be adjusted for inflation but will be prorated.

(4) Personal exemptions should be doubled, but should then begin to vanish after 40,000 pesos of taxable income at the rate of 1 peso for each 4 pesos of income. Filing requirements should be similarly raised.

(5) The deduction for payments to professionals should be disallowed, as should various forms of exempt income and other deductions.

(6) Personal income tax rates should be increased by 5 to 20 percent, depending on revenue targets, with the first bracket rate being raised to 4 percent and the highest rate to 55 percent.

(7) The rates of the net-wealth tax should be raised slightly, assets not capable of producing wealth and those held abroad should be taxed, and the deductibility of debts should be limited to those incurred in acquiring taxable assets.

Hard-to-Tax Groups (Chapter 3):

(8) All persons in certain activities (licensed professions, trade, service establishments, small manufacturing) should be made to file tax returns regardless of income.

(9) An elite auditing staff, with better salaries, should be established, and an intensive, well-publicized audit of selected groups should be undertaken using, as appropriate, external indices of income and wealth.

(10) The tax administration should be authorized to presume income on the basis of external indices where the taxpayer fails to supply adequate information.

(11) A presumptive income tax on farming should be established at a rate of 10 percent on cadastral value. The same should be done for cattle-raising.

Business Income Tax (Chapter 3):

(12) The excess-profits tax and the supplementary special taxes should be repealed.

(13) The present three-rate schedule on corporations should be replaced by a flat rate of from 44 to 46 percent, depending on revenue needs. Limited liability companies should be taxed like corporations.

(14) Partnerships (now taxed at 3 and 6 percent) should be taxed at 10 percent, with total profits taxable to owner. Closely held limited liability companies should be given the option of being treated like partnerships.

(15) The rate applicable to the first 50,000 pesos of net income of limited liability companies and corporations should be 20 percent.

(16) The dividend exclusion should be increased to 20,000 pesos, but included under the vanishing provision—mentioned in (4) above. There should be no further integration of the individual and corporate taxes.

(17) A five-year loss carry-forward should be introduced over a gradual transition period.

(18) The present depreciation system should be revised and liberalized by eliminating the 10 percent salvage requirement, by regrouping assets into a larger number of useful life categories, and by the optional use on new assets of declining-balance depreciation at twice the straight-line

rate. This mild acceleration should be introduced gradually, and there should be no general revaluation or replacement cost depreciation.

Tax Incentives (Chapter 4):

(19) The Law 81 incentives should not be extended beyond their scheduled termination date of 1969. No generalized tax incentive measures to raise the over-all level of capital formation are necessary at the present time. If any new incentives are granted, they might be related to sales rather than investment and should be better designed.

(20) The tax credit certificate for exports should be maintained, but it should be included in taxable income and based on value-added instead of sales.

Indirect Taxes (Chapter 4):

(21) The taxation of luxury consumption should be separated from the function of protecting domestic industry. Luxury tax rates should apply to imported and home-produced products alike. Increased luxury taxation should be accomplished through the sales tax by abolishing the 8 and 10 percent rates, moving the items formerly taxed at these rates to 15 percent, and taxing such things as automobiles, durable consumer goods, and jewelry at new rates of 25 and 50 (or 30 and 60) percent.

(22) The municipal tax on industry and commerce should be abolished, and replaced by a flat 2 percent retail sales tax (exempting small firms) in cities with over 100,000 inhabitants.

(23) The basic rate of the sales tax should be raised to 5 to 7 percent, depending on revenue requirements. In the long run the sales tax should be moved closer to the retail level and imposed at a uniform rate (with a separate set of luxury excise taxes).

(24) Gasoline tax revenue should be set to defray the cost of road maintenance by adjusting the petroleum exchange rate upward and lowering the tax rate. The present automobile registration taxes should be replaced by a uniform departmental tax on the value of vehicles.

(25) The present unwieldy array of stamp taxes should be reduced and simplified.

Local Government Finances (Chapter 5):

(26) A complete revaluation of property should be carried out rapidly, with provision for subsequent five-year revaluations and annual adjustments for price rises. Exemptions from property tax should be reduced where possible, and there should be no exemptions for private firms.

(27) A supplementary tax on luxury housing should be considered.

(28) Primary education should be expanded, the expansion being

financed by a surcharge on the property tax supplemented where necessary by national grants.

(29) Both responsibility for primary education and the property tax should, except for the largest municipalities, be transferred to the departments.

(30) There should be increased use of the valorization tax to finance urban development.

The quantitative impact of the Commission's main recommendations may be summed up briefly in the following table showing the percentage distribution of the proposed increase in revenues. The two left-hand columns assume a minimum 15 percent increase in revenues is needed; the right-hand columns assume a 20 percent increase is needed, partly to finance the proposed expansion of primary education:

Tax	Smaller increase		Larger increase	
	I	II	I	II
Personal income tax	13.8	19.0	29.4	32.9
Business income tax	14.0	14.0	10.6	10.7
Property tax	18.8	18.8	25.1	25.1
Indirect taxes	53.4	48.2	34.9	31.3

The set of recommendations most consistent with the discussion in the present book is that in the right-hand column, which allows for the expansion of primary education, and which relies relatively more on income- and property-tax increases and less on sales-tax increases. Adoption of these recommendations would give Colombia a more elastic, progressive, and growth-oriented tax system, which is what this book has demonstrated it needs. What the actual fate of the Commission Report will be in the turbulent Colombian political scene remains to be seen.

Bibliography | Notes | Index

Bibliography

Aaron, Henry. "Some Criticisms of Tax Burden Indices," *National Tax Journal*, XVIII (September 1965), 313-316.

Adams, Dale W., *et al. Public Law 480 and Colombia's Economic Development*. Medellín: Department of Agricultural Economics, Michigan State University, and Departamento de Economía y Ciencias Sociales, Facultad de Agronomía e Instituto Forestal, Universidad Nacional de Colombia, 1964.

Agudelo V., Hernando. *Cuatra etapas de la inflación en Colombia*. Bogotá: Ediciones Tercer Mundo, 1967.

Alonso, William. *Location and Land Use: Toward a General Theory of Land Rent*. Cambridge, Mass.: Harvard University Press, 1964.

Anales del Congreso (Bogotá).

Attir, Aryeh. *La reforma administrativa en Colombia*. New York: United Nations, 1962.

Baer, Werner, and Isaac Kerstenetzky, eds. *Inflation and Growth in Latin America*. Homewood, Ill.: Richard D. Irwin, Inc., 1964.

Banco Cafetero, *Carta económica* (Bogotá, monthly).

Banco de la República, Departamento de Investigaciones Económicas. *Atlas de economía colombiana*. 4 vols. Bogotá: Banco de la República, 1960-1964.

———— "Cuentas nacionales." Mimeographed, annual.

Banco Internacional de Reconstrucción y Fomento. "Evaluación del programa general de desarrollo económico y social de Colombia." Mimeographed; Bogotá: Departamento Administrativo de Planeación y Servicios Técnicos, n.d.

Banfield, Edward C., ed. *Urban Government: A Reader in Administration and Politics*. Glencoe, Ill.: Free Press, 1961.

Bank of London and Montreal Limited. *Economic Review* (London, bimonthly).

Barnes, William S., *et al.* "Analysis of Draft Law No. 462 and Evaluation of Comments on Income Tax Reform: A Report to the Minister of Finance of the Republic of Colombia." Mimeographed; Cambridge, Mass.: Harvard Law School, 1959.

Bauer, P. T., and B. S. Yamey. *The Economics of Under-developed Countries*. Cambridge: Cambridge University Press, 1957.

Bilsborrow, Richard. "The Structure of Tax Incentives in Colombia." Unpublished paper; Bogotá, 1966.

———— "The Tax Incentives for 'Basic' and 'Complementary' Industries." Unpublished paper; Bogotá, 1966.

Bird, Richard M. "A National Tax on the Unimproved Value of Land:

The Australian Experience, 1910–1952," *National Tax Journal*, XIII (December 1960), 386-392.

——— "A Note on 'Tax Sacrifice' Comparisons," *National Tax Journal*, XVII (September 1964), 303-308; and "Comment," XVIII (September 1965), 317-318.

——— "A Tax Incentive for Sales: The Canadian Experience," *National Tax Journal*, XVIII (September 1965), 277-285.

——— "A Value-Added Tax for Singapore: Comment," *Malayan Economic Review*, XII (April 1967), 39-41.

——— "Depreciation Allowances and Countercyclical Policy in the United Kingdom, 1945–1960," *Canadian Tax Journal* X (May–June and July–August 1963), 253-273, 353-380.

——— "Estimated National Government Revenues, 1965–1968, and the Public Sector in the Plan Cuatrienal." Unpublished paper; Bogotá, 1965.

——— "Income Distribution and Tax Policy in Colombia," *Economic Development and Cultural Change*, forthcoming.

——— "Local Property Taxes in Colombia," in Walter J. Kress, ed., *Proceedings of the 58th Annual Conference of the National Tax Association*. (Harrisburg, Pa., 1966), pp. 481-501.

——— "Revenue Requirements for Growth and Stability." Unpublished paper; Cambridge, Mass., 1967.

——— "Stamp Tax Reform in Colombia," *Bulletin for International Fiscal Documentation*, XXI (June 1967), 247-255.

——— "Tax-subsidy Policies for Regional Development," *National Tax Journal*, XIX (June 1966), 113-124.

——— "The Economy of the Mexican Federal District," *Inter-American Economic Affairs*, XVII (Autumn 1963), 19-51.

——— "The Need for Regional Policy in a Common Market," *Scottish Journal of Political Economy*, XII (November 1965), 225-242.

Bird, Richard M., and Oliver Oldman. "Tax Research and Tax Reform in Latin America—A Survey and Commentary," *Latin American Research Review*, III (Summer 1968), 5-28.

Boletín de la dirección nacional del presupuesto (Bogotá, irregular).

Boletín de información estadística sobre café (Bogotá, annual).

Break, George F., and Ralph Turvey. *Studies in Greek Public Finance*. Athens: Center for Economic Research, 1964.

Bridges, Benjamin, Jr. "Income Elasticity of the Property Tax Base," *National Tax Journal*, XVII (September 1964), 254-264.

Bruton, Henry J. "Productivity Growth in Latin America," *American Economic Review*, LVII (December 1967), 1099-1116.

Buron, Robert. *Decision-making in the Development Field*. Paris: Organisation for Economic Co-operation and Development, 1966.

Caldwell, Lynton K. "Technical Assistance and Administrative Reform in Colombia," *American Political Science Review,* XLVII (June 1953), 494-510.

Cano M., Augusto. "La planeación en Colombia." Mimeographed; Bogotá: Departamento Administrativo de Planeación, 1967.

Cepeda U., Fernando, *et al. Los grupos de presión en Colombia.* Bogotá: Ediciones Tercer Mundo, 1964.

Chelliah, Raja J. *Fiscal Policy in Underdeveloped Countries with Special Reference to India.* London: Allen & Unwin, 1960.

Comisión de Estudios. *Asuntos económicos y fiscales 1965.* Bogotá: Banco de la República, 1965.

Comité de los Nueve, Alianza para el Progreso. "Evaluación del programa general de desarrollo económico y social de Colombia." Mimeographed; Bogotá: Departamento Administrativo de Planeación y Servicios Técnicos, n.d.

Comité Interamericano de Desarrollo Agrícola. *Tenencia de la tierra y desarrollo socio-económico del sector agrícola: Colombia.* Washington, D.C.: Union Panamericana, 1966.

Consejo Nacional de Política Económica y Planeación, Departamento Administrativo de Planeación y Servicios Técnicos. *Plan cuatrienal de inversiones públicas nacionales 1961–1964.* Bogotá, 1960.

———— *Plan general de desarrollo económico y social.* 2 vols. Cali: Editorial El Mundo, 1962.

Contraloría General de la República, División de Análisis Financiero. *Informe financiero* (annual).

Crockett, Joseph P. "Apreciación del sistema del impuesto de Colombia derrarote la decada 1950–1959" and "Informe adicional." Mimeographed; Bogotá, n.d.

Currie, Lauchlin. *Accelerating Development: The Necessity and the Means.* New York: McGraw-Hill, 1966.

———— *Ensayos sobre planeación.* Bogotá: Ediciones Tercer Mundo, 1963.

———— *Una política urbana para los países en desarrollo.* Bogotá: Ediciones Tercer Mundo, 1965.

Currie, Lauchlin, *et al. Plan socio-económico para el Atlántico.* Bogotá: Imprenta Nacional, 1965.

———— *Programa de desarrollo económico del valle de Magdalena y notre de Colombia.* Bogotá, 1960.

Daza R., Alvaro. "La repartición de los ingresos," *Revista del Banco de la República* (July 1967), pp. 880-889.

"Declaración del espicopado colombiano sobre problemas socio-económicos de actualidad," *Revista del Banco de la República* (July 1966), pp. 835-836.

Delaplaine, John W. "The Structure of Growth in Colombia and Argentina." Economic Development Series Report No. 39. Multilith; Cambridge, Mass.: Harvard Development Advisory Service, 1966.

Departamento Administrativo de Planeación. "Algunos aspectos de la economía colombiana, 1961–65." Mimeographed; Bogotá, 1966.

——— "Programa de desarrollo regional para el departamento del Meta 1966–1969." Mimeographed; Bogotá, 1966.

Departamento Administrativo de Planificación (Bogotá). *Resumen de estudios adelantados hasta 1962.* Bogotá, 1965.

Departamento Administrativo Nacional de Estadística. *Anuario general de estadística* (annual).

——— *XIII censo nacional de población.* Bogotá, 1965.

Dosser, Douglas. "Tax Incidence and Growth," *Economic Journal,* LXXI (September 1961), 572-591.

Due, John F. *Sales Taxation.* Urbana: University of Illinois Press, 1957.

——— "The Retail Sales Tax in Honduras," *Inter-American Economic Affairs,* XX (Winter 1966), 55-67.

Dunkerley, Harold B. "Exchange-Rate Systems in Conditions of Continuing Inflation—Lessons from Colombian Experience," in Gustav F. Papanek, ed., *Development Policy—Theory and Practice.* Cambridge, Mass.: Harvard University Press, 1968, pp. 117-174.

Eckstein, Peter. "Accounting Prices as a Tool of Government Planning." Economic Development Series Report No. 53. Multilith; Cambridge, Mass.: Project for Quantitative Research in Economic Development, 1967.

Edel, Matthew D. "The Colombian Community Action Program: An Economic Evaluation." Duplicated; Cambridge, Mass., 1968.

Eder, George J., John C. Chommie, and Hector Julio Becerra. *Taxation in Colombia.* World Tax Series, Harvard Law School International Program in Taxation. Chicago: Commerce Clearing House, 1964.

El Tiempo (Bogotá, daily).

Encuentro Liberal (Bogotá, weekly).

Escuela Superior de Administración Pública. *La reforma tributaria de 1960.* 3 vols. Bogotá, 1961.

Fadul, Miguel. "El incentivo tributario como complemento a una reforma social agraria," *La nueva economía,* I (February 1961), 52-67.

Feldstein, M. S., and S. C. Tsiang. "The Interest Rate, Taxation, and the Personal Savings Incentive," *Quarterly Journal of Economics,* LXXXII (August 1968), 419-434.

Fluharty, Vernon Lee. *Dance of the Millions.* Pittsburgh: University of Pittsburgh Press, 1957.

Forte, Francesco. "Comment on Schedular and Global Income Taxes," in Richard M. Bird and Oliver Oldman, eds., *Readings on Taxation in Developing Countries.* Rev. ed. Baltimore: Johns Hopkins Press, 1967, pp. 137-138.

Friedmann, John. *Regional Development Policy: A Case Study of Venezuela.* Cambridge, Mass.: M.I.T. Press, 1966.

Galbraith, J. K. *Economic Development.* Boston: Houghton Mifflin, 1964.

Galvís Gaitán, Fernando. *El municipio colombiano*. Bogotá: Imprenta Departmental Antonio Nariño, 1964.

Goode, Richard. "Taxation of Savings and Consumption in Underdeveloped Countries," *National Tax Journal*, XIV (December 1961), 305-322.

——— *The Individual Income Tax*. Washington, D.C.: Brookings Institution, 1966.

Goode, Richard, George E. Lent, and P. D. Ojha. "Role of Export Taxes in Developing Countries," *International Monetary Fund Staff Papers*, XIII (November 1966), 453-503.

Hadley, George. "Some Characteristics of Colombian Industry." Mimeographed; Universidad de los Andes, Bogotá, 1965.

Hart, Albert G. *An Integrated System of Tax Information: A Model and a Sketch of Possibilities of Practical Application under Latin American Conditions*. New York: Columbia University School of International Affairs, 1967.

Head, J. G. "The Case for a Capital Gains Tax," *Public Finance*, XVIII (1963), 220-249.

——— "The Welfare Foundations of Public Finance Theory," *Revista de diritto finanziario e scienza della finanze* (May 1965), pp. 3-52.

Hinrichs, Harley H. "Dynamic-Regressive Effects of the Treatment of Capital Gains on the American Tax System during 1957–1959," *Public Finance*, XIX (1964), 73-83.

——— "Game Theory and the Rational Tax Evader." Unpublished paper; College Park, Md., 1965.

Hirschman, Albert O. *Journeys Toward Progress: Studies of Economic Policymaking in Latin America*. New York: Twentieth Century Fund, 1963.

——— "The Political Economy of Import-Substituting Industrialization in Latin America," *Quarterly Journal of Economics*, LXXXII (February 1968), 1-32.

Hofmeister, Ralph. "Observations on the Tariff Policies of the Electricity Supply Companies Affiliated with 'Electroaguas.'" Mimeographed; Bogotá: Los Andes–Minnesota Project, 1966.

Holland, Daniel. "The Taxation of Unimproved Value in Jamaica," in Walter J. Kress, ed., *Proceedings of the 58th Annual Conference of the National Tax Association* (Harrisburg, Pa., 1966), pp. 442-470.

Holt, Charles C., and John P. Shelton. "The Lock-in Effect of the Capital Gains Tax," *National Tax Journal*, XV (December 1962), 337-352.

Instituto Geográfico Agustín Codazzi. "Auto-avaluos." Unpublished study; Bogotá, 1964.

——— *Coeficientes para actualización de avalúos*. Bogotá, 1965.

International Bank for Reconstruction and Development. *The Agricultural Development of Colombia*. Washington, D.C., 1956.

————— *The Basis of a Development Program for Colombia.* Washington, D.C., 1950.

International Monetary Fund. *International Financial News Survey* (Washington, D.C., weekly).

————— *International Financial Statistics* (monthly).

Jarach, Dino. *El impuesto a la renta normal potencial.* Cuadernos de finanzas públicas. Washington, D.C.: Programa Conjunto de Tributación OEA/BID, Union Panamericana, n.d.

Joint Tax Program, Organization of American States, Inter-American Development Bank, and Economic Commission for Latin America. *Problems of Tax Administration in Latin America.* Baltimore: published for the Joint Tax Program by the Johns Hopkins Press, 1965.

Kaldor, Nicholas. "Economic Problems of Chile," in *Essays on Economic Policy.* 2 vols. London: Duckworth, 1964, II, 242-267.

Kling, Merle. "Taxes on the 'External' Sector: An Index of Political Behavior in Latin America?" *Midwest Journal of Political Science,* III (May 1959), 127-150.

Knorr, Klaus, and William J. Baumol, eds. *What Price Economic Growth?* Englewood, N.J.: Prentice-Hall, 1961.

Kravis, Irving B. "Relative Income Shares in Fact and Theory," *American Economic Review,* XLIX (December 1959), 917-949.

Kuznets, Simon. *Modern Economic Growth.* New Haven: Yale University Press, 1967.

Lascarro, Leopoldo. *Administración fiscal, presupuesto, decentralización.* Bogotá: Editorial Andes, 1965.

Laursen, Karsten. "Macroeconomic Relationships in Colombia." Unpublished paper; Bogotá, 1967.

Lauterbach, Albert. *Enterprise in Latin America: Business Attitudes in a Developing Economy.* Ithaca, N.Y.: Cornell University Press, 1966.

Lent, George E. "Tax Incentives for Investment in Developing Countries," *International Monetary Fund Staff Papers,* XIV (July 1967), 249-321.

Levin, Jonathan. "El ciclo de las importaciones y la política fiscal en Colombia," *Revista del Banco de la República* (June 1967), pp. 742-747.

————— "The Effects of Economic Development upon the Base of a Sales Tax: A Case Study of Colombia," *International Monetary Fund Staff Papers,* XV (March 1968), 30-99.

Lewis, W. Arthur. "Planning Public Expenditure," in Max F. Millikan, ed., *National Economic Planning.* New York: Columbia University Press for the National Bureau of Economic Research, 1967, pp. 201-227.

————— *The Theory of Economic Growth.* Homewood, Ill.: Richard D. Irwin, 1955.

Lipman, Aaron. *El empresario bogotano.* Bogotá: Ediciones Tercer Mundo, 1966.

Lipman, Aaron, and A. Eugene Havens. "The Colombian *Violencia:* An

Ex Post Facto Experiment," *Social Forces,* XLIV (December 1965), 238-245.

Lipset, Seymour Martin. *Political Man: The Social Bases of Politics.* New York: Doubleday, 1960.

Little, I. M. D. "Tax Policy and the Third Plan," in P. N. Rosenstein-Rodan, ed., *Pricing and Fiscal Policies.* London: Allen and Unwin, 1964, pp. 30-76.

MacBean, Alasdair I. *Export Instability and Economic Development.* Cambridge, Mass.: Harvard University Press, 1966.

McClelland, David C. *The Achieving Society.* New York: Free Press, 1967.

MacKinnon, Ronald I. "Export Expansion through Value-Added Taxation: The Case of Singapore," *Malayan Economic Review,* XI (October 1966), 1-27; and "Rejoinder," XII (April 1967), 42-46.

Mallon, Richard D. "Planning in Crisis." Economic Development Series Report No. 46. Multilith; Cambridge, Mass.: Harvard Development Advisory Service, 1966.

March J. G., and H. A. Simon. *Organizations.* New York: Wiley, 1963.

Martner, Gonzalo. *Desarrollo de las finanzas públicas de Colombia de 1950 a 1960.* Bogotá: Ministerio de Hacienda y Crédito Público, Dirección Nacional del Presupuesto, n.d.

Meade, J. E. "Mauritius: A Case Study in Malthusian Economics," *Economic Journal,* LXXI (September 1961), 521-534.

Ministerio de Educación Nacional. *Un programa de desarrollo para la educación en Colombia.* Bogotá, 1966.

Ministerio de Hacienda y Crédito Público. *Memoria de hacienda* (annual).

Ministerio de Hacienda y Crédito Público, División de Impuestos Nacionales, Subdivisión de Recaudación. *Informe financiero año fiscal 1965.* Bogotá, 1967.

Morag, Amotz. *On Taxes and Inflation.* New York: Random House, 1965.

———— "Some Economic Aspects of Two Administrative Methods of Estimating Taxable Income," *National Tax Journal,* X (June 1957), 176-185.

Morcillo, Pedro Pablo, and Humberto Castaño. "La administración y financiamiento de los municipios y de los departamentos, con referencia exclusiva al valle de Cauca." Unpublished paper; Cali, 1965.

Morgenstern, Oskar. *On the Accuracy of Economic Observation.* 2d ed. Princeton: Princeton University Press, 1963.

Musgrave, Richard A. *Revenue Policy for Korea's Economic Development.* Seoul: Nathan Economic Advisory Group, USOM/Korea, 1965.

———— *The Theory of Public Finance.* New York: McGraw-Hill, 1959.

Nelson, Richard R. *A Study of Industrialization in Colombia: Part I, Analysis.* Memorandum RM-5412-AID. Santa Monica, Calif.: RAND Corporation, 1967.

Netzer, Dick. *Economics of the Property Tax*. Washington, D.C.: The Brookings Institution, 1966.

—— "Local Government as a Development Instrument: The Colombian Experience." Mimeographed; New York, 1967.

—— "Some Aspects of Local Government Finances." Economic Development Series Report No. 51. Multilith; Cambridge, Mass.: Harvard Development Advisory Service, 1966.

Norr, Martin. "Depreciation Reform in France," *Taxes*, XXXIX (1961), 391-397.

Norr, Martin, and Pierre Kerlan. *Taxation in France*. World Tax Series, Harvard Law School International Program in Taxation. Chicago: Commerce Clearing House, 1966.

"Notas sobre las estadísticas de comercio exterior." Mimeographed; Bogotá: Proyecto Los Andes–Minnesota, 1966.

Ojha, P. D., and V. V. Bhatt. "Pattern of Income Distribution in an Underdeveloped Country: A Case Study of India," *American Economic Review*, LIV (September 1964), 711-720.

Oldman, Oliver. "Tax Reform in El Salvador," *Inter-American Bar Review*, VI (July–December 1964), 379-420.

Oldman, Oliver, et al. *Financing Urban Development in Mexico City*. Cambridge, Mass.: Harvard University Press, 1967.

Parra, Gustavo. "Reserva extraordinaria de fomento económico." Unpublished paper; Bogotá, 1968.

Peñalosa, Enrique. *Bases para una reforma de la tributación del sector agropecuario en Colombia*. Bogotá, 1963.

Pepper, H. W. T. "Instant Tax; An Appraisal of Enforcement Methods with Regard to Current Collection of Direct Taxes on Income," *Bulletin for International Fiscal Documentation*, XX (June and July–August 1966), 247-257, 323-329.

Please, Stanley. "Saving through Taxation—Reality or Mirage?" *Finance and Development*, IV (March 1967), 24-32.

Porter, Richard C. "Basic and Complementary Industry Tax Exemptions." Unpublished paper; Bogotá, 1968.

Poveda R., Gabriel. "Informe sobre inversiones y financiamiento de la industria (1958–1964)." Mimeographed; Medellín: Associación Nacional de Industriales, 1965.

Public Administration Service. *Strengthening Municipal Government in El Salvador*. Chicago, 1955.

Radhu, Ghulam Mohammed. "The Relation of Indirect Tax Changes to Price Changes in Pakistan," *Pakistan Development Review*, V (Spring 1965), 54-63.

Report on Japanese Taxation by the Shoup Mission. 4 vols. Tokyo: General Headquarters, Supreme Commander for the Allied Powers, 1949.

Reviglio, Franco. "Social Security: A Means of Savings Mobilization for

Economic Development," *International Monetary Fund Staff Papers,* XIV (July 1967), 324-347.

Revista del Banco de la República (Bogotá, monthly).

Revista del instituto colombiano de derecho tributario (Bogotá, biannual).

Rhoads, William G., and Richard M. Bird. "The Valorization Tax in Colombia: An Example for Other Developing Countries." Economic Development Series Report No. 50. Multilith; Cambridge, Mass.: Harvard Development Advisory Service, 1966.

Samper, Luis Eduardo. "Income-Market Problems of Basic Agricultural Commodities: The Case of Coffee." M.A. diss. Georgetown University, 1967.

Sazama, Gerald W. "Equalization of Property Taxes for the Nation's Largest Central Cities," *National Tax Journal,* XVIII (June 1965), 151-161.

Schydlowsky, Daniel M. "Short-run Employment Policy in Semi-Industrialized Economies." Economic Development Series Report No. 73. Multilith; Cambridge, Mass.: Harvard Development Advisory Service, 1967.

Sheahan, John. "El desarrollo de la producción de bienes de capital en Colombia," *Revista del Banco de la República* (July 1965), pp. 713-716.

———— "Imports, Investment, and Growth—Colombia," in Gustav F. Papanek, ed., *Development Policy—Theory and Practice.* Cambridge, Mass.: Harvard University Press, 1968, pp. 93-114.

Sheahan, John, and Sara Clark. "The Response of Colombian Exports to Variations in Effective Exchange Rates." Research Memorandum No. 11. Mimeographed; Williamstown, Mass.: Williams College Center for Development Economics, 1967.

Shere, Louis. "A Tax Program for Colombia." Mimeographed; n.p., n.d.

Shoup, Carl. "The Taxation of Excess Profits," *Political Science Quarterly,* LV (December 1940), 535-555, LVI (March and June 1941), 84-106, 226-249.

Shoup, Carl S., *et al. The Fiscal System of Venezuela: A Report.* Baltimore: John Hopkins Press, 1959.

Slighton, Robert L. *Urban Unemployment in Colombia: Measurement, Characteristics, and Policy Problems.* Memorandum RM-5393-AID. Santa Monica, Calif.: RAND Corporation, 1968.

Smith, Adam. *The Wealth of Nations.* New York: Modern Library, 1954.

Stolper, Wolfgang F. *Planning without Facts: Lessons in Resource Allocation from Nigeria's Development.* Cambridge, Mass.: Harvard University Press, 1966.

Sullivan, Clara K. *The Tax on Value Added.* New York: Columbia University Press, 1965.

Surrey, Stanley S. "Tax Policy and Tax Administration: Remarks at Inter-American Conference of Tax Administrators, Panama City, Panama, 1967." Mimeographed; U.S. Treasury Press Release F-900, Washington, D.C., 1967.

Tanabe, Noburu. "The Taxation of Net Wealth," *International Monetary Fund Staff Papers,* XV (March 1967), 124-156.

Tannenbaum, Frank. *Ten Keys to Latin America.* New York: Alfred A. Knopf, 1963.

Taylor, Lester D. "A Small Econometric Model of Colombia." Mimeographed; Bogotá, 1967.

Taylor, Milton C. "The Relationship between Income Tax Administration and Income Tax Policy in Nigeria," *Nigerian Journal of Economic and Social Studies,* IX (July 1967), 203-215.

Taylor, Milton C., *et al. Fiscal Survey of Colombia: A Report Prepared under the Direction of the Joint Tax Program.* Baltimore: published for the Joint Tax Program of the Organization of American States and the Inter-American Development Bank by the Johns Hopkins Press, 1965.

Thomas, Roger W. "Net Wealth Taxation." Mimeographed; Cambridge, Mass.: Harvard Law School Tax Program, Harvard–Chile Tax Project, 1967.

———— "Revaluation of Assets as an Adjustment for Inflation." Mimeographed; Cambridge, Mass.: Harvard Law School Tax Program, Harvard–Chile Tax Project, 1967.

United Nations, Economic Commission for Asia and the Far East. "Tax Potential and Economic Growth in the Countries of the ECAFE Region," *Economic Bulletin for Asia and the Far East, XVII* (September 1966), 29-48.

United Nations, Economic Commission for Latin America. *The Economic Development of Colombia. (Analyses and Projections of Economic Development,* vol. III.) Geneva: Department of Economic and Social Affairs, 1957.

———— *El desarrollo económico de América Latina en la postguerra.* New York: United Nations, 1963.

———— *El proceso de industrialización en América Latina.* New York: United Nations, 1965.

———— "Estudios sobre la distribución del ingreso en América Latina." (E/CN.12/770 and E/CN.12/770/ADD 1.) Mimeographed, 1967.

United States Department of Commerce, Bureau of the Census. *Property Taxation in 1962.* Washington, D.C., 1964.

United States Treasury Department, Internal Revenue Service. *Statistics of Income . . . 1962, Supplemental Report: Sales of Capital Assets Reported on Individual Income Tax Returns.* (Publication No. 458[10-66].) Washington, D.C., 1966.

———— *Statistics of Income—1964: Individual Income Tax Returns.* (Publication No. 79 [1-67].) Washington, D.C., 1967.

Universidad Nacional de Colombia, Facultad de Ciencias Económicas,

Centro de Investigaciones Económicas. *Balance económico y cálculo de la renta presuntiva de 6% para el año de 1964 en 488 fincas ganaderas de Colombia.* Bogotá, 1965.

Urdinola, Antonio, and Richard Mallon. "Policies To Promote Colombian Exports of Manufacturers." Economic Development Series Report No. 75. Multilith; Cambridge, Mass.: Harvard Development Advisory Service, 1967.

Vanek, Jaroslav, assisted by Richard Bilsborrow. *Estimating Foreign Resource Needs for Economic Development: Theory, Method and a Case Study of Colombia.* New York: McGraw-Hill, 1967.

Vega, Humberto, and Hernando Jiménez P. "Bases para una reforma tributaria." Mimeographed; Comité Operativo del Ingreso y la Cooperación Social, Bogotá, 1966.

Voz proletaria (Bogotá, weekly).

Watson, Andrew M., and Joel B. Dirlam. "The Impact of Underdevelopment on Economic Planning," *Quarterly Journal of Economics,* LXXIX (May 1965), 167-194.

Whiteford, Andrew H. *Two Cities of Latin America.* New York: Anchor Books, Doubleday, 1964.

Wildavsky, Aaron. *The Politics of the Budgetary Process.* Boston: Little, Brown, 1964.

Wingo, Lowden, Jr. *Transportation and Urban Land.* Baltimore: published for Resources for the Future, Inc., by the Johns Hopkins Press, 1961.

Yang, C. Y. "An International Comparison of Consumption Functions," *Review of Economics and Statistics,* XLVI (August 1964), 279-296.

Yates, Paul Lamartine. *El desarrollo regional de México.* Mexico, D.F.: Banco de México, 1961.

Notes

1. Public Finance and Development in Colombia

1. Calculated from Banco de la República, Departamento de Investigaciones Económicas, "Cuentas nacionales, 1950–1961" and "Cuentas nacionales, 1962–1965" (mimeographed; Bogotá, n.d.). (Hereafter cited as Cuentas nacionales 1950–61 and Cuentas nacionales 1962–65.)

2. The official average annual rate of population increase for 1951 to 1964, based on censuses in those years, is 3.2 percent (Departmento Administrativo Nacional de Estadística, *XIII censo nacional de población* [Bogotá, 1965]). There was considerable underenumeration in the 1951 census, however, so the actual average intracensal growth rate may have been as low as 2.8 percent, though the current rate of growth is probably even higher than 3.2 percent. The use of 3.0 percent for the 1950–1965 period seems a reasonable compromise.

3. For example, the Economic Commission for Latin America estimated (on the basis of admittedly poor data) that the average annual per capita growth in output over the 1925–1954 period was 2.5 percent. Per capita income was estimated to have increased at average rates of 4.6 percent in 1925–1929, 1.3 percent in 1930–1944, and 5.2 percent in 1945–1953 (United Nations, Economic Commission for Latin America (ECLA), *The Economic Development of Colombia* [Geneva: Department of Economic and Social Affairs, 1957], pp. 9, 11). Even in the depth of the world depression, at least according to these figures, Colombia did better than it has in the last decade.

4. Coffee prices from the *Revista del Banco de la República,* various issues.

5. For a more detailed analysis of this recent history, see John Sheahan, "Imports, Investment, and Growth—Colombia," in Gustav F. Papanek, ed., *Development Policy—Theory and Practice* (Cambridge, Mass.: Harvard University Press, 1968), pp. 93-114.

6. Percentage of gross domestic product at 1958 factor costs; includes livestock-raising, fishing, hunting, and forestry (Cuentas nacionales 1962–65, p. 32).

7. The national statistical department (DANE) classified a little over 50 percent of the Colombian population as "urban" in 1964, but many individuals thus classified were not urbanized in any meaningful sense. My estimate is based on Comité Interamericano de Desarrollo Agrícola, *Tenencia de la tierra y desarrollo socio-económico del sector agrícola: Colombia* (Washington, D.C.: Union Panamericana, 1966), p. 28, and on Dale W. Adams *et al., Public Law 480 and Colombia's Economic Development* (Medellín: Department of Agricultural Economics, Michigan

State University, and Departamento de Economía y Ciencias Sociales, Facultad de Agronomía e Instituto Forestal, Universidad Nacional de Colombia, 1964), pp. 70-71.

8. Lester D. Taylor, "A Small Econometric Model of Colombia" (mimeographed; Bogotá, 1967), p. 13.

9. Specifications of the Plan targets are from Consejo Nacional de Política Económica y Planeación, Departamento Administrativo de Planeación y Servicios Técnicos, *Plan general de desarrollo económico y social: Primera Parte—El Programa General* (Cali: Editorial El Mundo, 1962). (Hereafter cited as General Plan.) The realized figures are from Departamento Administrativo de Planeación, "Algunos aspectos de la economía colombiana, 1961–65" (mimeographed; Bogotá, 1966), and from other data obtained in the Planning Department and the Banco de la República.

10. For a detailed account of the background of the Plan and its "failure," see Augusto Cano M., "La planeación en Colombia" (mimeographed; Bogotá: Departamento Administrativo de Planeación, 1967), chaps. 2-4. The public-sector part of the Plan is discussed briefly in Chapter 2.

11. An expanded version of the study was subsequently published under the authorship of Jaroslav Vanek, assisted by Richard Bilsborrow, *Estimating Foreign Resource Needs for Economic Development: Theory, Method, and a Case Study of Colombia* (New York: McGraw-Hill, 1967).

12. My Table 2 shows the importance of capital and intermediate goods in imports; their vital position in the domestic economy is illustrated by the estimate that domestic capital-goods production, although expanding rapidly in recent years, still only supplies perhaps 20 percent of requirements (John Sheahan, "El desarrollo de la producción de bienes de capital en Colombia," *Revista del Banco de la República* [July 1965], pp. 713-716). Much of the modern industrial sector fostered by the import-substitution policy depends on imports for operation (materials, spare parts) as well as for new capacity.

13. This paragraph draws heavily on Sheahan, "Imports, Investment, and Growth."

14. This proposal, also labeled "Operation Colombia," was put forward by Lauchlin Currie in the early 1960's and elaborated in many publications, most recently in his *Accelerating Development: The Necessity and The Means* (New York: McGraw-Hill, 1966), Pt. II. In addition to Currie's own works, my discussion draws on the studies by Sheahan, Adams *et al.*, the Economic Commission for Latin America, and the Comité Interamericano de Desarrollo Agrícola cited earlier, as well as various publications of the Instituto Colombiano de Reforma Agraria (INCORA), the University of Wisconsin Land Tenure Center, and the Departamento Administrativo de Planeación. See also Gabriel Poveda R., "Informe sobre inversiones y financiamiento de la industria (1958–1964)"

(mimeographed; Medellín: Asociación Nacional de Industriales, 1965); George Hadley, "Some Characteristics of Colombian Industry" (mimeographed; Bogotá: Universidad de los Andes, 1965); and John W. Delaplaine, "The Structure of Growth in Colombia and Argentina" (multilith; Cambridge, Mass.: Harvard Development Advisory Service, 1966).

15. Overwhelming evidence supporting these statements may be found in the study of Colombian economic policy in 1960–1965 by Harold B. Dunkerley, "Exchange-Rate Systems in Conditions of Continuing Inflation—Lessons from Colombian Experience," in Gustav F. Papanek, ed., *Development Policy—Theory and Practice* (Cambridge, Mass.: Harvard University Press, 1968), pp. 117-174. Policy in 1966 continued along similar lines, culminating in a serious exchange crisis and the imposition of drastic direct controls, followed by another devaluation in 1967. See International Monetary Fund, *International Financial News Survey* (weekly) and Bank of London and Montreal Ltd., *Economic Review* (bimonthly) for a detailed chronology of government policy measures.

16. W. Arthur Lewis, *The Theory of Economic Growth* (Homewood, Ill.: Richard D. Irwin, 1955), pp. 379-380.

17. The Joint Tax Program group put their income figures together on the basis of the following items: (1) a 1958 distribution of taxpayers by brackets of net taxable income and a similar estimated distribution for 1962; (2) national-accounts data on employment and remuneration by sectors of the economy in 1961; (3) data on the income distribution of families of urban salaried and nonsalaried employees from a 1953 survey; (4) a 1962 survey of daily wages in agriculture (used as the basis of estimation for self-employed farmers also); (5) assumed distributions of unemployed and other self-employed (see Milton C. Taylor *et al., Fiscal Survey of Colombia* [Baltimore: Johns Hopkins Press, 1965], pp. 221-224—cited hereafter as Taylor Report—and the notes to my Table 3).

The degree of accuracy to be attributed to the final figures is obviously not too high. Nevertheless, there are no conceivable adjustments which would alter the picture of great inequality given in Table 3; so these figures are hereafter used as though they were accurate enough to serve as a basis for public policy, which they are.

18. International Bank for Reconstruction and Development (IBRD), *The Basis of a Development Program for Colombia* (Washington, D.C., 1950), p. 35.

19. See, for example, United Nations, Economic Commission for Latin America, *El desarrollo económico de América Latina en la postguerra* (New York, 1963), p. 56.

20. A similar phenomenon was noted in Chile in the early 1950's by Nicholas Kaldor, "Economic Problems of Chile," in *Essays on Economic Policy* (London: Duckworth, 1964), II, 242-250. The present analysis has benefited considerably from Kaldor's study. While it is true that industrial workers have gained relative to salaried employees, the evidence,

such as it is, does not seem to support the common complaint that the salaried middle class has suffered the most from the recent inflation (see, for example, Aaron Lipman, *El empresario bogotano* [Bogotá: Ediciones Tercer Mundo, 1966], p. 31), although they are no doubt the most vocal protesters. It is the relatively silent rural masses who have been the biggest losers.

21. Any inferences from these figures on factor income shares must be drawn with care since the results depend so much on the accounting framework within which the estimates are made. On the general problems of factor-share analysis, see Irving B. Kravis, "Relative Income Shares in Fact and Theory," *American Economic Review*, XLIX (December 1959), 917-949; Simon Kuznets, *Modern Economic Growth* (New Haven: Yale University Press, 1967), chap. IV. The refinements and methods of separating labor from nonlabor income suggested in these studies are not worthwhile given the basic weakness of Colombian national-accounts income data; and in any case changes of the order of magnitude involved in more refined analysis would not alter the trends discussed here. The use I have made of these crude estimates in interpreting the postwar period seems to be broadly supported by analysis of the percentage changes in labor and nonlabor income and by the more detailed studies of Albert Berry of the Yale Growth Center and of Robert Slighton of the RAND Corporation, to both of whom I am grateful for discussion of these matters.

22. Similarly unequal income distributions prevail in other Latin American countries: see United Nations, Economic Commission for Latin America, "Estudios sobre la distribución del ingreso en América Latina," E/CN.12/770 (mimeographed; 1967). In fact, the income distribution in Colombia appears to be among the less concentrated in Latin America, though it is much more concentrated than in either the United States or the United Kingdom. The more unequal income distribution in most Latin American countries (including Colombia) than in India is noteworthy (P. D. Ojha and V. V. Bhatt, "Pattern of Income Distribution in an Underdeveloped Country: A Case Study of India," *American Economic Review*, LIV [September 1964], 711-720).

23. An outstanding Colombian spokesman for this view was Camilo Torres, former Dean of Sociology at the National University, who was killed in 1965 while fighting with the guerrillas in the mountains; see, for example, his statements in Fernando Cepeda U. *et al., Los grupos de presión en Colombia* (Bogotá: Ediciones Tercer Mundo, 1964), and his speech to the University Students Federation (F.U.N.), April 22, 1965. A leading foreign commentator with rather similar views was the late Vernon Lee Fluharty, *Dance of the Millions* (Pittsburgh: University of Pittsburgh Press, 1957). Fluharty also argued that the increased strength of the middle class tended to perpetuate rather then relieve the basic inequities of wealth and power in that the middle class almost always

supported the conservative position of the wealthy (pp. 180, 187-191, 196).

24. See Currie, *Accelerating Development,* pp. 25-27, 45, 200, for a similar stress on the beneficial economic impact of income redistribution.

25. These figures are crude estimates based on Tables 3, 4, and 5, plus Cuentas nacionales 1950–61 and Cuentas nacionales 1962–65. The residual nature of the household savings figure and its extreme unreliability should be remembered. In particular, some recent evidence (see Taylor, "A Small Econometric Model of Colombia," p. 14) indicates that private saving may be consistently underestimated in the national accounts. (Table 5, for example, incorporates some substantial upward revisions in the 1960–1965 figures which were made in the 1966 accounts.) My calculation assumes that taxes take only the average ratio of the income of the richest group, so that their savings effort is slightly understated; but this effect is offset by the overstatement due to attributing all net saving to the very highest income class. On the other hand, both the income *and* the saving of the upper income group are probably understated by the method of estimation (mainly from tax returns). Thus the very approximate nature of the figures in the text should again be emphasized.

26. For a similar analysis for Venezuela, with somewhat similar conclusions, see Carl S. Shoup *et al., The Fiscal System of Venezuela* (Baltimore: Johns Hopkins Press, 1959), pp. 60-64. Although income appears to be even more unequally distributed in Venezuela than in Colombia (*ibid.,* pp. 20-41), this greater inequality appears to be offset by the higher saving of upper income groups in Venezuela. In this respect, Colombia more closely resembles the Chilean situation described in Kaldor, "Economic Problems of Chile," pp. 250-263.

27. The Taylor Report, p. 228, reaches the same conclusion but does not attempt to document it beyond showing the basic inequality of the income distribution. See also Alvaro Daza R., "La repartición de los ingresos," *Revista del Banco de la República* (July 1967), pp. 880-889.

28. For a similar argument, see George F. Break and Ralph Turvey, *Studies in Greek Public Finance* (Athens: Center for Economic Research, 1964), pp. 201-204. For the opposite point of view, that *private* saving is necessary for private investment, see Stanley Please, "Saving Through Taxation—Reality or Mirage?" *Finance and Development,* IV (March 1967), 24-32, where it is apparently assumed that the government is unable to exercise *any* choice as to the technique it may use in mobilizing and allocating financial resources. Note that for the moment my argument ignores the important point made earlier that imports, not saving, are what is really needed for investment in Colombia at the present time.

29. As the Taylor Report, p. 227, notes, the relative tax burden on the upper quartile is probably overstated because (1) untaxed capital gains and foreign income, which are not included in the income figure,

probably accrue mainly to this group; (2) the unreporting of income is probably more important in the higher brackets; (3) the retained earnings of corporations are not included in income; and (4) taxes probably borne in part by foreign owners are attributed to this quartile. More recent estimates of income distribution and tax incidence made by Charles McLure for the 1968 Commission for Colombian Tax Reform indicate a slightly more progressive tax system than shown in Table 6, but the differences are not significant.

30. These calculations are based on 1961 data in Table 6 and the Taylor Report, p. 225. The index used is $B = \frac{r}{y^\beta}$, where r = taxes as a percent of disposable income, y = per capita income, and β is a "progressivity parameter" of one. (For further discussion of all these concepts, in the context of geographical rather than income-class comparisons, see Richard Bird, "A Note on 'Tax Sacrifice' Comparisons," *National Tax Journal*, XVII [September 1964], 303-308; and in the same journal, Henry Aaron, "Some Criticisms of Tax Burden Indices," XVIII [September 1965], 313-316, plus Bird, "Comment," pp. 317-318.)

31. For a crude attempt to estimate the effect of government expenditures as well as taxes on income distribution, see the appendix to my paper on "Income Distribution and Tax Policy in Colombia," *Economic Development and Cultural Change,* forthcoming.

32. The fact is worth nothing that where most private saving is business saving, and where enterprises exercise considerable market power —both conditions largely true for Colombia—saving through corporations is as much an example of involuntary individual saving (through higher prices) as would be true if the same saving were achieved through forward-shifted corporate income or sales taxes. Some of the arguments of the more extreme anti-development-taxation writers therefore seem without foundation: see, for example, P. T. Bauer and B. S. Yamey, *The Economics of Under-developed Countries* (Cambridge: Cambridge University Press, 1957), chaps. XI, XII.

2. The Developmental Task of Tax Policy

1. See the General Plan, pp. 422-423. Chapter 6, pp. 373-465, of the Plan contains the public-sector analysis. More or less the same data and analysis may also be found in Gonzalo Martner, *Desarrollo de las finanzas públicas de Colombia de 1950 a 1960* (Bogotá: Ministerio de Hacienda y Crédito Público, Dirección Nacional del Presupuesto, n.d.); see also Consejo Nacional de Política Económica y Planeación, Departamento Administrativo de Planeación y Servicios Técnicos, *Plan cuatrienal de inversiones públicas nacionales 1961–1964* (Bogotá, 1960).

2. The only contemporary published criticism of the basic public-sector projections appears to be in Lauchlin Currie, *Ensayos sobre planeación* (Bogotá: Ediciones Tercer Mundo, 1963), p. 175. Although

the reviewing groups were apparently a little uneasy about the assumptions underlying these projections, they limited themselves to mild recommendations for slightly larger tax increases than those proposed (and assumed) in the Plan. See Comité de los Nueve, Alianza para el Progreso, "Evaluación del programa general de desarrollo económico y social de Colombia," p. 26, and Banco Internacional de Reconstrucción y Fomento, "Evaluación del programa general de desarrollo económico y social de Colombia," p. 6 (citations to mimeographed versions prepared in Departamento Administrativo de Planeación y Servicios Técnicos, n.d.).

3. While these figures indicate a much larger "public sector" than the figures usually cited (in the range of 10 to 12 percent), they should not be taken to measure the "size" of the public sector (a multidimensional concept), especially since they include the gross receipts and expenditures of many public enterprises. Two additional cautions seem in order: the data in Table 9 (and some subsequent tables) cannot be fully reconciled with the national accounts; and there are many difficulties in reconciling the public-sector figures themselves. For further discussion of some of these difficulties, see Appendix A and Dick Netzer, "Some Aspects of Local Government Finances" (multilith; Cambridge, Mass.: Harvard Development Advisory Service, 1966), pp. 129-147.

4. The total wage bill in real terms fell slightly in both 1964 and 1965, although the number of government employees apparently remained about the same (Contraloría General de la República, *Informe financiero de 1965* [Bogotá, 1966], p. 48). The other trends cited in the text are based on various unpublished sources cited in Table 9.

5. These statements are derived from detailed calculations (not shown here) using the standard formulas for point and arc elasticities, where

$$e_T = \frac{T_t - T_{t-1}}{T_{t-1}} \div \frac{Y_t - Y_{t-1}}{Y_{t-1}}$$

$$e_{T_{arc}} = \frac{T_t - T_{t-n}}{\frac{T_t + T_{t-n}}{2}} \div \frac{Y_t - Y_{t-n}}{\frac{Y_t + Y_{t-n}}{2}},$$

and T = taxes (or expenditures), Y = gross domestic product, and t and n are time subscripts. The data are from various sources in the Ministerio de Hacienda and the Banco de la República. Departmental and municipal current revenues (which include transfers from the national government) were markedly less elastic on average than central-government revenues. The conclusions are not substantially changed when real instead of current price data are used, when revenues are lagged a year, or when national income (which includes the effects of changes in the terms of trade) is used instead of gross domestic product.

6. A subsequent study carried out by Enrique Low and Aníbal Gómez for the Colombian Commission on Tax Reform indicates that in fact

the *ex ante* elasticity of national taxes in Colombia in the last decade was similar to the *ex post* elasticity of 1.1 cited in the text. This result arises mainly from the substantial tax reduction of 1961, however, and does not really modify the conclusion in the text.

7. This cycle is depicted in Dunkerley, "Exchange-Rate Systems in Conditions of Continuing Inflation." The same phenomenon was also noted after the 1957 devaluation by Martner, *Desarrollo de las finanzas públicas*, pp. 74-77. See also Vanek, *Estimating Foreign Resource Needs for Economic Development*, pp. 34-38, on the relation of taxes to foreign trade. While coffee-tax policy forms an important part of the picture being sketched here, it is best discussed separately and as a whole, as is done in Appendix B.

8. I have benefited greatly from the analysis of Jonathan Levin, "El ciclo de las importaciones y la política fiscal en Colombia," *Revista del Banco de la República* (June 1967), pp. 742-747. Something is said in Appendix B about the cyclical and long-term problem of maintaining real incomes in the important coffee-growing sector.

9. ECLA, *The Economic Development of Colombia*, p. 95.

10. This analysis is based on that in Richard A. Musgrave, *Revenue Policy for Korea's Economic Development* (Seoul: Nathan Economic Advisory Group, USOM/Korea, 1965), pp. 1-10, 44-56. In terms of the standard analysis of income determination: since $Y = C + I + G + NE$ and $Y = C + S + T$, then $S + T = I + G + NE$, and $T = I + G - S + NE$, where $T =$ government revenues, $G =$ government consumption, $I =$ total planned investment, $S =$ planned private savings, and $NE = X - M$ or net exports of goods and services (which if negative—net imports—is of course minus). In this formulation the needed level of public saving is independent of the division of investment between public and private sectors.

11. The detailed calculation of these particular ratios is not shown here. The values mentioned in the text are, for the most part, averages based on recent historical experience and are drawn from data in the Cuentas nacionales. For more elaborate macroeconomic models, see Taylor, "A Small Econometric Model of Colombia," and Karsten Laursen, "Macroeconomic Relationships in Colombia" (unpublished paper; Bogotá, 1967). See also Delaplaine, "The Structure of Growth in Colombia and Argentina," and C. Y. Yang, "An International Comparison of Consumption Functions," *Review of Economics and Statistics*, XLVI (August 1964), 279-296. (There is also a large relevant literature on the difficulties and dangers of using aggregate capital-output ratios and savings propensities for policy purposes.)

12. This crude estimate is derived from the following simple equation:

$$P_t = \frac{T_{1964} - T_{1960}}{Y_{1964} - Y_{1964}}.$$

The estimated propensity, like the elasticity estimate, includes not only the effects of the inherent responsiveness of the tax system to changes in income but also some measure of the past willingness and capacity to impose additional taxation. The estimate for Colombia of a marginal propensity to tax of 7.5 percent in 1960–1964 may be compared to estimates (based on simple regression analysis) ranging from 9.8 to 22.7 percent for eight (much poorer) Asian countries in the last decade. See United Nations, Economic Commission for Asia and the Far East, "Tax Potential and Economic Growth in the Countries of the ECAFE Region," *Economic Bulletin for Asia and the Far East,* XVII (September 1966), 29-48.

13. See, for example, Banco Cafetero, *Carta económica,* III (June–July 1966), 8-9, and Leopoldo Lascarro, *Administración fiscal, presupesto, decentralización* (Bogotá: Editorial Andes, 1965), p. 43.

14. Since the "estimate" figures used in calculating Table 14 are based on final official estimates (often made well after the fiscal year has begun), the table is really much too generous in appraising forecast error, especially because of the common past practice of deliberately underestimating revenues in the first version of the budget in order to avoid criticism and to provide room for an additional budget later. For comparison, it is of interest to note that the average gross estimating error of revenue forecasts in the United States federal budget in 1955–1967 was 5.6 percent, compared to the 12.3 percent for Colombia (calculated from data in First National City Bank, *Monthly Economic Letter* [December 1967], p. 141).

15. A "cash" budget is now prepared on a monthly basis by the central bank and is used for annual appraisals and projections of Colombia's economic performance by the international agencies. Unfortunately, it is as yet not possible to relate in a consistent way plans made on a cash basis to the budget figures required by law (and the Contraloría General) on either the tax or the expenditure sides. These difficulties have at times given rise to confusion both in Colombia and in the foreign lending agencies.

16. See George J. Eder, John C. Chommie, and Hector Julio Becerra, *Taxation in Colombia* (Chicago: Commerce Clearing House, 1964), pp. 505-513. (Cited hereafter as *Taxation in Colombia.*) For further outlines and discussions of these agencies, with particular stress on the "need" for greater coordination and control, see Aryeh Attir, *La reforma administrativa en Colombia* (New York: United Nations, 1962), pp. 31-93, and Taylor Report, chap. XII. Except in terms of their common dependence on the national budget, Colombia's diverse group of public agencies is not discussed in the present book.

17. This point is ignored in most criticisms of poor budgeting practices in developing countries—e.g., Andrew M. Watson and Joel B. Dirlam, "The Impact of Underdevelopment on Economic Planning," *Quarterly*

Journal of Economics, LXXIX (May 1965), 169. The only full treatment I have seen along the lines indicated here is Aaron Wildavsky, *The Politics of the Budgetary Process* (Boston: Little, Brown, 1964), in which the United States budgetary process looks not unlike that in Colombia. See also J. G. March and H. A. Simon, *Organizations* (New York: Wiley, 1963), and Edward C. Banfield, ed., *Urban Government* (Glencoe, Ill.: Free Press, 1961), for excellent relevant discussion.

18. Alasdair I. MacBean has recently argued that, in general, export instability is overrated as a cause of problems in poor countries (*Export Instability and Economic Development* [Cambridge: Harvard University Press, 1966]). His own data, however, show that exports relative to investment and government expenditure are considerably more important in Colombia than in most "large" underdeveloped countries (p. 60). Furthermore, although government revenues do not directly depend on foreign trade to such a large extent in Colombia as they once did, investment expenditures do, a factor which his analysis tends to neglect, although not ignore entirely (pp. 71, 74). In terms of MacBean's analysis, Colombia's relatively low taxes on exports, the low import content of its exports (most of which are agricultural), and the probably quite low percentage of export earnings sent abroad mean that the multiplicand (ΔX) is hardly reduced at all by leakages. Since the marginal propensities to tax and to save are also quite low, a change in export earnings might be estimated to have a substantial multiplier effect (perhaps about 3) on national income, assuming reasonable values for the coefficients. (The marginal propensity to import is high in part because of the nature of Colombian industry and its dependence on imported materials and capital goods). In short, as MacBean notes (p. 114), Colombia is a country of high export instability. It is also one in which fiscal fluctuations are associated closely—though not always consistently or necessarily—with fluctuations in foreign-exchange earnings.

19. This concept is taken from Richard D. Mallon, "Planning in Crisis" (multilith; Cambridge, Mass.: Harvard Development Advisory Service, 1966).

20. This discussion draws heavily on the analysis of Argentina in Mallon. The relation between monetary and fiscal policies in Colombia in recent years is analyzed in more detail in the study by Dunkerley cited earlier and in a study by Edgar Gutierrez C., in Hernando Agudelo V., *Cuatro etapas de la inflación en Colombia* (Bogotá: Ediciones Tercer Mundo, 1967).

21. Payments are delayed first by increased understating of income on private returns. These private assessments are then reversed by official assessments, and new tax bills go out after some months of delay. The effects of inflation and the private credit squeeze are at least in part indicated by the percentage increase of official over private assessments: 1960—8 percent, 1961—13 percent, 1962—15 percent, 1963—18 percent,

1964—34 percent, and 1965—55 percent (see Ministerio de Hacienda y Crédito Público, División de Impuestos Nacionales, Subdivisión de Recaudación, *Informe financiero año fiscal 1965* [Bogotá, 1967], p. xi). Even after the new assessments were issued, it was to the interest of the taxpayer to delay payment since he was in fact in most years subject to a negative real rate of interest on late payments. In any case, the penalty interest rate was much lower than that at which he could borrow privately.

22. For a similar point, see Henry J. Bruton, "Productivity Growth in Latin America," *American Economic Review,* LVII (December 1967), 1099-1116.

23. The traditional goal of "fiscal neutrality" thus has no place in a development-oriented fiscal system. Interestingly, neutrality has been strongly supported by a recent study on tax reform prepared for President Lleras Restrepo. This study states as an ideal that "government revenue should be obtained without interfering with productive activity and the normal development of the economy" (Humberto Vega and Hernando Jiménez Posada, "Bases para una reforma tributaria" [mimeographed; Comité Operativo del Ingreso y la Cooperación Social, 1966], p. 5). Such strict neutrality seems neither possible nor desirable in this imperfect world, though of course deliberate interference is to be avoided unless we are fairly sure of what we are doing.

24. In addition any redistributive policy effected through the tax system for socio-political reasons needs to allow for the relative rates of growth of income in different relevant sectors over time. On the concept of "dynamic incidence," see Douglas Dosser, "Tax Incidence and Growth," *Economic Journal,* LXXI (September 1961), 572-591, and the subsequent discussion between Bain, Prest, and Dosser in vol. LXXIII of the same journal (September 1963), 533-553.

25. Currie, *Accelerating Development,* p. 236, appears to stress simpler public administration as an end in itself, but it can also be justified on opportunity cost grounds.

26. That horizontal equity is not just an ethnocentric Anglo-Saxon (individualistic) judgment is indicated by the common discussion of "fairness" and "proportional sacrifice" with regard to taxes in Colombia. Its importance is also stressed in a statement by the Catholic hierarchy in Colombia: see "Declaración del espicopado colombiano sobre problemas socio-económicos de actualidad," *Revista del Banco de la República* (July 1966), p. 835. This interesting declaration also stressed the desirability of certainty and of higher direct personal taxes.

3. Growth, Equity, and the Income Tax

1. Since 1950, several additional taxes on income and wealth have usually been imposed for special purposes (housing, social security), and

in some years (1950–1953 and 1963–1966, for example) temporary income-tax surcharges have been levied. A detailed account of the income tax system may be found in Taylor Report, chap. II, and *Taxation in Colombia,* chap. II.

2. Ministerio de Hacienda y Crédito Público, *Informe financiero año fiscal 1965,* p. 55. Other data from Taylor Report, chap. II.

3. If T_t is the nominal tax calculated on income Y_t, $T_t = aY_t$, and $Y_{t+1} > Y_t$, then the real rate of tax collected in year $t + 1$ is $T_t = bY_{t+1}$, $a > b$. The faster the real growth rate and the rate of inflation, the greater the difference between the nominal and effective tax rates (a and b); if the inflation is accelerating, the real tax rate will be decreasing.

4. The 70 percent increase in the number of taxpayers in 1956–57 as a result of the temporary introduction of a partial withholding system indicates something of the potential of withholding in this respect. Evasion control rather than improved currency of payment has generally been the reason for recommending withholding in Colombia in the past: see Taylor Report, pp. 96-97; *Taxation in Colombia,* p. 98; Louis Shere, "A Tax Program for Colombia" (mimeographed; n.d.), pp. 91-93; William S. Barnes *et al.,* "Analysis of Draft Law No. 462 and Evaluation of Comments on Income Tax Reform" (mimeographed; Cambridge, Mass., 1959). This emphasis is true of other countries as well: see H. W. T. Pepper, "Instant Tax; An Appraisal of Enforcement Methods with Regard to Current Collection of Direct Taxes on Income," *Bulletin for International Fiscal Documentation,* XX (June and July–August 1966), 247-257, 323-329, for a useful review.

5. Wage and salary recipients already pay relatively more taxes than recipients of equal amounts of income in other forms simply because of the difficulties of taxing the latter; withholding on wages and salaries would accentuate this discrimination.

This sort of reasoning has been used to defend schedular tax systems, which impose different rates on different types of incomes partly in order to offset the greater ease of evasion for business and property income. See Francesco Forte, "Comment on Schedular and Global Income Taxes," in Richard M. Bird and Oliver Oldman, eds., *Readings on Taxation in Developing Countries* (rev. ed.; Baltimore: Johns Hopkins Press, 1967), pp. 137-138.

6. The attempt to impose a "perfect" system with a very imperfect administrative machine was one reason for the failure of the 1956–57 attempt at withholding. Similarly, since the general withholding decree passed in 1963 was totally unenforceable, it is not surprising it was never enforced (see *Revista del instituto colombiano de derecho tributario,* no. 1 [1965], pp. 29-36).

7. For example, most of the numerous obvious reforms in income tax base and rates outlined in the Taylor Report (and not discussed here in

detail) are worth adopting both on their own merits and to achieve the administrative simplification needed for an effective current-payment system.

8. For earlier (mostly equity) arguments in favor of stronger capital-gains taxes in Colombia, see IBRD, *The Basis of a Development Program for Colombia,* pp. 265, 554; Shere, "A Tax Program for Colombia," pp. 93-97; Barnes *et al.,* "Analysis of Draft Law No. 462," pp. 38-51; Joseph P. Crockett, "Apreciación del sistema del impuesto de Colombia derrarote la decada 1950–1959" (mimeographed; Bogotá, n.d.), p. 17; and Taylor Report, pp. 78-80.

9. The present treatment of capital gains in Colombia is outlined in more detail in *Taxation in Colombia,* chap. IX, and further discussed in *Revista del instituto colombiana de derecho tributario,* no. 3 (1966), pp. 13-39, and in Escuela Superior de Administración Pública, *La reforma tributaria de 1960* (3 vols.; Bogotá, 1961). In theory, "windfall" (unexpected or unintended) gains would seem the perfect base for high taxes without any adverse incentive effects—though the effect on private saving of tapping such transitory income may be greater than that of taxing regular income.

10. In the United States, for example, the top 10 percent of those who pay income tax receive less than one-tenth of total income but at the same time receive more than one-half of all capital gains, and these gains make up one-half of their gross income (estimated from United States Treasury Department, Internal Revenue Service, *Statistics of Income . . . 1962, Supplemental Report: Sales of Capital Assets Reported on Individual Income Tax Returns* [Publication No. 458 (Washington, D.C., 1966), pp. 3, 6]). The tendency for those who receive capital gains to improve their relative positions with growth and inflation in the United States has been documented by Harley H. Hinrichs, who labels the weak capital-gains tax in the United States a major dynamic-regressive element in the American tax system (see Hinrichs, "Dynamic-Regressive Effects of the Treatment of Capital Gains on the American Tax System during 1957–1959," *Public Finance,* XIX [1964], 73-83).

11. Actually, accrual taxation would appear more feasible in Colombia than in most countries because annual net-wealth statements are already required from most well-off taxpayers, though the accuracy of these statements is no doubt lamentably poor. This idea is not further pursued here, however, since I accept the conventional administrative case against accrual taxation in view of the limited capacity of the Colombian tax administration.

12. As usual, the arguments on both sides are more complex than indicated here. For a fuller rationale of the position adopted by me see J. G. Head, "The Case for a Capital Gains Tax," *Public Finance,* XVIII (1963), 228-230. The question of indexing the whole tax system (as sug-

gested in Amotz Morag, *On Taxes and Inflation* [New York: Random House, 1965], chap. VII) is not discussed here.

13. This point is closely related to the "replacement cost" argument on depreciation discussed below. Although authorities as respected as Musgrave have argued for deflating the nominal gain in order to tax only the "real" gain (see his *Revenue Policy for Korea's Economic Development*), any such adjustment in Colombia would not only be inequitable but undesirable in reducing the elasticity of the tax system, the improvement of which is a major aim of tax reform strategy.

14. This "lock-in" effect of capital-gains taxes is excellently treated in Charles C. Holt and John P. Shelton, "The Lock-In Effect of the Capital Gains Tax," *National Tax Journal*, XV (December 1962), 337-352, where it is shown to be normally small except when gains realized at death escape tax (as in the United States). For a discussion of the "lock-in" effect of the present stamp taxes on securities transactions in Colombia, see Richard M. Bird, "Stamp Tax Reform in Colombia," *Bulletin for International Fiscal Documentation*, XXI (June 1967), 247-255.

15. A full outline of a pro-rating system may be found in Richard Goode, *The Individual Income Tax* (Washington: Brookings Institution, 1966), chap. VIII.

16. United States Treasury Department, Internal Revenue Service, *Statistics of Income . . . 1964: Individual Income Tax Returns* (Publication No. 79 [Washington, D.C., 1967], p. 2).

17. One sample study of professionals in Bogotá indicated that at least 10 percent failed to file and that of those who did file doctors and lawyers were underreporting their income by at least 50 percent (Taylor Report, pp. 92-93).

18. Ministerio de Hacienda y Crédito Público, *Informe financiero año fiscal 1965*, p. v. The present 10-peso stamp tax on income declarations is sometimes justified as covering this processing cost. That tax should be eliminated, however, because "it is the opposite of logic to levy a charge, even a small one, on an activity such as the filing of income declarations which it is desired to facilitate rather than discourage. There are already too many lines in which a conscientious Colombian taxpayer must stand before complying with his legal duties to justify the addition of yet another before the stamp tax window" (Bird, "Stamp Tax Reform in Colombia," p. 252).

19. Taylor Report, pp. 63-70, 98.

20. For a detailed description of the present net-wealth tax, see *Taxation in Colombia*, chap. XIV. Net-wealth taxes in general and the Colombian tax in particular have recently been reviewed in two useful studies: Noburu Tanabe, "The Taxation of Net Wealth," *International Monetary Fund Staff Papers*, XIV (March 1967), 124-156; and Roger W.

Thomas, "Net Wealth Taxation" (mimeographed; Cambridge, Mass., 1967).

21. Corporate wealth has been excluded from the scope of the net-wealth tax since 1960, in part on the ground that taxing corporate wealth discouraged foreign investment (especially since the United States did not permit taxpayers to credit the wealth tax against their U.S. income-tax liabilities—*Taxation in Colombia*, p. 438) and in part on the ground that corporate wealth is reflected in the values of shares, which are supposed to be taxed as personal wealth. This "double taxation" argument is not particularly strong (see Thomas, "Net Wealth Taxation," p. 35, and Shere, "A Tax Program for Colombia," p. 177), especially since the first 100,000 pesos of shares are exempted from net-wealth tax in Colombia. On balance, however, since I accept the intermediate goal of promoting the corporate form of business enterprise, the 1960 reform was probably correct. Even the 100,000 peso exemption, undesirable as it is on equity grounds, can be defended on this argument.

22. Colombia appears to be the only country which exempts "unproductive" holdings from a net-wealth tax (Thomas, "Net Wealth Taxation," p. 42). My paragraph is based mainly on Thomas' comparative evaluation of the Colombian tax. Decree 1366 of July 1967 tightened this exemption and made some other improvements in the base of the net-wealth tax but has not solved the problem.

23. Another "inequity" which some authors (for example, Break and Turvey, *Studies in Greek Taxation,* pp. 175-177) have seen in net-wealth taxation is the failure to include "human capital" in the tax base. Apart from the incredible administrative difficulty of tackling this problem, the incentive effects of taxing "non-human" and exempting "human" capital would seem to be in the right direction for Colombia today.

24. For a fuller discussion of this alternative, see Ronald I. McKinnon, "Export Expansion through Value-Added Taxation: The Case of Singapore," *Malayan Economic Review,* XI (October 1966), 1-27; also, in the April 1967 issue of the same journal, Richard M. Bird, "A Value-Added Tax for Singapore: Comment," pp. 39-41, and McKinnon, "Rejoinder," pp. 42-46.

25. For a detailed discussion of the tax treatment of corporations and limited liability companies in Colombia and, to my mind, a complete justification of this conclusion, see Taylor Report, pp. 257-263. The absolute tax on partnerships should be raised slightly and put on a current payment basis like all business income, but essentially the present system of imputing partnership income to the partners and taxing it under the individual income tax should remain. The possibility of allowing small limited liability companies the option of being treated like a partnership might also be considered to avoid drastic changes in tax liability as a result of legal form rather than economic reality.

The effect tax changes can have on the form of business organization was made spectacularly clear in Colombia when corporate dividends were first subjected to taxation at the individual level in 1953. The number of domestic corporations, which had reached a high of 1,226 in 1953, fell at once to 1,024 in 1954 and continued to decline to a low of 885 in 1956. There was also a marked fall in the volume of transactions on the stock exchange. In 1963 there were still only 1,182 domestic corporations, though the largest 100 paid an estimated 40 percent of the *total* income tax assessed in that year. (Based on data obtained from the Superintendencia de Sociedades Anónimas and the Ministerio de Hacienda.)

26. For a theoretical argument that a dividend exclusion is likely to induce increased saving from small shareholders, see M. S. Feldstein and S. C. Tsiang, "The Interest Rate, Taxation, and the Personal Savings Incentive," *Quarterly Journal of Economics,* LXXXII (August 1968), 419-434. To reduce revenue loss and to restrict the benefits of the exclusion to relatively low-income shareholders, the exclusion might be made to vanish at higher levels of income (that is, for every additional peso or 2 pesos of income the allowable exclusion is reduced by a peso).

27. Profits taxation combined with full, immediate loss offset may, in theory, even lead to *increased* risk-taking rather than deterring risky investment (Richard A. Musgrave, *The Theory of Public Finance* [New York: McGraw-Hill, 1959], pp. 320-322). In Colombia, however, the government can hardly give refunds of taxes not paid; thus the carryover of losses is suggested. Furthermore, both to avoid the need for refunds and to favor new rather than old businesses, only the carry-forward of losses is recommended here (see also Taylor Report, p. 87).

28. See Shere, "A Tax Program for Colombia," pp. 88, 172-173, for a similar recommendation; also Carl S. Shoup, "The Taxation of Excess Profits," *Political Science Quarterly,* LV (December 1940), 535-555, LVI (March and June 1941), 84-106, 226-249, on the inherent arbitrariness and administrative difficulties of any excess-profits tax. The abolition of the corporate net-wealth tax in 1960 increased the difficulty of enforcing the excess-profits tax by removing any automatic penalty for overstating the net wealth basis on which the "excess" is computed.

29. Firms were allowed to deduct each year from net taxable income 15 percent of the historical cost of all plant and equipment purchased prior to June 1, 1957, until 100 percent of the cost was recovered. If firms immediately took advantage of this law in 1960, they could deduct from otherwise net taxable income 15 percent of the cost of such assets each year from 1960 through 1965 and the remaining 10 percent in 1966. Since this legislation did not remove the already existing regular depreciation allowances (10 percent a year for machinery for nine years, leaving a 10 percent salvage value), firms could depreciate up to 190 percent of the historical cost of qualifying depreciable assets: 10 percent of historical cost each year in 1958–59, 25 percent a year in 1960–1965, and 20 percent in 1966.

30. For a competent discussion of these matters, and especially of the technical difficulties encountered with revaluation schemes in various countries, see Roger W. Thomas, "Revaluation of Assets as an Adjustment for Inflation" (mimeographed; Cambridge, Mass., 1967). See also Taylor Report, p. 265.

31. For a much fuller discussion of the nature and workings of a system of accelerated depreciation, see Richard M. Bird, "Depreciation Allowances and Countercyclical Policy in the United Kingdom, 1945–1960," *Canadian Tax Journal*, X (May–June and July–August 1963), 253-273, 353-380. In addition to acceleration, steps might be taken to introduce a more realistic system of asset lives and to revise tax depreciation to accord more with accounting practices.

32. See Martin Norr, "Depreciation Reform in France," *Taxes*, XXXIX (1961), 391. Legally, depreciation at rates faster than the normal ten-year straight-line basis for machinery is already permitted in Colombia when depreciable property is in use more than ten hours a day, but this provision has apparently never been put into practice. Similar incentives for intensive use reportedly exist in Mexico and Peru (United Nations, Economic Commission for Latin America, *El proceso de industrialización en América Latina* [New York, 1965], p. 196).

33. These conclusions follow even if one makes the quite feasible assumption that the sharp division between businesses and individuals implied in my discussion is unrealistic for a developing country like Colombia. Higher personal taxation and constant business taxation—except for growing firms, for which taxes will be lower—tend to encourage retentions, especially in the favored firms, whether the firm and shareholder are considered as one or two decision-making units.

34. See International Bank for Reconstruction and Development, *The Agricultural Development of Colombia* (Washington, D.C., 1956); Ministerio de Hacienda, *Memoria de 1960* (Bogotá, 1961), p. 192; Enrique Peñalosa, *Bases para una reforma de la tributación del sector Agropecuario en Colombia* (Bogotá, 1963); Taylor Report, pp. 120-133. The Lebret Mission of 1958 also proposed this solution (see Ministerio de Hacienda, *Memoria de 1959* (Bogotá, 1960), III, 361-365), as did Miguel Fadul, "El incentivo tributario como complemento a una reforma social agraria," *La nueva economía*, I (February 1961), 52-67. Most of these proposals are summarized and discussed in Albert O. Hirschman, *Journeys toward Progress* (New York: Twentieth Century Fund, 1963), pp. 116-141.

35. Escuela Superior de Administración Pública, *La Reforma tributaria de 1960*, II, 33-34. It was apparently intended that the income tax on agriculture be suspended in favor of this presumptive tax.

36. For a clear statement of this argument, see Dino Jarach, *El impuesto a la renta normal potencial de la tierra* (Washington, D.C.: Union Panamericana, n.d.). Jarach's detailed proposal can serve as an illustration of all difficulties, conceptual and administrative, with tax

gadgetry in this field. Like most authors he tends to overemphasize the economic benefits and underestimate the administrative costs of his scheme.

37. Many of these points are based not only on Colombian experience but also on that of such an advanced country as Australia: see my "A National Tax on the Unimproved Value of Land: The Australian Experience, 1910–1952," *National Tax Journal*, XIII (December 1960), 386-392.

38. Although a presumptive tax on livestock alone is definitely *not* recommended in this book, it is of interest to calculate the yield of such a tax. If we assume there were 14 million cattle in Colombia in 1966, distributed as in the Censo Agropecuario of 1960 and with an average value of 1,000 pesos (a generous figure which should compensate for any underestimation of the herd size), the yield of the tax may be calculated at about 38 million pesos. The net yield, allowing for the inclusion of income from other sources on the one hand and for the replacement of the existing tax on the other, might be in the vicinity of 30 million pesos. In addition to its small yield, this tax would be much more difficult to administer than one based on land value (as well as less desirable in its economic effects), and so it is less likely that the full potential yield would be realized. It is unfortunate a limited form of presumptive livestock tax was in fact imposed in 1966.

39. See Hirschman, *Journeys toward Progress*, pp. 121-127. An extremely critical view of this decree, and of this sort of legislation in general, may be found in Lauchlin Currie *et al.*, *Programa de desarrollo económico del valle del Magdalena y norte de Colombia* (Bogotá, 1960).

40. Instituto Geográfico Agustín Codazzi, *Coeficientes para actualización de avalúos* (Bogotá, 1965). The Institute has since reworked its scheme as part of a proposed comprehensive revaluation.

41. Instituto Geográfico Augustín Codazzi, "Auto-avalúos" (unpublished study; Bogotá, 1964). For a further discussion of some of these matters, see Chapter 5 below and my "Local Property Taxes in Colombia," *Proceedings of the 58th Annual Meeting of the National Tax Association* (Harrisburg, Pa., 1966), pp. 481-501.

42. For such a study, see Universidad Nacional de Colombia, Centro de Investigaciones Económicas, *Balance económico y cálculo de la renta presuntiva del 6% para el año de 1964 en 488 fincas ganaderas de Colombia* (Bogotá, 1965). The study of 488 farms indicated that 366 made less than a 6 percent return, and 17 percent of them had no net profit at all. But much of this seems to result from variable inefficiency rather than fixed obstacles, since in every area studied some farms had returns over 6 percent, while 45 farms made over 12 percent and 16 over 18 percent.

43. On the use of such boards, see Oliver Oldman *et al.*, *Financing Urban Development in Mexico City* (Cambridge, Mass.: Harvard University Press, 1967), chap. II.

44. The yield of this tax in 1966 probably would have been about 100 million pesos (based on cadastral data in Chapter 5 and on an estimated distribution of the tax base and estimated tax rates in the Taylor Report, p. 131). Theoretically, this estimated figure is on the low side, since income from agricultural activities should be added to income from other sources before applying the tax rates. The yield of the tax may be perhaps doubled to about 200 million for this reason. On the other hand, in the late fifties the agricultural sector contributed about 4 percent of total income-tax yield, or, say, about 100 million in 1966, if we assume the same proportion held. If we assume *all* this amount is replaced by the presumptive tax, the net yield may be estimated, probably conservatively, as a little over 100 million pesos, or an increase of only about 4 percent in total income taxes collected—though perhaps a doubling of the present income taxes paid by agriculture.

45. Martin Norr and Pierre Kerlan, *Taxation in France* (Chicago: Commerce Clearing House, 1966), chap. VI, and Amotz Morag, "Some Economic Aspects of Two Administrative Methods of Estimating Taxable Income," *National Tax Journal,* X (June 1957), 181.

46. This kind of complicated approach has been suggested recently for use with handicraft industries and small merchants in Greece by Break and Turvey, *Studies in Greek Public Finance,* pp. 118-120.

47. See Netzer, "Some Aspects of Local Government Finances"; Departamento Administrativo de Planificación (Bogotá), *Resumen de estudios adelantados hasta 1962* (Bogotá, 1965), p. 102; and Chapter 5 below.

48. The Blue Return system was introduced in Japan in 1950 in order to improve bookkeeping practices and encourage honest self-assessment: see *Report on Japanese Taxation by the Shoup Mission* (Tokyo, 1950), II, 213, and IV, appendix, pp. D56-D59. Taxpayers who keep proper records are allowed to file their returns on a blue form which entitles them to such privileges as protection against arbitrary reassessment in accord with a "standard" or average (as is a common practice with other taxpayers) and the allowance of special deductions and reserves. Almost one-half of all business taxpayers now use the Blue Return, and it is thought to have been a considerable help in the successful adoption of self-assessment in Japan.

4. Taxation and the Allocation of Resources

1. See Raja J. Chelliah, *Fiscal Policy in Underdeveloped Countries with Special Reference to India* (London: Allen & Unwin, 1960), pp. 85-90, for a good discussion of the role of mass consumption taxation in development finance.

2. Calculated from data (all in 1958 prices) in the General Plan, p. 135, "Cuentas nacionales 1950–61," and "Cuentas nacionales 1962–63," tables 6-7.

3. This figure is a very rough estimate based on detailed calculations made for 1964 in current prices and assuming collection efficiency of 60 percent (see Table 18).

4. The miscellaneous nature of the items selected for high taxation is clear from a partial listing: the 5 percent rate originally applied to cosmetics, pens, sporting goods, stoves and heaters, dishes, jeeps and small trucks, motorcycles, bicycles, silk fabrics, bracelets, umbrellas, and domestically produced alcoholic beverages (later ceded in part to the departmental governments and consolidated with other sumptuary excise taxes); the 8 percent rate to radio and television sets, records, tape recorders, cameras, and various electrical consumer durables; and the 10 percent rate to jewelry, automobiles and boats, safes, watches, hair-dryers, tobacco products, Chiclets, imported dishes and glassware, imported olive oil, imported canned food, imported clothes, and imported liquors. In June 1966 the 5 percent rate was increased to 8 percent and the 8 and 10 percent rates to 15 percent, but no significant changes were made in the classification of taxable items. The administrative changes in this reform greatly increased the number of firms registered for sales tax purposes and improved tax yields for this reason as well. (See Taylor Report, chap. X, on other—mostly departmental and municipal—internal indirect taxes.)

5. An excellent summary of the classic arguments by Corlett and Hague and Lipsey and Lancaster on this point may be found in J. G. Head, "The Welfare Foundations of Public Finance Theory," *Revista di diritto finanziaro e scienza della finanze* (January 1965), section 3.

6. See also Richard Goode, "Taxation of Savings and Consumption in Underdeveloped Countries," *National Tax Journal,* XIV (December 1961), 305-322. Of course, any rate differentiation inevitably taxes people on the basis of their preferences rather than their ability to pay, for even when the consumption pattern of the well-off as a group is distinct, as is more or less true in Colombia, the individuals within the group will differ considerably in their tastes for taxed goods.

Instead of relying on indirect progressive taxes, why not impose a limited, moderately progressive direct tax on personal expenditures? The additional element of progressivity in the Colombian tax system would be most welcome. Despite the weakness of the tax administration, the expenditure tax could probably be effectively enough enforced to have some progressive impact, especially since net-wealth statements are already required as part of the income tax return for wealthy taxpayers. The usual administrative arguments against direct expenditure taxes overstress the case and tend to contrast the probable reality to some impossible perfectionist standard rather than to the equally wretched reality of other taxes. Nevertheless, I would not propose an expenditure tax for Colombia at the present time. I base my negative opinion primarily on the administrative grounds, first, that any gains in effective progressivity would be so small as not to be worth the peril and cost involved in an innovation of this magnitude, and, second, that the areas in which it would be most difficult to enforce the tax—and which would therefore become channels for evasion—are on the whole detrimental to the assumed goal of economic growth (for example, capital flight abroad). In short, something useful could be done with this tax, but at the cost of diverting scarce administrative resources from other pursuits and with some undesirable side effects. It seems unlikely the effort would be worthwhile at present. Conceptually, the idea of a direct progressive tax on personal expenditures remains an attractive one for a country where, at least in the long run, increased private investment and saving is a main concern of economic policy, and it deserves a closer examination in the Colombian context at some later date.

7. The scanty evidence available for most countries indicates a relatively low elasticity of substitution (apart from the substantial geographical shifts sometimes found with local sales taxes): see, for example, on India and Britain, I. M. D. Little, "Tax Policy and the Third Plan," in P. N. Rosenstein-Rodan, ed., *Pricing and Fiscal Policy* (London: Allen & Unwin, 1964), pp. 560-561.

8. This paragraph relies almost entirely on the much more detailed and refined analysis in the study by Jonathan Levin, "The Effects of Economic Development upon the Base of a Sales Tax: A Case Study of Colombia," *International Monetary Fund Staff Papers,* XV (March 1968), 60-74.

9. Ghulam Mohammad Radhu, "The Relation of Indirect Tax Changes to Price Changes in Pakistan," *Pakistan Development Review,* V (Spring 1965), 55.

10. See Levin, "Effects of Economic Development upon the Base of a Sales Tax," pp. 48-59.

11. The Taylor Report, p. 217, makes a similar point. Some income-elasticity estimates for consumer goods in Colombia are: foodstuffs, 0.6; processed foodstuffs, 0.9; other manufactured goods, 1.3; tobacco and alcoholic beverages, 1.0; services, 1.5 (ECLA, *The Economic Development of Colombia,* p. 67). See also Levin, "Effects of Economic Development upon the Base of a Sales Tax," pp. 48-59 for further relevant discussion. I have deliberately refrained from saying anything about the differential impact on savings of different degrees of progressivity, in part because of the lack of information and in part because the marginal propensity to consume is probably constant over fairly broad income ranges in Colombia as elsewhere.

12. Adam Smith's famous second canon of taxation would thus appear to be as applicable to Colombia in 1967 as to England in 1776: "The tax which each individual is bound to pay ought to be certain and not arbitrary. The time of payment, the manner of payment, the quantity to be paid, ought all to be clear and plain to the contributor, and to

258 | Notes to Pages 113-117

every other person. Where it is otherwise, every person subject to the tax is put more or less in the power of the tax-gatherer, who can either aggravate the tax upon any obnoxious contributor, or extort, by the terror of such aggravation, some present or perquisite to himself" (*The Wealth of Nations* [New York: Modern Library, 1954], p. 778). An informative handbook on Colombia's sales tax was finally published under private auspices in mid-1967, over two years after the tax went into effect.

13. Levin, "Effects of Economic Development upon the Base of a Sales Tax," pp. 75-93, discusses these points in detail and similarly concludes a wholesale level tax would be more suitable for Colombia. He would not, however, agree with the earlier proposal for a more selective excise-tax system, in part because his analysis of this possibility focuses on the shrinking tax base afforded by the traditional sumptuary items. See Netzer, "Some Aspects of Local Government Finance," pp. 92-123, for the best recent description and analysis of Colombian sumptuary taxes.

14. It might even be possible to go one step further and introduce a hybrid wholesale-retail sales tax like that in Honduras, though this possibility cannot be adequately discussed here. See John F. Due, "The Retail Sales Tax in Honduras," *Inter-American Economic Affairs*, XX (Winter 1966), 55-67.

15. The Taylor Report, p. 200, makes the same recommendation, but goes on to say (p. 217): "The introduction of a system of internal excises would facilitate this shift in emphasis [from import substitution to the development of exports] by increasing the prices of internally manufactured luxury and semi-luxury goods, which would, in turn, reduce their demand and channel investment funds to the production of more essential goods or exports." This form of the argument is not convincing. For example, the objection can be raised that some excises will be demand-absorbing, rather than demand-shifting, depending on price elasticities. Moreover, there is no guarantee that resources frustrated or deterred from investment in "undesirable" activities will be automatically invested in "desirable" activities—they may instead be consumed or sent abroad. (Similar objections can be made to the related argument in Chelliah, *Fiscal Policy in Underdeveloped Countries,* p. 89). In the text discussion it is assumed that the high duties on luxury imports can be enforced and that domestic production can, at least to some extent, provide adequate substitutes for imports. For an outline and appraisal of the Colombian tariff system, see Taylor Report, chaps. VIII-IX.

16. These remarks do not do full justice to the complex economic and political interplay of exchange-rate policy, tariff policy, quantitative import controls, export taxes, and internal indirect taxes, but my main concern here is simply to outline something of the role of the sales tax in this complexity.

17. John F. Due, *Sales Taxation* (Urbana: University of Illinois Press, 1957), p. 42.

18. *Ibid.*, pp. 271-273, discusses the two alternative exemption techniques mentioned in the text. Another alternative, which would also have the considerable merit of clearing up the present murky situation on the tax treatment of intermediate products such as fuels and lubricants, is to permit the crediting of taxes paid on all products incorporated (in a cost-accounting sense) in the final product against tax due on the sale of the final product. A partial move in this direction was made in the 1966 tax reform. This sort of problem can also arise with exporters and importers and could, if desired, be resolved in the same way.

19. This point is developed at length in Clara K. Sullivan, *The Tax on Value Added* (New York: Columbia University Press, 1965), chap. I.

20. The offsetting effect of the tax on capital goods is somewhat weakened by the fact that the sales tax paid on a depreciable asset can be written off, according to prevailing depreciation schedules, against income tax. Also, although the treatment of contractors under the sales tax is obscure, it appears that while most building materials are taxed, the labor costs of construction are not. Investment in real property as compared to other forms of capital investment is thus made relatively more attractive by the tax. Though biased correctly toward labor-intensive, low-import investment, such a provision goes too far in creating an incentive to do what conditions in Colombia dictate anyway.

21. For extensive discussion, see Robert L. Slighton, *Urban Unemployment in Colombia: Measurement, Characteristics, and Policy Problems* (Santa Monica: RAND Corporation, 1968).

22. Richard R. Nelson, *A Study of Industrialization in Colombia: Part I, Analysis* (Santa Monica: RAND Corporation, 1967), p. 22. See also Bruton, "Productivity Growth in Latin America," p. 1112.

23. See *ibid.*, p. 1115. There are other government policies—wage laws, import licensing, etc.—which probably have more important effects on factor choice than do taxes; but, as usual, only the tax system is being studied here.

24. The output incentive is most fully discussed in Klaus Knorr and William J. Baumol, eds., *What Price Economic Growth?* (New York: Prentice-Hall, 1961). Some of the difficulties with applying this idea are noted in my "A Tax Incentive for Sales: The Canadian Experience," *National Tax Journal*, XVIII (September 1965), 277-285. No developing country appears to use such an incentive: see, for example, George E. Lent, "Tax Incentives for Investment in Developing Countries," *International Monetary Fund Staff Papers*, XIV (July 1967), 249-321. Occasionally, countries do require that some employment criterion be satisfied as a condition for receiving tax benefits, but on the whole the stress is very clearly on subsidizing capital and capital-intensive methods of production.

25. Slighton, *Urban Unemployment in Colombia,* p. 58.

26. For such a proposal, see J. E. Meade, "Mauritius: A Case Study in Malthusian Economics," *Economic Journal,* LXXI (September 1961), 521-534.

27. See Slighton, *Urban Unemployment in Colombia,* pp. 62-65, for an interesting discussion of this and the technology problem discussed in the next paragraph.

28. For a good discussion of the case for attempting to correct market prices (rather than just using shadow prices in planning) and of the revenue constraint on subsidy policies, see Peter Eckstein, "Accounting Prices as a Tool of Government Planning" (multilith, Cambridge, Mass.: Project for Quantitative Research in Economic Development, 1967).

29. This aspect of social security financing is nowhere mentioned in a recent extensive study by Franco Reviglio, "Social Security: A Means of Savings Mobilization for Economic Development," *International Monetary Fund Staff Papers,* XIV (July 1967), 324-347. There are, of course, other aspects of the problem which are not mentioned here. I have assumed that the exact incidence of payroll taxes is not important for the choice of factors, that there will be no substantial effects on saving (or population growth) from using this source of financing, and that the distributive effects of the system are not so important or beneficial as to outweigh its distorting allocative effects.

30. See Currie, *Accelerating Development,* pp. 46, 212, 219 for a negative appraisal; also the Taylor Report, pp. 87-91 (which comments on some minor incentives not discussed here). The 1957 ECLA study, *The Economic Development of Colombia,* p. 112, outlines the history of tax incentives in Colombia, some of which date back to the 1930's. (For more favorable evaluations of tax incentives than my own, see this ECLA study as well as Colombia's General Plan, II, 367-373.)

31. It is assumed throughout this section that the government has decided the private sector can make better use of the tax revenue foregone than the government itself. This assumption allows me to concentrate on appraising opportunity costs in terms of other conceivable forms of subsidies to private activities. In a country like Colombia, where the private sector has been and is likely to continue to be the main engine of development, this assumed decision is perhaps not unrealistic. It is also consistent with the earlier discussion of the likely need for transferring public saving into private investment.

32. This statement and much of the other material in these paragraphs is based on two unpublished 1966 papers by Richard Bilsborrow, "The Structure of Tax Incentives in Colombia" (Bogotá, 1966) and "The Tax Incentives for 'Basic' and 'Complementary' Industries" (Bogotá, 1966). I have also drawn upon unpublished papers by Richard C. Porter, "Basic and Complementary Industry Tax Exemptions" (Bo-

gotá, 1968) and Gustavo Parra, "Reserva extraordinaria de fomento económico" (Bogotá, 1968).

33. The most systematic study of the environment for making business decisions in Latin America is Albert Lauterbach, *Enterprise in Latin America: Business Attitudes in a Developing Economy* (Ithaca, N.Y.: Cornell University Press, 1966). I have also benefited from access to unpublished interviews with Colombian businessmen carried out by Richard Bilsborrow in Bogotá, Cali, and Medellín in 1965–66.

34. If, as noted earlier, firms use a payback-period criterion, a higher initial allowance—say, 25 percent instead of 15 percent—might be more effective because it would increase cash flow more in earlier years, although the present value of the allowance's revenue cost would remain the same to the extent it had to be paid back through reduced depreciation allowances in later years. This and numerous other points on investment incentives are discussed at length in my "Depreciation Allowances and Countercyclical Policy in the United Kingdom, 1945–1960."

35. See Feldstein and Tsiang, "The Interest Rate, Taxation, and the Personal Savings Incentive."

36. On the short-run effectiveness of altering exchange rates to induce minor exports, see John Sheahan and Sara Clark, "The Response of Colombian Exports to Variations in Effective Exchange Rates" (Williamstown, Mass.: Williams College, 1967); also Antonio Urdinola and Richard Mallon, "Policies To Promote Colombian Exports of Manufactures (multilith; Cambridge, Mass.: Harvard Development Advisory Service, September 1967). There is some question on the long-run as opposed to short-run effectiveness of higher profits in achieving higher exports, but we cannot explore this complex issue further here.

37. Both Sheahan and Clark and Urdinola and Mallon, make a similar point; see also Daniel M. Schydlowsky, "Short-Run Employment Policy in Semi-Industrialized Economies" (multilith; Cambridge, Mass.: Harvard Development Advisory Service, 1967).

5. Local Government Finance

1. This summary of Netzer's views is based on his "Local Government as a Development Instrument: The Colombian Experience" (mimeographed; New York, 1967), pp. 3-5. My disagreement with these arguments does not alter my considerable indebtedness to Netzer's previously cited pioneering study, "Some Aspects of Local Government Finances."

2 According to Mathew D. Edel, "The Colombian Community Action Program: An Economic Evaluation" (duplicated; Cambridge, Mass., 1968), in some rural areas local community development programs have been quite successful in mobilizing both resources and entrepreneurial talents and in efficiently allocating them. I do not explore this possibility at length here, however.

3. For a respectable psychological argument that this result may ensue, see David McClelland, *The Achieving Society* (New York: Free Press, 1967), pp. 431-437.

4. Persuasive general argument along similar lines may be found in W. Arthur Lewis, "Planning Public Expenditure," in Max F. Millikan, ed., *National Economic Planning* (New York: Columbia University Press, 1967), pp. 201-227. See also Wolfgang F. Stolper, *Planning without Facts* (Cambridge, Mass.: Harvard University Press, 1966), p. 12. Stolper (like Edel) also stresses the advantage of special local knowledge in coping with local needs and problems.

5. John Friedmann, *Regional Development Policy: A Case Study of Venezuela* (Cambridge, Mass.: M.I.T. Press, 1966), p. 7.

6. Shoup *et al.*, *Fiscal System of Venezuela*, p. 313.

7. Spearman's coefficient of rank correlation for the two rankings (based on slightly different data than those in Table 21) when tested by Student's t-distribution proved to be significant at the 99 percent level of confidence. That is, a strong positive correlation exists between the ranking of departments by welfare and the ranking by per capita local revenues. The rank correlation between per capita income-tax collections and local revenues was also significant.

8. On Mexico, see Paul Lamartine Yates, *El desarrollo regional de México* (Mexico, D.F.: Banco de Mexico, 1961), especially p. 99 (for a welfare index similar to that constructed for Colombia in Table 21). An estimate of regional income for Brazil may be found in ECLA, "Estudios sobre la distribución de ingreso en América Latina." The latter ranks Colombia as having a greater degree of regional inequality than Brazil, but this seems unlikely in view of the careful analyses of Marabelli and Netzer (summarized in Table 21).

9. Netzer, "Some Aspects of Local Government Finance," p. 38.

10. Cited in *Taxation in Colombia*, p. 19.

11. See, for example, Shoup *et al.*, *Fiscal System of Venezuela*, pp. 315-319; Oldman *et al.*, *Financing Urban Development in Mexico City*, chap. I; Public Administration Service, *Strengthening Municipal Government in El Salvador* (Chicago, 1955).

12. For examples of these, see Lascarro, *Administración fiscal, presupuesto, decentralización*, pp. 174-178; Fernando Galvís Gaitán, *El munnicipio colombiano* (Bogotá: Imprenta Departmental Antonio Nariño, 1964), pp. 167-177; and Attir, *La reforma administrativa en Colombia*, pp. 70-72.

13. See *Encuentro liberal*, September 9, 1967, p. 14. I have expounded my views on regional fiscal and development problems at some length in numerous other publications: see esp. "The Economy of the Mexican Federal District," *Inter-American Economic Affairs*, XVII (Autumn 1963), 19-51; "The Need for Regional Policy in a Common Market," *Scottish Journal of Political Economy*, XII (November 1965), 225-242; and "Tax-

Subsidy Policies for Regional Development," *National Tax Journal,* XIX (June 1966), 113-124.

14. The data in this and the surrounding paragraphs are taken from the sources cited in Table 25.

15. See the interesting study on the Cali area by Pedro Pablo Morcillo and Humberto Castaño, "La administración y financiamento de los municipios y de los departmentos, con referencia exclusiva al valle de Cauca," (unpublished paper; Cali, 1965).

16. A study of the situation in the Special District of Bogotá (not included in Table 24) showed that 49.5 percent of the total exempt property there was government-owned and 10.5 percent church-owned in 1962 (Lauchlin Currie, *Una política urbana para los países en desarrollo* [Bogotá: Ediciones Tercer Mundo, 1965], p. 165). For more details on the nature of exemptions, see *Taxation in Colombia,* pp. 129-132.

17. These estimates are probably low, since one would expect exempt properties to be undervalued relative to taxed properties. The "urban" and "rural" classifications are those of the census, which calls any area with over 1,500 inhabitants "urban."

18. For a more detailed depiction of the complicated rate structure in Bogotá, see *Taxation in Colombia,* p. 146. That same work, pp. 138-140, outlines the special tax on unimproved values in urban areas (not discussed here).

19. See United States Department of Commerce, Bureau of the Census, *Property Taxation in 1962* (Washington, D.C., 1964), p. 191; also Gerald W. Sazama, "Equalization of Property Taxes for the Nation's Largest Central Cities," *National Tax Journal,* XVIII (June 1965), 151-161.

20. The two studies cited in note 19 indicate that a ratio of less than 0.30 is quite common in the United States.

21. See Taylor Report, p. 146, on Bogotá; also a report by the National Planning Department on Meta, the report on Cali and Valle cited in note 15 above, and information obtained from the CAR (Regional Corporation for Bogotá and the Sabana) on various municipalities in Cundinamarca.

22. This elasticity may be estimated as 0.8 in current prices. The comparable figure for the United States for the 1956-1961 period is 1.4 (see Benjamin Bridges, Jr., "Income Elasticity of the Property Tax Base," *National Tax Journal,* XVII [September 1964], 255). The same method as used by Bridges, p. 254, n. 4, was used with Colombian data. As Bridges notes (p. 264), the elasticity method is not a particularly reliable means of forecasting the growth of a tax base, but it is the only one that can be used in Colombia at present. If inflation slows down, the elasticity of the tax base in real terms might be as high as 0.7 instead of the historic 0.1 to 0.4 that can be estimated from Table 25.

23. At various times in the past assessment has been carried out on a much more decentralized basis, and at any given moment there is usually

some agitation to allow at least the larger cities to carry out their own assessments (as do Bogotá and Medellín). For a recent proposal along these lines, see Proyecto de Ley número 69 de 1965 (*Anales del Congreso*, August 27, 1965). Though this topic perennially comes up at meetings of the National Association of Municipalities, there is probably not much likelihood of further decentralization in the future, nor should there be.

24. For further stimulating (or perhaps depressing) thoughts on this subject, see Aaron Lipman and A. Eugene Havens, "The Colombian *Violencia:* An *Ex Post Facto* Experiment" *Social Forces*, XLIV (December 1965), 238-245; see also Edel, "The Colombian Community Action Program."

25. See Lascarro, *Administración fiscal, presupuesto, decentralización*, pp. 37-38, and Break and Turvey, *Studies in Greek Public Finance*, pp. 102-107, for examples of the usual arguments. A proposal along the lines suggested in the text was made in Ministerio de Educatión Nacional, *Un programa de desarrollo para la educación en Colombia* (Bogotá 1966).

26. The figure of 6.2 percent applies only to Medellín proper and reflects the fact that that city alone among major Colombian cities has a significant (one-quarter) of its metropolitan area population living outside the central city. The growth rate for the Medellín metropolitan area in its entirety was somewhat higher.

27. See the different theoretical models in Lowdon Wingo, Jr., *Transportation and Urban Land* (Baltimore: Johns Hopkins Press, 1961); and William Alonso, *Location and Land Use* (Cambridge, Mass.: Harvard University Press, 1964).

28. Among recent authors, Dick Netzer, *Economics of the Property Tax* (Washington, D.C.: Brookings Institution, 1966), p. 205, and Daniel Holland, "The Taxation of Unimproved Value in Jamaica," *Proceedings of the 58th Annual Conference of the National Tax Association* (Harrisburg, Pa., 1966), p. 457, have accepted this argument.

29. This argument assumes that there is no "Veblen effect"—that is, it is not considered *more* prestigious to hold out of use land whose productive value has risen. Also, if the benefit exceeds the tax, the income effect will tend to increase all consumption, including that of land used for prestige purposes.

30. These factors are well discussed by Holland in "The Taxation of Unimproved Value in Jamaica," pp. 457-460. The effect of valorization taxes on the amount of land held for speculative purposes is uncertain: if the increase in land values due to the public improvements leads speculators to believe that the land has matured and is ready for development, the amount of land held for speculative purposes might increase. This question is not further discussed here.

31. This part of the analysis is based on numerous personal interviews and visits in Colombia. A detailed account of the Colombian experience, together with a briefer look at the less happy experience with similar

taxes in Ecuador and Mexico, may be found in William G. Rhoads and Richard M. Bird, "The Valorization Tax in Colombia: An Example for Other Developing Countries" (multilith; Cambridge, Mass.: Harvard Development Advisory Service, 1967). This detailed study also discusses the use of valorization financing for rural improvements.

32. According to a recent report, largely for political reasons the valorization program has been rather small in Barranquilla, Colombia's fourth largest city. See Lauchlin Currie et al., Plan socio-economico para el Atlántico (Bogotá: Imprenta Nacional, 1965), pp. 200-209.

33. The exemption of publicly owned property is sometimes justified on the ground that the property has no commercial value. While this position may recognize the realities of political life, it has no basis in economic analysis. The use of land for public rather than other purposes has an opportunity cost equal to its highest value in alternative uses, and increases in this cost due to public works should, in theory, be explicitly recognized in making decisions on the location of public facilities.

34. As noted earlier, such authorities as Netzer appear to favor a land-value increment tax over the valorization tax recommended here: that is, they prefer a tax assessed on benefits actually received as a result of the work to one on benefits that it is presumed will arise in the future. To repeat, the valorization tax is preferable in developing countries despite its arbitrary nature because of the lack of a capital market for financing public works, the more favorable attitudes of taxpayers to benefit taxes, and the growth-inflation cushion of rising property values.

35. Even at this more advanced stage there is still a role, though a lesser one, for valorization taxes in the financing of works with an irregular local-general benefit split. For example, a recent analysis of pricing for electric utilities in Colombia by Ralph Hofmeister of the University of Minnesota, "Observations on the Tariff Policies of the Electricity Supply Companies Affiliated with 'Electroaguas'" (mimeographed; Bogotá, 1966), points out that the costs of local distribution systems for utilities are joint costs that cannot be assigned to individual users and that the local distribution system is best considered a "Samuelsonian" public good whose costs should be covered by taxation. He recommends more use of special assessments to cover those costs.

6. Taxing for Development

1. This paragraph is based on a substantial amount of detailed quantitative research carried on during and after my stay in Colombia and reported in two unpublished papers, "Estimated National Government Revenues, 1965–1968, and the Public Sector in the Plan Cuatrienal" (Bogotá, 1965), and "Revenue Requirements for Growth and Stability" (Cambridge, Mass., 1967). Some results from these papers are summarized at various points in this study, but I have decided not to clutter up the

argument with elaborate descriptions of simple statistical manipulations since the results are invariably those mentioned.

2. For a general argument to this effect, see W. Arthur Lewis, "Closing Remarks," in Werner Baer and Isaac Kerstenetzky, eds., *Inflation and Growth in Latin America* (Homewood, Ill.: Irwin, 1964), pp. 23-24.

3. Interestingly, the two previous attempts at domestic sales taxation (in 1914 and 1942) also occurred when wartime cuts in foreign trade created an urgent need for increased domestic revenues (Levin, "Effects of Economic Development upon the Base of a Sales Tax," pp. 2-4).

4. For a sweeping proposal for stamp-tax reform, see my "Stamp Tax Reform in Colombia," pp. 247-255.

5. This account is based on Fluharty, *Dance of the Millions,* pp. 237-238, 242-244, and on ECLA, *The Economic Development of Colombia,* pp. 111-112.

6. See, for example, *Voz proletaria,* January 21, 1965, p. 16 (full-page advertisement in socialist-realism style, saying "Down with the tax on consumption"—a slogan which also appeared on walls all over Bogotá at this time); in addition a leaflet was circulated which managed to blame the Yankees, declaring that the sales tax was necessary only "to satisfy the Colombian exploiters and the gringo monopolists."

7. Official statement of the two labor groups (the UTC and the CTC), reproduced in *El Tiempo,* January 9, 1965, p. 7.

8. Comisión de Estudios, *Asuntos económicos y fiscales 1965* (Bogotá: Banco de la República, 1965), p. 211.

9. For example, the 1967 income-tax "reform" had to be softened in its treatment of the cattle industry in order to win acceptance in the Senate (*El Tiempo,* July 6, 1967).

10. A recent clear statement of this view is Albert O. Hirschman, "The Political Economy of Import-Substituting Industrialization in Latin America," *Quarterly Journal of Economics,* LXXXII (February 1968), 10-11. Merle Kling in an earlier attempt to evaluate Colombian tax data for evidence on political behavior concluded Colombia was a good instance of "interest group politics," a conclusion which differs from my own partly because his analysis is mistaken in ignoring the pronounced cycle in tax revenues from foreign trade. See Merle Kling, "Taxes on the 'External' Sector: An Index of Political Behavior in Latin America?" *Midwest Journal of Political Science,* III (May 1959), 127-150.

11. On these questions, see Fluharty, *Dance of the Millions,* pp. 159, 172-173; Seymour Martin Lipset, *Political Man* (New York: Doubleday, 1960), p. 51; Frank Tannenbaum, *Ten Keys to Latin America* (New York: Knopf, 1963), pp. 120-121.

12. For an even stronger statement of the political, social, and administrative requirements for effective developmental decision-making, see Robert Buron, *Decision-making in the Development Field* (Paris: Organisation for Economic Co-operation and Development, 1966).

13. The question is paraphrased from one in Milton C. Taylor, "The Relationship between Income Tax Administration and Income Tax Policy in Nigeria," *Nigerian Journal of Economic and Social Studies,* IX (July 1967), 203-215, a useful article which answers this question in much the same way I do.

14. Harley H. Hinrichs has provided an interesting analysis of the "game" of tax evasion in "Game Theory and the Rational Tax Evader" (unpublished paper, 1965), which stresses the importance of changing the rules of the games by higher and better-enforced penalties for evasion. As David McClelland (*The Achieving Society,* p. 399) has noted, nothing is so useful in developing "market morality" as some well-publicized sanctions for immorality.

15. Much confusion exists on this question in part because of the propensity to treat illegal tax evasion and perfectly legal tax avoidance as similarly heinous crimes. A good example of this confusion is a powerful statement in 1967 by President Lleras attacking "tax evaders," most of whom seem, judging from the examples in his speech, to be taking advantage in a quite legal fashion of the numerous loopholes and exemptions in present Colombian tax law. This distinction is important since, as noted below, structural defects in the law can be much more quickly and effectively remedied than basic administrative weaknesses arising from underdevelopment and a set of values which does not foster voluntary compliance.

16. See Albert G. Hart, *An Integrated System of Tax Information: A Model, and a Sketch of Possibilities of Practical Application under Latin American Conditions* (New York, 1967), for a stimulating discussion of the importance of this task.

17. J. K. Galbraith, *Economic Development* (Boston: Houghton Mifflin, 1964), preface. Albert Hart, whose work is cited above, is an excellent example of an originally ambitious fiscal reformer who has really taken this lesson to heart as a result of sobering experiences in Latin America.

18. Currie, *Accelerating Development,* p. 236, sums up the present state of Colombian public administration well when he says: "The country simply cannot hope to achieve the desired economic goals without modernizing its manner of conducting public business and making it much more efficient. . . . The whole system of multiple responsibility (in which no one is responsible), multiple signatures, endless shuffling about of papers, preaudit, and postaudit . . . , monthly budget allotments, archaic tax enforcement methods, and complete disregard for the convenience of the public, is costing the country heavily in unnecessary bureaucracy, unnecessary delays, and a great waste of time on the part of anyone who has anything to do with government, which includes practically everybody." A different aspect, corruption in the sense of the need for political connections to get a government job, is stressed by Andrew H. Whiteford, *Two Cities of Latin America* (New York: Double-

day Anchor Books, 1964), pp. 216-217, though outright bribery of public officials is much less widespread by all accounts in Colombia than in many other developing countries.

19. See Lynton K. Caldwell, "Technical Assistance and Administrative Reform in Colombia," *American Political Science Review*, XLVII (June 1953), 494-510. Incidentally, my appraisal of the prospects for successful reform in Colombia in 1968 is *much* more optimistic than Caldwell's was in 1953.

20. For an excellent brief discussion of the relation between administration and policy, see Stanley S. Surrey, "Tax Policy and Tax Administration" (mimeographed; Washington, D.C., 1967).

21. ECLA, *The Economic Development of Colombia*, pp. 96, 108-111, 136, 269.

Appendix B.   Coffee Tax Policy

1. *Boletín de información estadística sobre café*, no. 40 (1966), pp. 33, 35, 45. The *Boletín* is published in Bogotá by the Federación Nacional de Cafeteros.

2. *Ibid.,* p. 42.

3. Since, for my purposes, the distinction between the Fund and the Federation is of no importance, I shall hereafter refer to these two entities as if they were the same, though it is the operations of the Fund which are my main concern here.

4. While most studies support this assumption, indicating elasticities as low as 0.2 to 0.3, there may well be substantial elasticity of demand for Colombia's premium mild coffee in place of Brazil's. The International Coffee Agreement precludes price-cutting, however, and the question is not really germane here; so the subject is not further pursued.

5. This estimate is based on data in *Boletín de información estadística sobre café*, no. 40, pp. 18, 32, 48. Owing to the confusing way in which different size units and types of coffee are recorded for different purposes, this figure is only a crude estimate. The Federation does not publicize the size of its stocks. Preliminary indications are that about the same proportion of the 1966–67 crop went into stocks. In 1967–68, however, it appears that there was virtually no new net addition to stocks, possibly in part reflecting a lagged supply response to earlier sales problems.

6. In 1965, for example, there were at least eight major changes in coffee policy: in February the surrender price was lowered; in March the internal purchase price was lowered, the coffee exchange rate was raised, and the retention tax was raised; in May the surrender price was lowered again; in September the surrender price was raised; and in November the coffee rate and retention tax were both raised. This kind of up-and-down movement has been common in the past ten years.

7. For a useful discussion of these taxes, see Luis Eduardo Samper, "Income-Market Problems of Basic Agricultural Commodities: The Case of Coffee" (M.A. diss. Georgetown University, 1967), pp. 74-86. The coffee tax system in 1964 is also described in *Taxation in Colombia*, pp. 39-40, 174-176. I have further benefited from an unpublished study by Michael Kuczynski of the International Monetary Fund staff and from discussions with William G. Rhoads, Jonathan Levin, and William E. Breidenbach.

8. Banco Cafetero, *Carta económica*, III (October–November 1966), 5.

9. From May to September 1967, for example, the internal support price was raised six times (presumably to keep the Federation competitive with private exporters).

10. It should be remembered that most Colombian coffee is grown by farmers with very small holdings: a 1955 study found 235,000 coffee farms with an average (both mean and modal) size of 3.3 hectares—barely enough to produce a subsistence income even at the then-prevailing record prices (Banco de la República, *Atlas de economía colombiana*, vol. IV).

11. Export figures from *Boletín de información estadístico sobre café*, no. 40, p. 36; budget figures from *Boletín de la dirección nacional del presupuesto*, no. 53, p. 94; additional information from Table 29.

The "tax" as defined in Table 29 can also be calculated from the following formula:

$$[d(1+a) - [c(1-b)\ (1-e) - ef]\ ]/d(1+a),$$

where a = retention tax as a percent of value exported, b = ad valorem export tax, c = coffee exchange rate, d = other exchange rate used in calculation, e = percentage difference between required surrender price and actual cash receipts in dollars, and f = rate at which dollars can be bought (or sold). In Table 29, $d = f$ as a rule, except for 1967 when $d = c$ and f is the capital market rate.

It must be emphasized that these "tax" calculations are illustrative and, to some degree, inherently arbitrary. Not only are unweighted averages and other questionable data freely used but also the way in which I have chosen to calculate the "tax" is open to some question. An alternative calculation by W. E. Breidenbach of the "tax" for the 1966-67 coffee year (a period not covered in Table 29), for example, yields "tax" estimates of 32 to 38 percent: those interested in more details on the complexity of the required calculations should consult the seventeen pages used to derive the Breidenbach estimates in United States Embassy Airgram A-771 of May 22, 1968.

12. I have assumed throughout this discussion that the incidence of the major coffee taxes, given the relative inelasticity of demand, almost certainly falls on the growers. In recent years, owing to the Federation's price policy, it is perhaps possible that some of the tax burden has been shifted to the private exporters, who are now in more severe competition with one another. The income of growers is also subject to the regular

income tax, although the scanty data available indicate that (in part no doubt owing to the great proportion of coffee income going to small growers) coffee income accounted for less than one-tenth of 1 percent of income tax revenues in 1959, the most recent year for which this information is available. In these circumstances there seems no point in pursuing the suggestion sometimes put forth that the coffee export tax should be made creditable against income tax due on coffee income (see, for example, Oliver Oldman, "Tax Reform in El Salvador," *Inter-American Bar Review,* VI [July–December 1964], 405).

13. The strength of the Colombian coffee sector against taxation was also noted in the early 1950's in ECLA, *The Economic Development of Colombia,* p. 107. Curiously, the contrary conclusion appears to emerge from another recent study: see Richard Goode, George E. Lent, and P. D. Ojha, "Role of Export Taxes in Developing Countries," *International Monetary Fund Staff Papers,* XV (November 1966), 6, 8.

14. "Notas sobre las estadísticas de comercio exterior" (mimeographed; Bogotá, 1966), p. 9. Of course 1963 was, according to Table 29, a year of relatively low coffee "taxation," and one might expect more smuggling when the rewards are higher, as in 1965 and 1967.

15. Dunkerley, "Exchange-Rate Systems in Conditions of Continuing Inflation," p. 165.

Index

Acción Comunal. *See* Community development

Acerías Paz del Río, S.A., 134. *See also* "Complementary" industries, incentive for

Administration, tax. *See* Tax administration

Agency for International Development, 8. *See also* Foreign aid

Agriculture: importance of, 4, 237; in Currie Plan, 9, 10; taxation of, 54, 88-96, 188, 197, 220, 255; effects of sales tax on, 107-108. *See also* Coffee; Currie Plan; Land taxes; Livestock industry; Politics, of tax reform; Presumptive taxation

Alcoholic beverages, taxes on, 106, 107, 108. *See also* Sales tax; Sumptuary taxes

Alliance for Progress, 27

Antioquia, Department of, 150, 151; and property tax, 163, 164

Argentina, 246

Assessment. *See* Land taxes; Real property tax

Atlántico, Department of, 151

Australia, land tax in, 254

Autonomous agencies (of national government): importance of, 12, 28, 29, 48; control of, 49, 51, 167, 245; in Cali, 178. *See also* Earmarking of revenues

Avoidance, tax. *See* Erosion, tax

Balance-of-payments problems, 4. *See also* Foreign-resources gap; Foreign trade

Barranquilla, city of, 157; valorization tax in, 265

"Basic" industries, incentive for, 133-134, 138, 141. *See also* Incentives

Bearer securities: withholding on, 63; abolition of, 70

Benefit taxation, 172, 181. *See also* Earmarking of revenues; Valorization tax

Betterment taxes. *See* Valorization

"Blue Return," in Japan, 100, 255

Bogotá, Special District of: fiscal powers of, 151, 155; taxes in, 157, 162, 263; assessment in, 163, 264; growth rate of, 169; valorization tax in, 177, 178, 180, 183; tax evasion in, 199, 250

Borrowing, government: limitations on, 37; forced debt placement, 37, 193. *See also* Coffee Fund; Deficit financing

Brazil, 35, 150, 268; regional differences in, 151, 262

Breidenbach, William E., 269

Budget, government: relation to plan, 46; cash budgeting, 47, 245; politics of, 49-50, 245; "contingency" budget, 50-51. *See also* Revenue forecasting

Business, taxation of. *See* Corporations; Depreciation; Dividends; Excess-profits tax; Limited liability companies; Loss offset; Partnerships; Small business

Cadastre. *See* Land taxes; Real property tax

Caldwell, Lynton K., 268

Cali, city of, 157, 159, 263; taxes in, 162; growth rate of, 169; valorization tax in, 177-178.

Capital gains, taxation of, 65-73, 188, 219, 249; and concept of income, 65-66; and progressivity, 66, 249; on real property, 66, 172, 194; realization basis, 67; at death, 67-68; and inflation, 68-69, 219, 250; effects on saving and investment, 69-70, 72, 73; "roll-over" of, 70-71; pro-rating of, 71-72. *See also* Income tax

Capital goods: imports of, 5, 238; low utilization of, 10, 86, 128; sales

taxes, 60, 83; of property tax, 167-168, 192, 221-222. *See also* Autonomous agencies; Benefit taxation; Valorization tax

Econometric studies, and policy, 8-9, 11, 25-26. *See also* Data, weakness of

Economic Commission for Latin America, 40, 202, 237

Economic development reserve, 135-136; 138. *See also* Incentives

Economic growth: rate of, in Colombia, 3, 237; and task of tax policy, 41-44

Edel, Matthew, 262

Education: tax allowance for expenditures on, 129; earmarking of taxes for, 167-168, 192, 221-222

Elasticity: importance of, 12, 34-35, 53, 187, 189; assumed in 1962 Plan, 25; defined, 31-32, 243; estimated, 32, 43, 244; of local governments, 41; of income tax, 60, 65, 111; of sales tax, 111; of property tax, 157, 164-166, 263. *See also* Foreign-resources gap; Inflation

Erosion, tax, 73, 75, 267

Evasion, tax: importance of, 34, 199; in income tax, 60, 73-74, 250; in agriculture, 90; in small business, 96; countermeasures to, 101-102, 201-202, 220; confused with avoidance, 267. *See also* Tax administration

Excess-profits tax, 59, 81; abolition recommended, 83-84, 86, 128, 130, 220; and net-wealth tax, 252. *See also* Income tax

Exchange rates, 20n; and choice of technology, 120-121; and export subsidization, 143; and coffee taxes, 213, 214, 218. *See also* Devaluation; Foreign trade

Excise taxes. *See* Alcoholic beverages, taxes on; Gasoline taxes; Sales taxes; Sumptuary taxes; Tobacco taxes

Exemptions, personal, 219; in presumptive tax, 94-95. *See also* Income tax

Expenditure tax, 141, 256-257

Exports: importance of, 3, 4; subsidization of, 35; taxes on, 116, 246; incentives for, 142-144, 189, 261. *See also* Coffee; Foreign-resources gap; Foreign trade; Incentives

Federation of Coffee Growers, 211, 213, 214, 217, 268

Finance, Ministry of. *See* Ministry of Finance

Fluharty, Vernon Lee, 240

Forced loans. *See* Borrowing, government

Foreign aid: in 1962 Plan, 25, 26; relation to budget, 35, 42-43; relation to growth, 35, 42-43, 45; agency policies criticized, 117, 192, 245. *See also* Foreign-resources gap; Foreign trade

Foreign-resources gap: as constraint on growth, 5, 8-9, 45, 123; and Currie Plan, 10-11; and budget, 34-35; and tax reform, 54

Foreign trade: cyclical influence on government finance, 35-39, 51, 193, 246; taxes on, 35-36, 39, 193. *See also* Coffee; Exports; Imports; Tariffs

Foreign travel, taxation of, 108, 111, 196

Forfait system of taxation, 112

France, 86, 96, 112

Galbraith, J. K., 199

Gasoline tax, 111, 123, 188, 196, 221

General strike, and sales tax, 195, 196

Geographic Institute, 93, 161, 163

"Hard-to-tax" sectors, 88, 220. *See also* Agriculture; Presumptive taxation; Small business

Hart, Albert G., 267

Hinrichs, Harley H., 267

Hirschman, Albert, 91, 92

Honduras, 258

Housing: earmarked tax for, 83, 247; taxes on, 89, 111, 123; incentives for, 139, 140, 141, 161

Imports: importance, 5; composition